In Search

Peter Reason tackles huge themes with clarity and intelligence. Through his own private pilgrimage he asks, how a modern citizen can live on good terms with the rest of nature's glorious republic? And what can we do to honour the four-billion-year-old miracle that has given us all the gift of life? This is an important and challenging work.

Mark Cocker, author of *Crow Country* and *Claxton: Field Notes from a Small Planet*

Peter Reason puts to sea in a purposeful wandering. This man in a boat is on an ecological pilgrimage and apart from having the skills and temperament to avoid capsize and deadly rocks, to weather storms and just not drown in a wild ocean that has us landlubbers shaking in our boots, there is work to do. How do you explore a deeper connection with the wild, the more-than-human world? How can a spiritual response to Nature support the pragmatic prevention of those destructive impulses that are causing such a dreadful state of affairs in the natural world? How do you articulate an experience of those unexpected and spontaneous sacred moments? This account from the liminal edge between these notions goes much further than anyone contemplating a sightseeing voyage would dare.

Paul Evans, author of *Field Notes From The Edge: Journeys Through Britain's Secret Wilderness*

In an age of ecological crisis, perhaps humanity itself needs a pilgrimage. Perhaps we need to seek out the truth of who we are and what we have done, and leave a space for some kind of transformative grace to enter. Peter Reason's journey may show

some of us the way. His book is both brave and necessary.
Paul Kingsnorth, author of *The Wake* and *Beast*

In his years at the University of Bath, Peter Reason rose to promi-
nence as a brave pioneer of Action Research—a participative
approach to scholarly and whole-life inquiry that refuted narrow
reductionism. Now, in this meditatively written and richly inter-
woven account, he takes his inquiry further. Sailing his boat
around the seas of Celtic lands, he gleans insights into these our
troubled times, as glimpsed through the cracks of a deeper grace
belonging to this planet Earth.
Professor Alastair McIntosh, author of *Soil and Soul* and
Poacher's Pilgrimage: An Island Journey

How do we create a new healing relationship between the human
and the more-than-human world and discover a new sense of
what it means to be a responsible species? These are urgent
questions for us all, if we going to learn how to change from
destroying the planet to restoring it. Peter Reason is a poetic
story-teller, a courageous pilgrim, a questioning philosopher and
an explorer of the emergent, who beautifully and generously
shares his 'moments of grace' at home and at sea.
Professor Peter Hawkins, author of *Leadership Team Coaching*

In Search of Grace

An ecological pilgrimage

In Search of Grace

An ecological pilgrimage

Peter Reason

EARTH

BOOKS

Winchester, UK
Washington, USA

First published by Earth Books, 2017
Earth Books is an imprint of John Hunt Publishing Ltd., Laurel House, Station Approach,
Alresford, Hants, SO24 9JH, UK
office1@jhpbooks.net
www.johnhuntpublishing.com
www.earth-books.net

For distributor details and how to order please visit the 'Ordering' section on our website.

Text copyright: Peter Reason 2016

ISBN: 978 1 78279 486 8
978 1 78279 487 5 (ebook)
Library of Congress Control Number: 2016954749

A CIP catalogue record for this book is available from the British Library.

Design: Stuart Davies

Printed and bound by CPI Group (UK) Ltd, Croydon, CR0 4YY, UK

We operate a distinctive and ethical publishing philosophy in all
areas of our business, from our global network of authors to
production and worldwide distribution.

CONTENTS

Other books by Peter Reason

Spindrift: A Wilderness Pilgrimage at Sea
Stories of the Great Turning (edited with Melanie Newman)
Leadership for Sustainability (with Judi Marshall and
Gill Coleman)
SAGE Handbook of Action Research (edited with Hilary Bradbury)
Human Inquiry in Action
Participation in Human Inquiry
Human Inquiry: A Sourcebook of New Paradigm Research (edited
with John Rowan)

Moments of Grace

To recover from ecological disaster, we humans must transform our sense of who we are, so we experience ourselves as part of, rather than apart from, the community of life on Earth.

Moments of grace occur when a crack opens in our taken-for-granted world, and for a tiny moment we experience a different world that is nevertheless the same world. It is a world that is not fixed in form, but forever changing: no longer divided into separate things, but one dancing whole.

Pilgrimage

A pilgrimage is a journey of moral or spiritual significance, undertaken in response to deep questions and a yearning for answers from a realm beyond the everyday. A religious pilgrimage can be described as a search for a holy realm and a direct encounter with that which is sacred. An ecological pilgrimage can be seen as a search for an experience of deep participation with the Earth and her creatures.

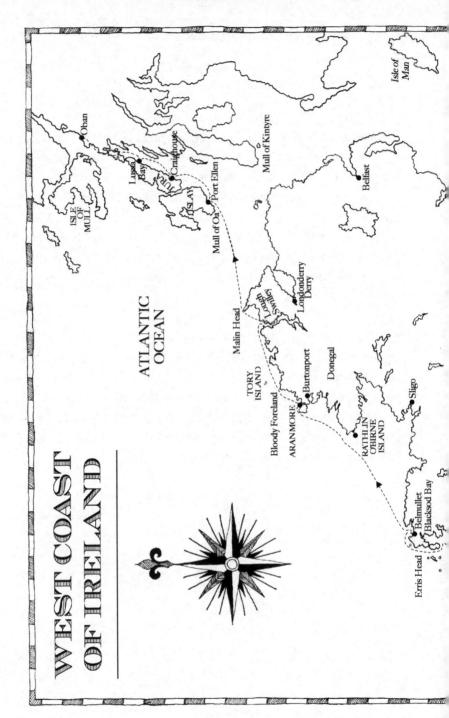

WEST COAST OF IRELAND

ATLANTIC OCEAN

Isle of Man

Belfast

Mull of Kintyre

Oban

ISLE OF MULL

Lussa Bay

Craighouse

ISLAY

Port Ellen

Mull of Oa

Malin Head

Lough Swilley

Londonderry
Derry

TORY ISLAND

Burtonport

Donegal

Bloody Foreland

ARANMORE

RATHLIN OBIRNE ISLAND

Sligo

Belmullet
Blacksod Bay

Erris Head

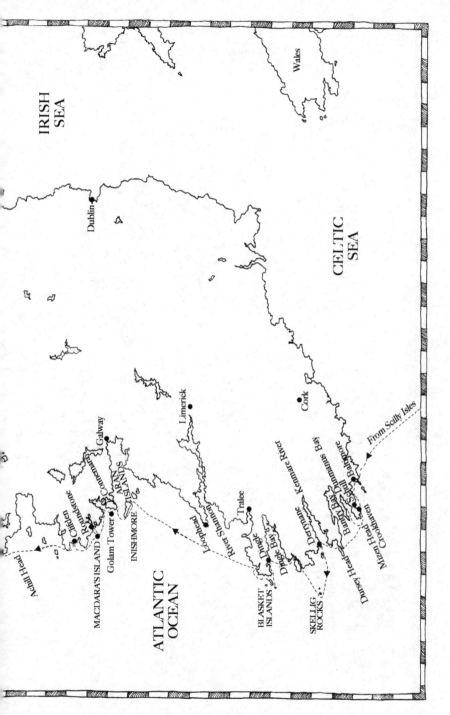

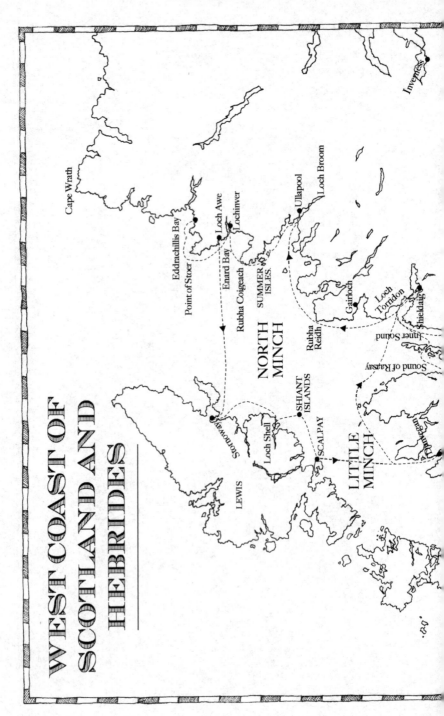

WEST COAST OF SCOTLAND AND HEBRIDES

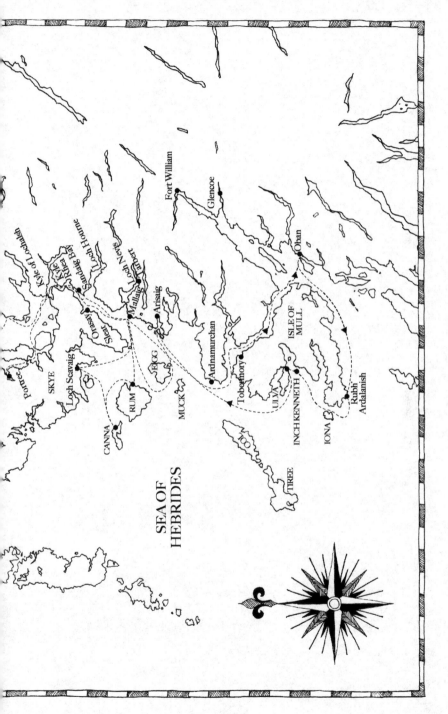

Chapter One

The Questions

It's all a question of story. We are in trouble just now because we do not have a good story. We are between stories. The old story, the account of how the world came to be and how we fit into it, is no longer effective. Yet we have not learned the new story... A radical reassessment of the human situation is needed...
Thomas Berry
The Dream of the Earth

Early one winter morning I pulled up the blinds and looked out into the dark. Our house stands high on the hills on the south side of Bath with a panoramic view over the city. From the top floor window I traced the streetlights that spread across the floor of the valley and meandered westward toward Bristol, where they cast an orange glow into the sky. Beyond, on the farther side of the River Severn, another patch of lights — probably the little town Chepstow — shimmered delicately through the dark.

I stood for a few moments gazing at the lights, remembering how our visitors the previous evening had been drawn to the window and looked out at the lights with wonder. "What a fantastic view!" they said. "It's like coming to land in an aeroplane." And it *is* a spectacular scene: the orange sodium lights follow the lines of the streets, interspersed with bright security lights, occasional intense blue from advertising signs and the flashing lights of pedestrian crossings.

A recent news report came into my mind: photographs of Earth at night taken by a NASA satellite showed something similar but on a grander scale: the blue night-time glow of the atmosphere studded with artificial light. Bright clusters covered much of North America, Europe, and Japan as well as big chunks

1

of India and China. The more isolated cities such as Johannesburg, Rio, Sydney, Lagos stood out from darker patches. The whole of the Nile valley and delta was picked out in a ribbon of light, as was the Indus snaking up through Pakistan. I found it an astounding image: the reflection of a marvellous human accomplishment, in equal parts beautiful and terrible.[1]

When I pull up the blind and see the city lights, when I look at these satellite pictures, I do marvel; yet also have a sinking feeling in my stomach, a rising sense of panic and helplessness. For what I see is the accumulated fossil energy store of the planet leaking into the atmosphere, as if Earth is suffering an internal bleeding. When I link what I see to what I know about carbon emissions and climate change, I wonder to myself, "What are we doing to our planet?"

After I had stood at the window for a few moments I turned away and put on the kettle to make tea. Everyday normalness took over and I got on with my day.

Our house is one of seven that make up a small Georgian crescent on the southern hills above Bath. Now surrounded by 1930s suburbia, when built in the 1790s it was a little way out of the city, designed to be self-sufficient: a shared driveway leading to a courtyard with coach houses that now serve as garages; underground cisterns to collect rainwater; a communal 'pleasure garden' overlooking the City; and a row of seven stone-walled vegetable gardens reaching westward from the end of the crescent itself. We are fortunate to own two of these; one was attached to the house when we bought it, in which my wife Elizabeth has created a flower garden.

The adjoining garden we bought more recently; it had been a flourishing vegetable plot, then was neglected for seven years. We worked hard to clear the overgrown brambles and old man's beard, dig up the self-seeded ash and buddleia trees, and take piles of disintegrating building materials to the recycling centre.

We planted fruit trees surrounded by flowering meadow grass. All the trees needed winter pruning. It was easy to give the new ones a light trim. But there were three old Bramley's Seedling cookers that needed serious attention: they had a lot of dead wood and a tangle of overlapping branches, although the biggest problem was that they had been smothered by the overgrowth and in their struggle toward the light had become misshapen.

I had been working on them whenever the winter weather permitted, taking the pruning slowly, learning as I went along. That afternoon I took along my pruning saw and loppers to finish the job. After several hours' work the trees were more nearly the recommended wineglass shape, compact, open in the middle 'so you could throw your hat through' as the old saying goes.

All this work set me thinking again about the relationship between humans and the 'more-than-human' world.[2] For these trees are not at all 'natural': they have been selected, grafted on to an appropriate rootstock, transported to the orchard, planted and tended over the years. Prior to that, in ancient times, apple pips, fruit and trees were transported westward along the traditional routes between the orient and the occident, so that a tree that evolved in Asia is now cultivated worldwide.[3]

Philosopher of science Bruno Latour tells us that our world is a proliferation of 'hybrids', networks that are simultaneously 'real, social and narrated'. In particular, nothing can be seen as either 'nature' or 'culture' but rather forms a seamless fabric of 'nature-culture'. The apple tree is a wonderful example of this. Or rather, I should say, the relationship formed between the apple tree, as a representative of nature; me, as a representative of culture; and the story I tell about it, is such an example. For it is out of this network of relationships, through the interactions of the apple tree's 'heterozygosity' (its ability to produce seeds that may grow into completely new different apple trees), and the learned human culture of selection and grafting, that the hybrid form we call 'Bramley's Seedling' has emerged. But if the grown tree is neglected, as has happened to mine for the past seven years, it grows 'out of shape'. The 'proper' shape for the tree emerges in the interaction of the creative capabilities of the species, cultural choices, the inherent qualities of 'Bramley's Seedling', and my pruning and care. I can influence this, but I cannot radically change it.[4]

Another way of looking at this is through the idea of evolutionary symbiosis. Biologist Lynn Margulis shows us that symbiosis is 'crucial to understanding evolutionary novelty'. Of course there is always struggle for space and nutrients, but competition, 'nature red in tooth and claw', is not the primary driver: Margulis describes how new species continually emerge from symbiotic mergers. Dissimilar individuals come together to make larger and more complex beings: freshwater hydra join with photosynthetic partners called Chlorella to create a symbiont capable of both swimming and producing food; prokaryotes (cells without nuclei) join together to form eukaryotes (complex cells with nuclei). We humans would not survive without the symbiotic relationship with bacteria in our gut that help digest food.[5]

We cannot separate ourselves from the natural world, nor can we see that world as separate from us. We are all part of each other: linked in a network of hybrids, all symbionts on a symbiotic planet.

I spent maybe an hour pruning the trees while these thoughts ran through my mind, so absorbed in my work and my reflections that I was surprised to see how many branches and twigs now lay on the ground. It took me quite a while to collect them all into piles of kindling. It would soon be time for another bonfire. I noticed that some of the twigs showed little red dots, flower buds just emerging from their protective winter covering. I selected three from the pile of cuttings and put them in water in the warmth of the house. I wondered whether they would flower.

I watched carefully over two weeks. Slowly, the red dots fattened, added a hint of green and grew into little round balls, tightly folded in their sepals. One morning the sepals were cracked open, revealing creamy petals, still overlapping snugly. After a long wait, they unfolded to show first a hint, then a deeper flush of pink. As the flowers opened fully, the pink disappeared leaving each petal crisply white, spoon-shaped, its surface faintly granular. A minute black speck crawled along the edge of one petal, emphasizing its sharp fragility. And in the middle of each flower, a cluster of yellow stamens reached out to make contact with the world.

The sparse arrangement of dark brown twigs and contrasting white flowers looked fine in a tall glass vase, rather like a Japanese Zen arrangement, both natural and arranged. Outside the March fog held on into the afternoon, filling the valley. The chestnut trees outside my window showed only as black skeletons. I guessed that in the garden buds on the apple trees were still showing only that little hint of red.

We humans may be part of a hybrid, symbiotic network, but we certainly don't behave as if we are. Modern humans have enclosed themselves in an apparently self-sufficient culture with little attention to the consequences of their actions.[6] The Biblical book of Ecclesiastes tells us, 'What has been will be again, what has been done will be done again; there is nothing new under the sun'. But it seems that this ancient book is now proved wrong: what has been is no longer; an unprecedented instability threatens complex life on Earth. The human destruction of the ecology that supports us is taking place at an alarming new scale.

The crisis we face is not just another challenge within the human story, like poverty, war and famine, but a challenge to the continuation of the story itself. Human civilization arose over the past thousands of years in a benign environmental context, a period of stability that our own actions may be bringing to an end. Climate change is just the most dramatic of a nexus of issues that include the loss of soil, the acidification of oceans, the overuse of water, the disruption of ecosystems and the extinction of other life forms on the planet. The list is endless, depressing, terrifying, all brought about by needs — and rampaging overconsumption — of vast numbers of human beings. We live in times of astonishing loss.

My own life has been overshadowed by this gathering crisis. I have a childhood memory, strangely both clear and hazy, that was an intimation of things to come. As a small boy in the 1950s I am sitting at the kitchen table turning the pages of a weekly magazine — possibly *Life* or *Picture Post*. I come on a double-page spread featuring a dramatic black and white photo of a filthy smokestack, illustrating an article pointing toward a future environmental crisis. I ask my mother about it, and her reply brushes my concerns aside as if forbidding even the thought behind the question, "You don't want to think about that, dear." But clearly the notion that life on Earth was precarious lodged in my mind. Through my adult life this early intimation was reinforced: in 1962 by Rachel Carson's *Silent Spring*; in 1968 by Buckminster Fuller's challenging proposal that we live on 'spaceship Earth'; in 1972 by the Club of Rome's *Limits to Growth* report pointing to overshoot and collapse; and in the 1990s by Al Gore's movie *An Inconvenient Truth*; in the new century by the series of increasingly alarming reports from the Intergovernmental Panel on Climate Change; and now daily in reports of rapidly melting of icecaps, record temperatures, violent storms, the bleaching of coral reefs, all indicating that the crisis is on us even faster than even the pessimists thought.[7]

I remember conversations with activist colleagues in the 1990s, agreeing, "We have another ten years to address this, then it will be too late." Yet here we are now, halfway through the second decade of the new millennium, with so little that has really changed. Is it *still* nearly too late, or has the moment, if indeed it existed, actually slipped from our collective grasp? Developments in our ecological understanding, the sustainable technologies that these bring with them and the nascent sense of a global community suggest that so much is possible. There are many proposals, conservative, moderate and radical, about how we might change our politics and economics so as to live more sustainably. Yet so very little has been achieved.

I look in the face of an environmental catastrophe that should overwhelm all other concerns. What does a responsible citizen do in the face of this approaching calamity? How, I ask myself, am I to live in these times in a way that makes some contribution to healing, however small that may be? These questions take me beyond the realm of everyday, practical or political responses to the need for a new account of human life on Earth.

I recall the conversation I had with Thomas Berry, the priest who called himself a geologian or Earth scholar. 'It's all a question of story', he wrote in *The Dream of the Earth*. 'We are in trouble just now because we do not have a good story... of how the world came to be and how we fit into it'. When I met him I asked him, "When there are so many good ideas around about new forms of economics, radically efficient methods of production, renewable energy and so forth, why do we need a new story?" And I remember how he looked me straight in the eye and replied, "Because, Peter, if we don't have a different vision of who we are in relation to the Earth, we won't have the psychic and spiritual energy needed to make the profound changes needed." In addition to practical action, significant change toward sustainability requires a new account of human identity, a fundamental shift in our sense of who we are in relation to the planet that sustains us.[8]

If it all begins with story, the story we are offered in modern times is inadequate. Once upon a time, in the European world, humans understood themselves as placed on Earth in the image of their God. Life may have been brutish and short for many, but they had a secure identity in the scheme of things, in a stable hierarchy, above the animals and below the angels. In the Renaissance a new story emerged of man as the measure of all things, a story captured beautifully in Leonardo's drawing of *Vitruvian Man*. But when Copernicus showed that the Earth circled the Sun along with the other planets he began a movement that displaced human from the centre of things. Copernicus was followed by Descartes and Newton, who envisaged a world of objective matter and blind cause and effect. Two centuries later Charles Darwin and Alfred Russel Wallace showed that humans evolved along with other life on Earth; Nietzsche declared that God is dead. In the late twentieth century modern cosmological science portrays Earth as a tiny planet orbiting an unexceptional star in a medium-sized galaxy in a cosmos that contains more galaxies than there are grains of sand on Earth. All these new understandings have undermined the stories that told us who we came to be and what is our place in the scheme of things: are we still the measure of all things or a chance speck in an uncaring universe?

There is a new story of human identity emerging among ecological thinkers like Thomas Berry and his colleagues Brian Swimme and Mary Evelyn Tucker that tells of the human, along with all other beings, as emerging as part of an evolving planet within an evolving universe. This story tells of the visible universe flaring forth in what is commonly known as the Big Bang and developing over eons of time in ever-greater diversity and complexity. The lighter elements hydrogen and helium emerged early on; the heavier elements necessary for life were created in the explosions of early stars. As second- and third-generation stars were formed, conditions where life might be possible emerged in the planets that circulated on them. One of those stars we call Sun, and one of those planets is Earth, where we know that life began its evolution some 2–3 billion year

It is possible to see this story as one of human insignificance. we are the outcome of random physical processes on a small rocky planet circling a minor star in an insignificant galaxy. That is to continue the story of alienation that Copernicus' work set in train. Or we can see that human emergence, with reflective consciousness and intellectual, emotional, aesthetic capabilities are an outcome of an evolutionary, self-generating universe. We are part of the community of life on Earth, an aspect of the universe aware of itself, reflecting on itself, and celebrating itself. In this view, the human presence brings both enormous creative opportunities and alongside these substantial threats to the well-being of life on Earth.

Part of the problem is that our reflective consciousness is so thoroughly self-absorbed: our interest and attention is focussed almost exclusively on ourselves and those close to us. At our best, we may feel part of a fellowship of humanity or a human family. While our understanding of evolution and ecology tells us that we are also part of the community of life on Earth, we rarely feel that in our bones or our hearts. However much we may assert that we are all part of the same universe, that we are part of the evolution of life on Earth, we still find it difficult to overcome a sense of estrangement, of otherness. As philosopher David Cooper puts it, 'Shouting about humankind being part of nature may mask a fear that it is nothing of the sort'.[10]

In medieval times it was virtually impossible not to believe in the existence of God. That belief was foundational, axiomatic. The shift to a secular society involved a transition from a society in which belief in God was unchallenged and unproblematic to one in which it is one option among many. In modern times, since the Enlightenment, I suggest it is virtually impossible not to experience the world as a collection of objects available to humans as 'natural resources'. While we are beginning to accept that some may have sentience—for example, we are learning that trees communicate though huge fungal networks that connect their roots; and research is casting new light on the extraordinary intelligence of corvids—I think the cultural norm is to accept that humans stand at the top of the evolutionary tree, alone in possessing self-reflective consciousness and destined to have dominion over the Earth and her creatures.[11]

What would it take for we modern humans to fully experience ourselves as part of the whole, in the same fashion that medieval people experienced the existence of God? What does it take to deeply experience the damage to ecosystems as damage to ourselves? "I am not protecting the rainforest," activist and writer John Seed tells us, "I am part of the rainforest protecting myself."[12]

The one thing I am sure of in these confusing times is that we need to shift in our relationship to the planet. This is a practical shift: we must stop wrecking the ecosystems that support our lives. It is a shift in our ways of thinking from seeing a world of separate objects to an interconnected whole. And it is a moral shift, a shift from seeing the Earth and her living and non-living communities as resources for humans to exploit toward seeing the living world as of value for its own sake regardless of its value to humans; and toward seeing humans as part of the community of life on Earth.

Chapter Two

Ecological Pilgrimage

To be a pilgrim is to be connected. We are all connected, we are all related, there is no I and the other, I am the other, the other is me— that is what makes me a pilgrim in life and a pilgrim of the Earth. My pilgrimage is not going somewhere; my pilgrimage is to be one with the universe. I am the universe, and the universe is me.
Satish Kumar
Earth Pilgrim

One morning in early winter, as I walked up the lane from the house to the orchard, I again found these questions about the place of humans on Earth turning over in my mind. "It's time for another pilgrimage at sea," I told myself. It had been a full two years since my last long voyage in my little yacht Coral. I had been guided by Thomas Berry's lament that we modern humans are only talking to ourselves: 'if we do not hear the voices of the trees, the birds, the animals, the fish, the mountains and the rivers, then we are in trouble', he wrote, calling for a renewed 'great conversation' with the more-than-human world.[1] I wrote about that voyage and the many things I had learned from it in my book *Spindrift: A Wilderness Pilgrimage at Sea*.[2] But there was more to learn, and I was drawn again to the challenge and adventure of single-handed sailing.

Immediately, the many reasons why I shouldn't go came flooding over me. I worried about leaving Elizabeth on her own; I knew we would miss each other's company. I would be neglecting the house and the orchard. And maybe as I approached 70 I was getting too old for challenging adventures. I remembered how tired, uncomfortable, lonely and homesick I had been at times on my last long voyage and asked myself why

I didn't stay in the comfort of home. I thought about the dangers of storms and shipwreck, imagining Coral shattered against rocks or sunk without trace far offshore. But still I wanted to go.

This time, I told myself, I would take two years: the first summer I would sail right round the west coast of Ireland and leave Coral for the winter on the west coast of Scotland; the second year I would sail round the north of Scotland and return back to the west coast through the Great Glen and the Caledonian Canal. And I would take all these questions about the place of humans on Earth with me.

As my plans took shape in my mind, I began to think about my journeys as ecological pilgrimages. I thought of myself as travelling along the 'western edge' — the western extremes of the British archipelago, but also the 'edge' of the Western mindset. While I was going on a real physical journey with all the adventure that entails, I also had a wider purpose in seeking illumination of my questions: how we modern humans may deepen our sense of being participants in the ecology of the planet. I expected that adventure and pilgrimage would be intertwined and overlaid one with the other; that special experiences would occur at quite unexpected moments.

And so it turned out. There was that day when Coral lay at a visitors' buoy at Craighouse on Jura in the Western Isles of Scotland for two days and two nights while the northwesterly gale blew. Fierce squalls came gusting down through the mountains, bringing heavy rain rattling on the deck and sprayhood. For the past month I had been sailing from Clifden on the west coast of Ireland, mostly on my own. The weather had been particularly difficult: there had been good sailing days but these were nearly always followed by strong winds and high seas that kept Coral at sheltered anchorages. I had been away long enough and was keen to get to her winter berth near Oban.

Eventually the gale blew through. Overnight the wind

dropped away to nothing. In the grey dimness just before dawn I dropped the lines on the mooring buoy and steered Coral out of the bay. The green and red navigation lights that mark the channel between Goat Island and the underwater reefs flashed reassuringly. Once clear of the island I turned Coral north up the Sound of Jura, intent on catching the last quarter or so of the flooding tide north toward Oban. I had it all worked out: the tide times, the landmarks, the alternative anchorages along the coast.

When the tide turned against me, I took Coral into Lussa Bay, tiny, south facing, twelve miles or so north from Craighouse, and tucked her in behind a rocky peninsula out of the stream. A lone cormorant stood sentinel on the tip of the rocks. Low cloud enveloped the hilltops and mist descended to sea level, full of dampness that now and again turned into light rain. The ensign hung soggily from the backstay. Through the mist the tones of the land were subdued: a sharp green scrub, russet brown bracken, punctuated by the black silhouettes of windblown trees; rocks dark and wet at the waterline, lighter above. In contrast to this wildness, at the head of the bay I could just see a little pocket of cultivation: a house showing white amid a cluster of mature trees; a bridge over a stream; a meadow where a brown horse was grazing.

Once I was sure the anchor was secure, I cut the engine. Its mechanical grumble and the churn of the propeller had filled my ears for two hours. Once it stopped, I felt the silence as a tangible presence inviting me to open to my surroundings. Gradually my ears cleared of engine noise and I could hear the subtle watery sounds around me: the background burbling of the tidal stream out in the sound; the deeper, hollow percussion of wavelets slopping against the rocks; the occasional creaks from the engine as it cooled down; above all these the faint patter of fine rain on the deck and sprayhood that came and went as showers blew through the bay, punctuated by the thud of larger drops falling from the boom.

As I stood in the companionway out of the rain, looking across the bay, I heard a guttural call. I looked around and saw a raven flapping its wings to land among the rocks, the inky black of its feathers penetrating the rain mist and standing out strongly against the grey of the rocky shore. I watched as it searched the foreshore. Then another movement caught my eye, across the water this time: an otter, maybe, but more likely a seal. I searched the surface hopefully, but saw no further sign.

I came into this bay for the purely practical purpose of waiting out the adverse tide. But I was enchanted. I spent hours watching, listening, scribbling incoherent notes as I searched for the right words. The quiet of this bay silenced my mind. I was absorbed with just being there.

By mid-afternoon the ebb had weakened. It was time to get going again so as to reach the tidal race at the Sound of Luing at slack tide. I started the engine, hauled up and stowed the anchor, edged Coral round the low rocky headland that had sheltered us and continued northwards.

Through the winter before I set out I looked into the notion of pilgrimage. There is a longstanding tradition in most human societies of making a more or less arduous journey away from the comforts and familiarities of home in search of new insights and deeper understandings. This practice may be as old as the human species: Mesolithic peoples in Europe certainly made long journeys to the sacred sites marked by stone circles; the Aboriginal people of Australia still take extended walks along 'songlines', re-enacting the journeys of 'creator-beings' during the Dream Time.

The idea and practice of pilgrimage was systematically forged in a religious context. I read of the requirement of good Muslims to undertake the Hajj at least once in their lives; of the Christian pilgrimages of the Middle Ages and the continuing contemporary practice; the vast numbers of Hindu devotees who travel to sacred sites on the River Ganges; and of Buddhists who walk the difficult path to circumambulate Mount Kailash. In modern times the word has perhaps become devalued, it has become customary to speak of pilgrimage in a secular sense: a Wagner devotee may describe a trip to the Bayreuth *Festspielhaus* as a pilgrimage, as might a cricket lover a visit to Lords.[3]

The English term 'pilgrim' originally comes from the Latin word *peregrinus* (*per*, through plus *ager*, field, country, land), which means a foreigner, a stranger, someone on a journey, or a temporary resident. It can describe a traveller making a brief journey to a particular place or someone settling for a short or long period in a foreign land. *Peregrinatio* was the state of being or living abroad; and of course all Christians were seen as temporary residents in this world, 'strangers and pilgrims in the Earth', travelling toward 'a heavenly country'. Here on earth, wrote St Augustine, Christians wander 'as on pilgrimage through time looking for the Kingdom of eternity'. This contrasts with an ecological view that we are indigenous Earthlings first: we are not just passing through; we evolved with and profoundly belong to this planet. Our place is not in heaven, but here. As Aldo Leopold, one of the originators of the modern ecological movement, put it, we are plain members of the biotic community.[4]

In modern times, the idea of pilgrimage falls within so many cultural and spiritual traditions that it holds no single meaning. However, it usually entails a long journey in search of qualities of moral or spiritual significance, a journey across both outer physical and inner spiritual landscapes. A pilgrim separates herself from home and familiars, may join with a group of like-minded seekers, sometimes wearing special clothes or other marks that indicate their pilgrim status. In an important sense the pilgrim leaves the everyday and familiar, and journeys through an in-between space toward some transcendent purpose. The Hindu concept of the *tirtha*, a Sanskrit term for a ford or intersection between two realms, expresses this well. Places where two ecosystems meet, such as the brackish water of lagoons, are rich with lifeforms and ecological adaptation. As the Catholic writer Douglas Christie puts it, 'The liminal space of the pilgrimage journey offers a fluid and imaginative space between the human and the more-than-human worlds, between matter and spirit, body and soul, heaven and Earth, humanity and divinity'.[5]

I studied many accounts of religious pilgrimages, learning how the faithful travel to sacred sites in order to encounter a holy realm for worship and the affirmation of faith, in search of illumination and for healing. I began to draw parallels with my idea of ecological pilgrimage as seeking a primal, heartfelt connection with the Earth itself and the community of life that has evolved on Earth. It is also an ongoing celebration of that connection and an act of homage, honouring the Earth as the more-than-human world of which we are a part, existing for itself rather than for human use. By taking the pilgrim away from the habits of civilization and by disrupting the patterns of everyday life, pilgrimage offers an opening to a different view of the Earth of which we are a part.

It was straightforward, coming from the east, to find the point of Rubh' Ardalanish toward the southwest corner of Mull. The pilot book gave directions for an anchorage amongst the rocks just inside the headland: do not cross the twenty metre sounding line until you have identified the double-headed rock Sgeir an Fheidh; then line up the eastern edge of the rock with the stream at the head of the bay until the anchorage opens clear to starboard.

But on my own it was quite tricky. I had to get the mainsail down and stowed, to lift the anchor on to the bow roller ready for dropping, and to make sure the chain was running free, while Coral rolled extravagantly in the cross swell. All that done, I approached the bay cautiously, keeping an eye on the depth sounder. Feet braced each side of the cockpit, holding the pilot book in one hand and the tiller in the other, I talked myself into the opening. "Which rock is Sgeir an Fheidh? That one? No, it must be that other one, although it looks much bigger than I imagined. Ah, there is the stream tumbling down a little valley." As so often happens, what I could see and what was sketched on the chartlet suddenly fell into place.

There were steep cliffs ahead and rocks all around so I took her in steadily, just fast enough to keep steerageway. "Is that the way in to starboard? It looks very narrow!" Closer and closer to the shore, wondering still if Coral was in the right place, then the anchorage opened up, a wider entrance than I feared. I swung the tiller over to take Coral between the rocks into still, deep water with plenty of room for a little boat like her to swing. I circled round to check depths, chose a spot and soon had her securely anchored.

Then I looked around. The anchorage was landlocked in all directions except due west, where the rocks and reefs I had just negotiated gave shelter. Immediately, I felt blessed: this little bay was safe, almost cosy; and even in the drizzle that had started to fall, breathtakingly beautiful. The shoreline all around was a tumble of granite boulders, most of them showing clearly the pink tint they carry at this westerly end of the Ross of Mull. Just a few metres away from Coral's stern, along the shore lay a line of boulders, their faces criss-crossed with fissures set by the stresses created when the granite spewed molten out of the Earth. They show no identifiable pattern, but I remember how my old friend and complexity theorist Brian Goodwin described these as following a mathematically chaotic form; he thought that such natural forms, in contrast to the sharp angles of urban environment, stimulated relaxation in the brain. As I gazed at this chaotic fissured tumbling I felt my mind come into a sense of peace and quiet.[6]

Is it necessary to go on a long and arduous journey to open such experiences? Satish Kumar, who as a young Jain monk made an 8,000-mile pilgrimage for peace, walking from India over the Himalayas to Paris, suggests that pilgrimage is not necessarily about travel, but that its essence lies in its deep commitment to life, here and now on the Earth. He writes that: 'A pilgrim is someone who keeps their mind and heart open for whatever is emerging—it is that openness that puts you on a pilgrimage, not how many miles you physically travel'. While I accept this important point, the significance of travel is that it takes you out of the taken-for-granted structures and habits of everyday life: work, family, relationships, play, news, entertainment, all of which shape consciousness into a conformity that is conducive to modern life. It is not easy to move across the boundaries between worlds when locked in everyday familiarity: the practical challenges of pilgrimage spin the human heart and mind into new realizations.[7]

I thought of the ecological pilgrim as journeying into the wild, whether the distant wild of the seas or mountains or the more immediate wild of a meadow flower. The wild in this sense can release us from the constraints of everyday consciousness. The ecological pilgrim starts from a sense of the importance and legitimacy of unmediated, direct experience of the more-than-human, independent of any benefits that might arise out of that experience. Poet and wilderness writer Gary Snyder describes the wilderness pilgrim's 'step-by-step, breath-by-breath' progress into the wild, whether the wild of mountains or ocean or meditation as 'an ancient set of gestures', that bring a sense of joy. It's a joy that arises through 'intimate contact with the real world' and so also with oneself. While the modern eye may see pilgrimage in its traditional sense as full of superstition, self-delusion and even mass hysteria, if we look beyond these preju-dices to the 'ancient set of gestures', to the underlying archetype, we may discover how practices of pilgrimage can inform the development of ecological sensitivity and responsiveness.[8]

So pilgrims are travellers in life, rather than tourists. I mean this in the sense that the veteran travel writer Paul Theroux used it: Tourists don't know where they've been; travellers don't know where they're going. Theroux was, of course, being mischievous, but he touches on an important truth: most us live our lives half asleep (as the spiritual teacher Gurdjieff, among many others, has pointed out). Pilgrimage is one attempt to wake up. In particular, we modern humans think we know where we are going, but actually we don't: an important dimension of the crisis of ecology is that, with our interconnected, global and increasingly virtual society, we do not know how to live well on the Earth. It may be that small groups of humans still do, or once did (although the evidence is that humans started what is now known as 'the sixth extinction' as soon as we got effective hunting tools; and impoverishing the land as soon as we started agriculture). So the ecological pilgrim is on a journey of inquiry that is potentially relevant to all humanity, not just the privileged West.[9]

This is why pilgrimages into the wild world are one response to the ecological crisis of our times. They are not, of course, a sufficient response, for we also urgently need a whole range of political, financial, technological and cultural initiatives that would change society as we know it. I think they are nevertheless a necessary response that may inform these practical and political concerns. Opening oneself to the wild world and describing what one finds with love and passion is a political and spiritual act.

Christian writer Martin Palmer tells us that to undertake a pilgrimage is to place yourself at risk: not just the physical risks, but the risk that you may not return the same person as you set out. He also warns that the pilgrim may even be risk being surprised by joy.[10] Alone at sea I was often disoriented from the taken-for-granted realities of the social world and open to a more naked sense of what it was to be a human being. At such moments it was as if a crack in the cosmic egg opened and for a tiny moment I experienced a different world that is nevertheless the same world. This was a world not fixed in form, but forever changing: no longer divided into separate things, but one dancing whole. I realize that these tiny moments also occur in everyday life, but they are easy to overlook, to see as insignificant. I have come to call these experiences 'moments of grace', a recovery of the sacred dimension of being. In this book I explore more deeply these moments of grace, how they may arise in the terror of tumultuous seas as much as in the wonder of the night sky. I also explore those times I fall from grace—moments of 'disgrace', maybe—when I lose my centre, my sense of purpose and everything looks like a failure.

Chapter Three

Getting Ready

It was only towards the end of last autumn that I returned from rambling along the coast. I barely had time to sweep the cobwebs from my broken house on the River Sumida before the New Year, but no sooner had the spring mist begun to rise over the field than I wanted to be on the road again to cross the barrier-gate of Shirakawa in due time. The gods seemed to have possessed my soul and turned it inside out, and roadside images seemed to invite me from every corner, so that it was impossible for me to stay idle at home. Even while I was getting ready, mending my torn trousers, tying a new strap to my hat, and applying moxa to my legs to strengthen them, I was already dreaming of the full moon rising over the island of Matsushima.

Matsuo Basho
The Narrow Road to the Deep North

I travelled down to Plymouth to see Coral in mid-February. The previous autumn I had seen her lifted out of the water and settled ashore on timber props. I had taken off all the soft furnishings and other things that might deteriorate over the winter to store at home. Now my mind was full of the jobs that needed to be done before she could be launched and ready for a long voyage: build a new hatch cover for the gas locker, varnish the bright woodwork, take the batteries home to recharge them. I needed to scrub the decks clean, polish the topsides, renew the antifouling, and grease the seacocks.

It was a bitterly cold but bright late winter day. Light clouds were blowing in from the northwest on a blustery wind, bringing dry but near freezing air from Scandinavia. I could see the treetops tossing about as I drove down the motorway. Early daffodils nodded around at the service station where I stopped for coffee, and the feathers on the crows lurking around for scraps of food were raised up by the wind.

The boatyard was packed with yachts resting in their cradles or chocked up with timber props. I found Coral hemmed in next to an old wooden fishing boat, recently worked timber showing where a repair was underway, and a large yacht with husband and wife in overalls painting on antifouling. Coral looked forlorn. The antifouling below the waterline was faded and chipping off; the white topsides grubby and smudged with red from the bootline; the teak toerail green with algae. I had not been near her in four months. I unlocked the ladder and climbed up to deck level—some ten feet above ground—and stood in the cockpit looking around. Through the jumble of cabins and masts I could see down to the familiar Cattewater—the navigable lower reaches of the River Plym. A few yachts were afloat on the lines of moorings, presumably belonging to brave souls who continue to sail through the winter months. Further downstream a cargo ship was unloading at the commercial quay, a crane scooping sand from the hold and dropping it into huge lorries that shuddered under the increasing load.

Coral's decks were grubby after the winter ashore. Stripped of sails and running rigging she looked strangely naked. But it didn't take much for me to imagine her afloat and fully rigged, to remember how she heeled over to meet the wind and lifted her bows to the waves. At just under 32 feet long, narrow of beam, she is compact compared with most modern yachts. A Rustler 31, designed and built in the 1960s, her hull is a classic wineglass shape, curving into a long, deep keel, ballasted with several tons of lead. All this means she rides deep in the water and is extremely seaworthy—as we discovered the first year we had her when caught out in a gale in the middle of the Bay of Biscay. I looked forward beyond the mast to the fine bows, remembered how they cut through the water, sometimes throwing up sheets of spray.

But this was no time for reverie; I was high up, exposed and getting very cold. The sharp wind grasped my attention, howling through the masts and wire rigging of the hundreds of boats clustered together in the yard. A continual low moan filled my ears, overlaid with screeches of banshee wailing that built and diminished as the squalls came and went. The wind rattled the halliards against hollow metal masts in a regular percussive beat that rose a hysterical commotion in the squalls.

I opened the companionway and climbed down into the cabin, which was chilly and unwelcoming with all the soft uphol-stery removed for the winter. But at least I was out of the wind. I shook the kettle and found it had enough water for a cup of tea, so I lit the gas ring and, while waiting for it to boil, looked around. Coral's main cabin is small; some would say cramped. At the foot of the companionway the galley area is to port, with a two-burner stove and racks for crockery and cooking pans. To starboard is the navigation table, with storage place for charts underneath, a bookcase for almanacs, tidal charts and sailing directions, and an array of instruments. Further forward is the main living area, with bunks to port and starboard that also serve for daytime seating, and an additional pilot berth higher on the port side. There are lockers of various shapes and sizes wherever the boat builder could fit them in; and a table that folds down from the bulkhead. All the bunks are narrow, equipped with a lee cloth or board so you don't fall out when asleep at sea. Forward through a sliding door is the heads, a cramped space for the sea water toilet and opposite a hanging space for wet wear. Tucked up in the bows is the forecabin, which has two more bunks for occasional use; while sailing shorthanded I use it as a storage space.

Even without milk, my mug of tea warmed me up, and I managed to do the essential jobs, going up on deck for the shortest periods possible. I measured up for the hatch cover, unbolted the power lines from the batteries and carefully lowered them over the side and down to the ground. Most important, I had a good look at Aries, the wind steering gear mounted on the stern.

Without Aries, long distance single-handed sailing would be impossible. In most winds I can set it to steer Coral for hour upon hour, making continual adjustments, never tiring, never getting distracted, always following the wind. Particularly going to windward, Aries will steer better, more consistently and in stronger winds than most human beings, and certainly for longer. It consists of a solid cast aluminium frame, is strongly bolted to the transom, supporting a windvane above and a paddle deep in the water below, connected to the tiller by a clever set of gears and pulleys. But its gearing had been pulled out of true when the mooring line got wrapped around it toward the end of last season, and I needed some pictures to send to the manufacturer so they could tell me how to correct it.

By the time I had taken a few pictures my hands were rigid with the cold, clumsy every time I tried to do something delicate, and hurting badly when I knocked them against a hard object. I did the minimum needed, locked up again and retreated to the car. The big jobs of cleaning up and antifouling would have to wait for warmer weather.

Over the next weeks I felt I was just waiting: waiting for spring to arrive and the daffodils to come out; waiting for it to be warm enough to get Coral ready for my voyage; waiting to get on with my plans. This waiting created a space that amplified all my worries and fantasies about the voyage: anxiety seems to breed in this empty gap between present and future. At times I wondered what on Earth I was up to.

Preparations for a pilgrimage also demand attention to what was left behind. As well as practical preparations for the voyage, I had been making sure all the jobs that needed my attention in the house, garden and orchard had been completed. More importantly, I was concerned to leave relationships in good order. In particular I was leaving my wife Elizabeth on her own. Maybe inevitably those left behind will feel bereft as one departs, feeling deserted for some cause that was seen as more important. And one may feel some degree of responsibility, if not guilt, for leaving them. These issues cannot be resolved, but do need careful attention.

What had to be given up was also important. Many little things: while I would probably catch the best of the apple blossom before I left, I would miss the burgeoning of the 'upstart Spring' in our garden. Since I planned for Coral to be away from her home port for two, maybe three years, I decided to give up the familiar mooring she had occupied for the last fifteen years, give away the hard dinghy I no longer needed to row out from the shore. In the greater scheme of things this was no big deal, but letting go was strangely upsetting. And more than this: my intention was that at the end of this voyage I would sell Coral and let her go to a new owner. By then I would be in my early seventies, time enough to hang up my waterproofs. To give up my identity as a sailing person would involve a huge shift in my sense of who I am and how others see me.

All these personal worries about the voyage rubbed up against my concern for the state of the Earth, and climate change in particular. The winter had been long and hard. Persistent high pressure had brought northerly winds and arctic weather over the country for weeks on end. Would we ever move beyond this extended winter, this long cold spring? If changes in the climate brought a southerly extension of the Arctic weather systems, would we ever again have a proper maritime climate? Would rain-bearing depressions ever again come in from the Atlantic, bring their wet warmth to our islands? What did the future hold and, more immediately, was the weather now so unpredictable to make it unwise to undertake a long voyage in a small yacht?

But there was more to do than worry: practical things needed attention. I had conceived of the voyage looking at small-scale passage charts; now I needed detailed charts and sailing directions for the whole of the west coast of Ireland and on through the Western Isles of Scotland. Charts are expensive, so I was fortunate to be able to borrow many of those I needed from the chart collection of the Rustler Yacht Association. I also needed to begin to familiarize myself with the waters where I would be sailing: I knew the Irish coast as far as Dingle from previous voyages, but beyond that all was unfamiliar. I spent many evenings reading sailing directions and checking them against the charts.

Then there was the question of crew. I intended to be alone for much of the voyage. I had set Coral up for single-handed sailing, enjoyed being on my own, and on the whole felt a lone pilgrimage offered better opportunities for addressing the questions I was exploring. But it seemed wise to have someone with me on the overnight passage across the Irish Sea, and my friend Steve agreed to come with me for the first two weeks. Steve is very practical, a motor engineer with lots of sailing experience, although mainly on the sheltered waters of the Solent.

In the previous autumn I was invited to join a residential week with students in outdoor education at the University of Edinburgh, to run some sessions on creative writing in response to the landscape of the Cairngorms. I enjoyed our conversations, and thought it would be interesting to have some younger people with outdoors experience on board. I suggested that some of them might like to join me on Coral for a week during my voyage. Suzy and Gib agreed to join me in July; Susi and Dave in September.

After weeks of penetrating cold, a series of proper Atlantic depressions swept across England bringing warm southwesterlies, several days of rain, then a spell of sunny weather over Easter. At last the primroses were out and there was a hint of pink on the apple trees. Blessed relief! I could at last get down to Plymouth to get Coral ready for launching. It is amazing how much work it takes to turn her from a grubby lump of fibreglass sitting on its props in the boatyard into a working and homely yacht. I installed the batteries that had been on charge at home, followed the manufacturer's advice about adjusting the Aries steering gear, cleaned the cruddy marks along the waterline, painted on two coats of antifouling and made sure everything was sound below the waterline. It was a physically exhausting day, but doing something practical was an immense relief.

Once she was ready to launch, the yard crew put slings under her keel, lifted her off her props with their massive forklift truck, carried her to the dock and lowered her gently in the water alongside the pontoon. This was, as always, a moment of minor and quite unnecessary anxiety: will she float? I scrambled on board and checked the seacocks and propeller shaft: there were no signs of leakage, so the slings could be released. Once she was safely moored, I carried three trolley loads of equipment and stores from the car down to the pontoon and heaved them on board, finishing quite late at night.

The following morning I awoke, feeling rather cold, to a cabin in complete chaos. Nothing was in the right place: the second bunk was a heap of bedding and bags of clothes, the pilot berth was still full of boxes of victuals, the forecabin was a muddle of goodness knows what. Through the morning I worked to stow everything, which often meant moving things from one wrong place to another wrong place in order to put something else in the right locker. It was as if there had to be more chaos along the way to finding order. Eventually the pile disappeared, leaving just one or two things yet to find a home.

After I got the cabin in order I set to work on the deep lockers in the cockpit: how to get two containers for diesel and two for fresh water stowed safely in a way that I could still access the heavy anchor that lives at the bottom of the port locker? I took everything out, re-coiled ropes so they were ready for use, and eventually managed to find a place for everything. Once that was done there were the sails to get out of their bags and rigged. Finally, I got out the bosun's chair and climbed halfway up the mast to attach the lazy jacks that support the sail when it is lowered.

At times I was close to tears—there was so much mess, so much to do, and I was so tired. At other moments I had a glimpse of the delights of being aboard and was strangely happy. Eventually I let go the lines, motored down river and tacked to and fro across Plymouth Sound, gradually getting back into the feel of Coral under sail. I found a quiet place to anchor in Jennycliff Bay. With a warm supper and bottle of beer inside me, I watched the sun go down in a completely clear sky, the street lamps flicking up one by one on the waterfront, and the house lights showing dimly in Cawsand and Kingsand on the far side of the Sound. As darkness gathered deeper, I lit the Tilley lamp, set up the anchor light, tied the halliards away from the mast so they didn't rattle in the night and walked round the deck to make sure everything was in order. The green starboard hand marker at the easterly extreme of the deep shipping channel flashed green every five seconds. All was well. I climbed early into my bunk.

The following day I sailed around Plymouth Sound, putting Coral through her paces and making sure everything was in working order. All seemed well until I came to furl the genoa, hauling on the line that runs forward from the cockpit and round a drum at the bottom of the forestay. The first half of the sail rolled up easily, then it jammed: it would neither furl further nor pull out again. Squinting up the mast I could see the wire halliard had somehow wrapped itself around the top of the furling gear.

Back in the shelter of Jennycliff Bay, I got out the bosun's chair and climbing ascenders and, after making sure everything was secure, hauled myself up the spinnaker halliard to the top of the mast. I have watched young riggers swarm up a mast in no time at all, but I took my time: sit back in the bosun's chair, pull up the foot strop and let the cam in the ascender grip the rope; stand in the strop and raise the chair; sit back in the chair and repeat the process. Foot by foot, then awkwardly over the cross trees, to where the shrouds close in at the masthead. Coral's mast is not so very high, but nevertheless, from up there the deck looked a very long way down, and the height of the mast exaggerated the slight roll of the boat.

The wire halliard was not only horribly twisted around the rotating forestay but also tangled around itself. The hard wire was harsh on my cold hands, and as I worked on it I had to let go of the mast, lean back from the bosun's chair and stretch out to the forestay with my legs clutching around the mast. Once the wire was free, I let myself back down the mast. This I always find trickier than going up because the cams on the ascenders grip the rope very tight: each has to be freed up then lowered. Back on deck my hands were sore and my legs were trembling, but I was pleased with myself, and even more pleased to have found the problem in the calm of Plymouth Sound rather than in the open sea. Before I left for Ireland, I would need to install a new halliard.

Later that day, back on the mooring, going over all the work I had done in the last two days, I heard a quiet voice in the back of my mind. It was as if some internal Zen Master was speaking me, saying, "Of course, if this really is a pilgrimage these things that are thrown at you are part of the process. Step by step, breath by breath, one challenge after another. Every contingency is an opportunity for you to be awake to the moment." Very true, although these internal voices can be very annoying.

Chapter Four

Leaving

This longing to retreat just at the point of achieving your heart's desire... Certain men do an about-face at the crucial moment. I'm afraid I might be one of them.
Sylvain Tesson
Consolations of the Forest

As the date Steve and I had set for leaving for Ireland approached, the Met Office issued a warning for a period of strong winds and rough seas. It had been a lovely spring weekend, but a deepening area of low pressure was closing in on the high that brought the sunshine; squeezed between the high and the low, the westerly winds intensified. The seas were forecast to be not just 'rough' but 'very rough, becoming high'. 'High' is such an unusual term in a summer shipping forecast I had to look it up: it refers to wave heights of six to nine metres. Coral is only nine metres long. I delayed departure: we were not going sailing.

The waiting amplified my diffuse anxiety about leaving. I wanted to get on my way, to see all my plans unfold. At the same time, I didn't want to go, didn't want to leave my everyday life behind, didn't want to deal with the challenges of being at sea. Above all I wanted to get over the dreadful ambivalence of waiting. I knew that patience was what was needed, patience, respect and careful judgement about when it would be safe and sensible to sail. But I was irritated and restless.

Eventually the winds moderated and we slipped out of Plymouth for the short hop down channel to Fowey. The following morning we picked up the first of the west-going tide to round Dodman Point, then hardened the sheets and set off close-hauled down the coast toward Falmouth. It seemed at first that we might make it on one tight tack. But through the afternoon the wind freshened, became squally and backed against us. Sailing became seriously cold and unpleasant. Coral plunged into steep waves, throwing up sheets of water that crashed on to the deck and sprayhood. The wind pushed Coral out toward the Lizard rather than into Falmouth Bay. We tacked round and headed inshore, seeming to make up the lost ground, but when we turned again the wind had freshened again and backed even more.

The last few miles were really hard work. The wind blew the tops off the waves, covering the sea surface with white horses. As we tacked back and forth, tired, huddled miserably under the sprayhood, my anxiety returned. I imagined that the whole voyage would be like this, a fight against contrary winds. I felt the wind was trying to drive me back home, to tell me that this was all folly. Why, oh why, was I doing this?

At last we reached the shelter of Falmouth Bay. The sea smoothed out as we turned to make a final tack between the castle and Black Rock into Carrick Roads, then motor safely into the Yacht Haven. But the weather was not finished with us. That evening, as groups of skippers gathered on the pontoons, chatting over the latest forecast and discussing options for the following day, a wild squall blew downriver. Within minutes the boats moored in the open river were tossing about in sharp waves. Inside the Yacht Haven boats moored on the windward side were blown hard against the pontoons, their fenders squashed flat; some even threatened to blow right over the pontoon. Those moored to leeward were more fortunate, simply blown to the end of their mooring lines—although some were so far out that their crews were unable to get back on board. It became difficult to walk safely on the bucking pontoons. The wind howled through the rigging, reading fifty knots on my wind indicator (other skippers say they recorded nearly sixty).

We were reasonably safe, but this was a terrifying warning of what the weather could do. Then, as quickly as it had started, the wind dropped away.

The next day brought more challenges. We caught the morning tide around the Lizard, but as we crossed Mount's Bay the wind again freshened and headed us. Not wanting to tack all through the night to the Scillies, as we passed Wolf Rock Lighthouse I started the engine and we motorsailed westward. The motion was horrible. For hour after hour we plunged on, forcing Coral directly over the waves until Steve, more used to the sheltered waters of the Solent, was on the edge of being seasick. As evening approached and the light faded, low cloud covered the sky; thankfully only a little rain spat at us.

It was a relief when at last, through the gloom, we picked out Peninnis Head lighthouse, then the three quick flashes of the cardinal buoy marking Spanish Ledges in St Mary's Sound. By the time we were alongside the buoy it was completely dark, and we had to pick our way along the line of flashing red lights on the port-hand buoys marking the sound. After passing the last buoy I turned Coral to starboard toward the harbour; suddenly rocks loomed out of the night in front of us, a patch of darker black with a line of white foam at the foot. I realized that in my impatience to get on to a mooring, I had cut the corner and gone too close to the unlit coast of St Mary's. I sheered off quickly into deep water and kept well clear of the shore until we saw the leading lights into Hugh Town. In the brightly lit harbour it was then easy to pick up a mooring.

The following day the weather was fine: a lovely day in the Scillies, with azure water, golden beaches, and fresh green grass and trees, just like the travel brochures. We should have been able to rest and prepare for crossing to Ireland. But other things start to go wrong. First of all, the outboard started dripping petrol, leaving nasty oily patches on the water. We spent about an hour stripping down the carburettor, not finding anything obviously wrong, but somehow solving the problem.

Once that was sorted, Steve went ashore to explore while I stayed on board to rest. When I tried to light the stove to make tea, I found the gas bottle had run out. The spare was stored in the depths of the cockpit locker: I had to haul everything out, including the heavy containers of water and diesel, and pile them untidily round the cockpit while I dug out one of the two full bottles and replaced the empty one. After I had packed everything back in the locker I tried to light the stove for a cup of tea. No gas came out, even though the new cylinder was heavy, as if full. Everything had to come out of the locker again to get the other spare bottle. This one worked, but why didn't the first one? I tried one, then the other, then the first one again, getting hot and sweaty as I hauled heavy bottles around. I began to feel a bit crazy, as if the world was playing tricks on me but when Steve came back on board he had the same result as me. I *knew* I had two spare bottles, more than enough for the summer. But only one bottle worked and that was not enough; we couldn't sail without being able to make hot food and drink. I was pretty sure that the Irish bottles are bigger and have a different connection. It was like the metaphorical nail missing in the horse's hoof: this could wreck the whole trip. What would I do in a boat with no gas on the west coast of Ireland?

I woke that night in the very early hours needing to pee, as I so often do. I climbed out of my bunk and tiptoed across the creaking cabin sole to the head, hoping that pumping out the sea toilet would not wake up Steve. Back in my bunk I snuggled down again, trying to get warm again after meeting the night chill. But I was wide awake. I checked the time: only four thirty in the morning, although already quite light. I was desperate for more sleep: I lay on my left side, then my right, worming round in the narrow bunk. I rearranged the pillow. Still no sleep. Maybe I should get up and make a cup of tea, but the clank of the kettle would really wake Steve up. "Oh god," I said to myself. "It's much easier on my own and I can be as noisy and grumpy as I like."

With the repetitive anxiousness that so often comes in the small hours, I went over the events of the past days: the strong contrary winds, the howling squall in Falmouth, the close shave with the rocks, the misbehaving outboard, the gas problem. I lost all sense of why I was on this journey; all sense of pilgrimage disappeared. I tossed around in my bunk, uncomfortable, feeling almost sick, "I don't want to be here, I want to go home." And we could go home! Here in the Scillies we were at the point of no return. With the northwesterly winds we had been battering into, it would be easy to sail back to Plymouth, give up this silly idea of pilgrimage. This was the last opportunity I really had to stop, change my mind, return home. After we had got to Ireland there was no option but to go on. My night thoughts went on and on, round and round.

Then I remembered Coral was now homeless: I had given up the mooring that she had been on for so many years. If I went back I would have to put her in an expensive marina. We just had to keep sailing, on to places where we could anchor for free. Then again, I remembered I had decided to sell Coral after this voyage. However much I hated the present moment, she was part of my identity. This cabin was so familiar, so homely... and so uncomfortable, so cramped. Again the thoughts ran around my mind, "I don't want to go sailing, I don't want to start the crossing, I want to go back to Plymouth, going straight to the boatyard, get them to lift Coral out of the water and put her on the market. That's the answer."

And another voice replied, "No it's not! You'd be so disappointed! And anyway, how could you explain that to all the people who have made arrangements to fit in with yours? You are just having a panic, like you always do at the start of a long sail. You thought you had confronted all your fears as part of the preparation for the voyage, but you hadn't and you couldn't. The experience is never the same as the anticipation. It will be fine once you are underway, and afterwards you will look back on this as part of the whole voyage."

When Steve woke up I made tea for both of us and tried to tell him about my fears. I found him infuriatingly cheerful, refusing to hear me. "We can't go back now," he said. "You've got this big voyage planned." Somehow I couldn't make him realize that the 'big voyage' was exactly the problem. I lay in my bunk, nursing my warm mug of tea, utterly miserable and dejected.

But with the gathering warmth of the morning, something inside me began to turn: the weather would change, we could get the outboard fixed, and surely there would be a way around the gas problem. Steve was right: this long sail was something I had wanted to do for years.

I hauled myself out of my bunk and checked the weather forecast: the winds had moderated, northeasterly for a while backing northerly later. If we left this morning we should be able to make a course north by west to Baltimore on the southwestern corner of Ireland. Suddenly I was energized: I worked out a course that gave us the option of alternative landfalls at Schull or Crookhaven. My optimism returned: if the wind held favourable we might even stay at sea a second night and go all the way to Bantry Bay.

The routine of getting ready—porridge and more tea, setting waypoints in the GPS, making sure everything was safely stowed, starting the engine, loosening the sails ready to hoist, dropping the line from the buoy and motoring north out of New Grimsby Sound—all seemed to help me to drop my panic and my grumpiness and simply get on with the business of sailing. In the cold, bright morning sun the sea looked inviting for a small yacht. The wind was just right for the passage. I started to enjoy myself.

In the first phase of the *rite of passage* that is pilgrimage, the pilgrim is separated from their social milieu. This separation can be joyful, but also experienced as a wrench in leaving the comforts of home and launching into adventure. Things fall apart. There is loss of faith, struggle, doubt and hope: the whole venture appears foolish, ridiculous. What is the point?

It is not uncommon for travellers to feel resistant at the point of setting out. For years the French writer and traveller Sylvain Tesson had wanted to spend the winter in a small cabin in Siberia. In *Consolations of the Forest* he writes about the challenge of even rousing himself from bed on the morning he is to set out, and wonders if he will undermine his own desire. In *The Snow Leopard*, Peter Matthiessen describes the calamitous weather and uncertainty about porters at the beginning of his trip into the Himalayas. The forthcoming journey is losing all sense of reality, and he asks, 'where did I imagine I was going, where and why?'[1]

I suspect that in order to gather the energy for a significant journey we have to idealize it in our minds beforehand. There has to be some grand purpose to make it all worthwhile. So I had described my voyage as a pilgrimage (rather than as a sailing cruise). I had thought of it as a 'deep ecology homage'; I considered my pilgrimage as a contribution to the ecological challenge of our times. But once I set off, these worthy ambitions ran up against the unrelenting and sometimes frightening reality of the wild world. The high-minded purposes become meaningless and difficult to hold on to. The pilgrimage is not all plain sailing, not all peak experience. We can only engage with the world on its own terms, terms that include inclement weather, the contingency of plans, and the unreliability of equipment. And they meet with my fragility as a human being: my mistakes, my indulgence in emotions, my fear, the gap between my high expectations and the reality.

There is something of the ridiculous in this. I boldly wrote that on pilgrimage we leave the comforts and habits of home in order to meet the more-than-human world more directly. But I was discombobulated when I had to live through what this actually meant in practice. The grand purposes with which the pilgrim sets out will only survive and deepen as they are tested against experience.

Speaking about his journeys in Africa, Paul Theroux points out, 'Part of travel writing is about the miserable and the difficult and the inhospitable'. Having a bad time on a trip is helpful: it gives perspective on the wonderful times. But obviously, it doesn't feel like that.[2]

I knew from experience that as the pilgrimage unfolded I would develop a greater resilience. With a more balanced eye, the gloom of the gathering night and lowering clouds would have their own beauty. I would watch Coral plunging through the waves and delight in the elegance of her design. I would look back at the two of us cowering wet and cold in the cockpit and laugh at our misery. But this resilience does not develop until we have lived through the moments of loss of faith, struggle, doubt and hope; these are essential aspects of pilgrimage. They mark the point at which home is really left behind and the pilgrim faces the contingencies of the journey. It is inevitable that at some point the whole venture will appear foolish, impossible. The question of continuing or turning back will arise, and pilgrims, like Eliot's Magi on the way to see the Christ Child, will hear voices in their ears saying that the whole enterprise is folly.

Chapter Five

Moments of Grace

As their eyes met, a bird sang aloud in the branches of the tree. In that moment, Ged understood the singing of the bird, and the language of the water falling in the basin of the fountain, and the shape of the clouds and the beginning and end of the wind that stirred the leaves: it seemed to him that he himself was word spoken by the sunlight. Then that moment passed, and he and the world were as before, or almost as before.

Ursula Le Guin

A Wizard of Earthsea

After our early breakfast Steve and I motored Coral out of Old Grimsby Sound between Tresco and Bryher into the Celtic Sea and sailed north by west through a bright, sunny, but chilly day. Coral danced through the waves, travelling at a good speed toward Ireland on a brisk northeasterly. As usual, we made ourselves comfortable in the cockpit, taking turns to go below and cook up our morning coffee, then lunch, then supper, wedging ourselves safely against the bulkhead next to the cooker while we did so.

Early in the day the sun's low light gave form and texture to the ocean; as it rose higher through the morning and early afternoon, the stronger light flattened out the details and blurred the horizon. With the approach of evening, as the sky turned an ever-darker shade of blue, the waxing half-moon, which had risen in the afternoon as a faint presence, began to dominate the sky.

Around eight we started a formal watch system. Steve took the first three-hour stint, while I went below, settled myself comfortably into the leeward bunk, pulled over my duvet and slept well. When I woke to relieve Steve at eleven it was dark, the moon shining through the cabin windows. After plotting our position on the chart I went on deck, to find him really cheerful, having enjoyed watching the sun set and the day close. "I've been sailing through this lovely night," he told me happily. "No ships to report, nothing in sight but sea and moonlight." Once my eyes had got accustomed to the darkness, I too saw that the sky was still clear, and the moon had moved across the sky toward the west, shining through the sails and casting a shifting silver path across the waves toward us.

Steve went below, and settled into his bunk. I began the familiar routine of a night watch: wedge myself into the corner of the cockpit under the sprayhood out of the wind; get up and look about for ships and fishing boats every fifteen minutes or so; on the hour, go below, note our position from the GPS and plot our progress across on the chart; snack on apples and chocolate. It's a familiar routine that I use to sink into a strange kind of contentment, a quiet, almost thoughtless contemplation of my surroundings.

Coral continued sailing on a starboard tack, now more gently heeled and rocking away in a slight sea. There was nothing big to bang into, just the gentle rhythm of one wave after another passing under the hull, with a deeper note as she breasted a steeper one. The winds so far had been very kind to us: we had kept up well over five knots through the passage so far, sometimes as much as seven, although that had been a little uncomfortable compared with this easy amble through the waves.

It was that kind of beautiful night sailing when everything is only vaguely coloured. In the just-light I could make out, or maybe imagine, the red of my waterproofs, the yellow of the lifebuoy and the silver of the outboard. Looking forward, I could see the moon glinting on the pulpit rails up in the bows, casting lumpy shadows in the troughs between the waves and catching the occasional luminescent breaking peak. When I stood up to look out for ships, my attention was arrested by the path of the moonlight across the sea, fragmented by the waves into tiny flickering points of light so it appeared to be flowing toward me. The cold light sharpened the line between sea and sky in the west and north, while leaving an indistinct blur in the south and east. It lit up Coral's sails and illuminated Aries, the steering gear, showing the windvane moving this way then that as it constantly adjusted Coral's course to keep to the same angle to the wind.

Then, following the sun, the moon began to sink toward the horizon, gradually turning from cold white to a deep yellow, almost orange. As it dropped and changed colour, the world changed with it, becoming darker, less clearly articulated, more mysterious. And in the ever-darkening sky, gradually the stars appeared: first one or two right above me, then a handful, eventually more than I could ever count.

About one in the morning, suddenly and unexpectedly, the wind dropped away and backed northerly. Coral's speed fell back to three knots, two, then practically nothing. Aries, following what little wind there was around, steered her on to a westerly course, away from Ireland and out into the Atlantic. I lost my attention for the moon and stars and started fussing with the sails, the steering, the course. It made no difference: Coral wallowed around uncomfortably, getting nowhere, the boom banging about, the sails flapping aimlessly. What to do? Should I start the engine? But that would wake Steve and I remembered how he hated the movement when Coral was motoring. Should I drag out the big genoa, take it forward on the deck and set it? But it would be silly to work alone on the deck in the middle of the night; stomping around on the deck would also disturb Steve. If the wind stayed light it probably wouldn't do much good anyway.

So I decided to do nothing, just wait, see what happened, and enjoy the night. By this time, with the moon fully set, plunging everything into deeper darkness. The sea now merged with the sky at the horizon so all that was left was the increasing starlight to contrast with the lurking quietness of the sea. I tipped back my cap, and looked up past the green loom of the masthead light into the night sky. Just as I stopped worrying about our progress, something happened that loosened my attention from the multitude of individual stars, even the patterns between them. I looked behind the bright stars into the smoky haze of starlight that filled the sky, faint but dense, profoundly dark and brightly lit at the same time. And with the gazing I was drawn into the infinity of the space above me, so that I felt I was both disappearing into and becoming part of the whole of everything. I am not sure how long this sensation lasted, maybe a few seconds, maybe minutes. But even now as I write it feels like it might well have lasted forever.

It seemed to me, having watched the sun and then the moon traverse the sky through the day, that they create a perceptual firmament, delineate a boundary to our planet, a sense of finiteness. In the daytime the white light of the sun is scattered as it passes through the atmosphere, giving us the illusion of a bowl of blue sky curving from horizon to horizon. Moonlight scatters too, creating a profoundly blue night sky and a similar, though subtler, sense of sky as boundary. But in the profound darkness of a moonless night, particularly when one looks beyond the bright stars and planets into the infinite haze—into what we have learned very recently is not just billions of stars but billions of galaxies—this sense of a boundary disappears. There is not a sphere up there that is 'the sky'. You look beyond and through into some other reality.

The faithful embark on religious pilgrimage in search of a holy realm; my ecological pilgrimage takes me away from the habits of civilization and disrupts the patterns of everyday life in search of an experience of being more fully part of the community of beings on Earth. The theologian Richard Niebuhr suggests pilgrimage reinterprets the word 'experience' for us. In its weak form, he writes, experience just means the flow of moments scarcely distinct one from another. But in its strong form, experience can mean much more:

> ... the passage into ourselves of places and beings previously unfamiliar and an accompanying enlargement of ourselves. With these increments to our being, we are made new, made more thorough kin to the Earth, its elements, and its peoples. Pilgrimage experience is radical experience: exposure to trial and peril, the making of perilous passages from a world grown comfortable and too confining into a world whose vastness we had only dimly surmised. Pilgrimage experience deports us from home; it exports us abroad into an hitherto unimaginable reality.[1]

As William Blake asks, 'What is the price of Experience?' He answers, '... it is bought with the price | Of all that a man hath...'[2] These stronger meanings of experience open up quite unexpectedly, as on that night when I stopped fussing about the technicalities of sailing and opened my attention to the sky. They arise in 'moments of grace', an idea I take from Gregory Bateson's particular brand of systemic thinking. Bateson was one of my intellectual heroes since I first read his book *Steps to an Ecology of Mind* in the early 1970s. He was one of the first to link the environmental crisis with the way humans experience and understand the world. There is, he told us, something fundamentally wrong with our ways of knowing; the conscious, purposive human mind is necessarily damaging to the ecological whole.[3]

Bateson describes how an unspoiled natural ecology consists of a network of many creatures, each of which has the capacity for runaway growth in population. A frog, for example, produces far more spawn than is needed to replace the adult population; some is eaten by newts, some by fish; those that become tadpoles and baby frogs are prey for birds; and so on. Without the predators, frogs would overrun their habitat; without the frogs, the predators would starve. The ecosystem's balance is maintained because the diverse members live in an intricate network of collaboration and competition that is dynamically stable.

In contrast, Bateson argues that the human mind is driven by conscious purpose. It is concerned not with long-term stability but with pursuit of short-term goals. If we poison the slugs in our garden to protect our plants, we also kill the frogs that eat the slugs; then we wonder why we have so many slugs, and where the birds have gone. Conscious purpose is a short-cut device that allows you to get quickly at what you want without regard for the consequences for the wider whole. It cuts through the balancing circuits and undermines the ecosystem's stability.

Some would say that this is a consequence of Western culture. But if it is true that as soon as early humans arrived in a new territory they quickly wiped out the large herbivores, and that agriculture seriously reduced ecological complexity, then this characteristic reaches back into prehistory. In modern times, when conscious purpose is coupled with powerful technology and the reduction of everything to monetary market value, the outcome is often even more devastating. We modern humans have created a world in which destructive error is embedded and in which we now have to live.

Since the environmental crisis is rooted in our ways of thinking, it is not possible to think ourselves out of it, however ingenious we may be. The answer, Bateson proposed, lies not in more rationality but in a reintegration of the 'pattern which connects' — a favourite phrase of his — in particular reconnecting that which is unconscious. The way back to the experience of interconnectedness and intimate interdependency we have lost is through aesthetic, artistic process, both as creative activity and active appreciation. Art, because it is not subject to purposive, language-bound rationality, is capable of re-linking us with our context. He called this the recovery of the grace of embeddedness in the natural world, the sacred dimension of our being:

> I do not know the remedy but there is this: that consciousness can be a little enlarged through the arts, poetry, music and the like. And through natural history. All those sides of life which our industrial civilization tries to mock or put aside.
>
> Never vote for a man who is neither a poet nor an artist nor a birdwatcher.[4]

The word 'grace' is itself ambiguous, appropriately so for such an elusive notion. The word itself derives from the Latin *gratus*, meaning pleasing or thankful; in Spanish *gracias* means both thank you and gratitude.[5] At its simplest it means smoothness and elegance of movement or form: animals in their natural state show grace in the elegance, naiveté and simplicity of their movement. In a social sense, 'grace' includes good manners and a special favour. Grace also holds a special place in Christian theology, although it is the subject of fierce disputes. It conveys the sense of an unmerited and unearned divine assistance, a salvation for sinners. This is beautifully expressed in the traditional Christian Benediction, 'May the grace of the Lord Jesus Christ, the love of God and the Fellowship of the Holy Spirit be with you all.'

Thomas Berry uses the term 'moments of grace' to refer to those privileged periods when great transformations take place. He uses it to describe irreversible moments in the evolution of the universe, such as when the solar system condensed out of the wreckage of an exploding star; to moments in evolution of life on Earth when new forms of life appeared; and to times of major change in human culture—such as the present moment when humans are making an impact on the planet of a geological scale. The poet Carol Ann Duffy uses the same phrase to point to occasions when an individual life is 'shaken', as by first love, so that 'in moments of grace | we were verbs'.[6]

Drawing on this diversity, I use 'grace' to speak of that capacity that integrates the diverse parts of the experience: the physical with the mental, the conscious mind with the unconscious and the human with the more-than-human. We experience grace when intellectual understanding and aesthetic appreciation come together and there is a loosening of the boundary that separates self from the wider whole. Bateson was fond of quoting the Enlightenment mathematician Blaise Pascal, who is famous for observing, "Le coeur a ses raisons que la raison ne connaît point." Moments of grace occur when, *contra* Pascal, the reason of the heart is at one with the reason of reason.

As I sat in Coral's cockpit and gazed at this infinite sky I recalled an earlier experience when the night sky had opened my sense of myself and my world. For several years I was one of thirty Apprentices in the Dreamweavers' Lodge, exploring Earth-based spirituality through Native American Medicine Wheel teachings. Our explorations took us through a series of ceremonies, starting with the Night on the Mountain, a twenty-four-hour vision quest alone on a hillside; and continuing through increasingly challenging encounters with natural and spirit teachers. My Night on the Mountain took place on the cliffs of Ramsey Island in Wales, where I watched the world go to sleep and reawaken with the dawn. I became so quiet that I could hear the wind rustling through the feathers of martins as they flew low over my head to their nearby nests. What I remember most is my experience of the startling beauty of the world around me.

According to Cheyenne writer Hyemeyohsts Storm, the Medicine Wheel teaches that everything on Earth has spirit and life, including the rivers, rocks, Earth, sky, plants and animals. Storm explains that the Medicine Wheel can be understood as a mirror in which everything is reflected: 'Any idea, person or object can be a Medicine Wheel, a Mirror, for man. The tiniest flower can be such a Mirror, as can a wolf, a story, a touch, a religion or a mountain top…'[7]

All beings know their harmony with other beings within the Wheel—except humans. But humans are alone in having a determining spirit, and can find our place in the circle of beings only through direct, intense physical and spiritual encounter with our brothers and sisters. We each can discover our gifts and character, our 'giveaway', through our reflection on the world we live in.

The culmination of the first ceremonial cycle was the Sacred Name ceremony. This took place after several years of practice, once the Apprentice had built their own Medicine Wheel of sacred objects and gone some way to discover their core gifts and qualities. The challenge of the ceremony was to find and confirm a Name to represent this 'sacred essence'. It was not a name to be used every day—I already had been given the Medicine Name Wolfheart—but between oneself and Great Spirit, to serve as a reminder as to who one truly was, and a challenge to live this fully.

I searched for many months for an indication of what my sacred name might be. When the time came for the ceremony, I took my sacred objects, the crystals and icons representing my allies and teachers, along with my staff up to the summit of a hill in mid-Wales in the middle of the night. I laid everything out around me in a Medicine Wheel, called the powers of the Four Directions, and settled down in the middle with my prayers.

My instructions for the ceremony were like this. Having set up the Wheel, I was to call my Name—or what I imagined was my Name—loudly in each of the sacred directions and listen for a response from the world around. The response might be a stirring of the trees, the calling of an owl, or just an inner experience of a reply. If and when there was such a response the second stage was to conjure a sign from the Universe—usually a shooting star—to confirm this. Conjuring involved chanting that would build power to reach through the 'circle of law', which holds all things in their everyday place, and summon this extraordinary event.

My first attempt at calling my Name into the darkness produced no response of any kind at all. There was nothing but a dull silence from all directions. Feeling foolish and crestfallen, I returned to the centre of my Medicine Wheel. What did I expect? Whatever doubts and scepticism I had brought up the hill with me were confirmed: why would the world and spirit respond to me? And what was so special about a name? What was I doing with this New Age nonsense? My rational mind and scientific education ran riot, explaining to myself why this was all so misguided. I sat in the middle of my Medicine Wheel in the dark, feeling profoundly silly. I must have fallen asleep. When I awoke I found I had dreamed a new version of the Name that felt more right, more powerful. And so I called this new Name in the eight directions, and this time had an altogether different feeling, as if something out there was stirring in response.

So, holding myself between hope and scepticism, I went back to the centre and took up my Wolfheart staff. I chanted the words of the conjuring as loudly as I could, swung my staff in a spiral to build a cone of power up into the sky, called out my Name loudly and confidently and pulled my staff in a line across the sky from east to west. And then, full of doubts, still by no means convinced by my own performance, I lay back to see what happened.

The moment my head touched the ground a brilliant star streaked right across the sky above me, from east to west, just as I had commanded. Was this an illusion? No, I was wide awake, fully present: this was a real star that I experienced incontrovertibly as responding to my call. I just lay there for a while, amazed and thrilled. Then, after thanking and releasing the Powers I had called, I collected my ceremonial items together and made my way back down the hill to rejoin the others in the

Lodge.

I was in a most extraordinary state of elation and confusion. To this day my hair stands on end when I recount this story. What I remember most was that I couldn't stop grinning.

For a long while after I didn't tell anyone other than my teacher. I saw all this as private; that it was between me and the cosmos, between me and Great Spirit. I didn't want to seem to be boasting about my spiritual or shamanic capacities. But more recently I have regarded this experience as a teaching that I should share with others. How could this happen to a rational European male like me? For this extraordinary event cuts right through everything we take for granted about the nature of the world. And it seems central to the questions of who we are as humans and our relationship to this world and universe we inhabit.

There is an old Buddhist story of a monk who is having terrible difficulty with his meditation practice over many years and is forever arguing with his teachers. One day he storms out of the meditation hall in disgust. After a while trudging through the woods, he comes across a stream with a bridge over it, and as he crosses the bridge he looks over the side and catches sight of his own reflection. In a moment of enlightenment experience he exclaims, "Ha! I am not it, yet it is all of me!"[8]

The point, very simply, we are already part of it all. We don't have to work at it. We belong in the cosmos, always in relation to each other and the more-than-human world, glorious and flawed yet temporary centres of awareness and action within an inter-connected whole. And since we are part of it all then the moral and practical issue for all humans is to learn to live in a way that does justice to this participation.

The lull in the wind allowed me plenty of time for these memories, but within an hour it picked up again, carrying Coral toward the coast of County Cork. We made landfall at Baltimore in the early morning but carried on through the islands to Schull, where we knew we could rest after the overnight passage. We spent a further week exploring Long Island and Dunmanus Bays, then returned to Schull to leave Coral on a visitors' buoy. I was to return a month later, but this was the end of Steve's contribution although he was to join me again the following year in Scotland.

Chapter Six

Sacred Places: Skellig Rocks

Now we can rethink what sacred land might be. For people of an old culture, all their mutually owned territory holds numinous life and spirit. Certain places are perceived to be of high spiritual density because of plant or animal habitat intensities, or associations with legend, or connections with human totemic ancestry, or because of geomorphological anomaly, or some combination of qualities. These are places through which one can — it would be said — more easily be touched by a larger-than-human, larger-than-personal, view.
Gary Snyder
The Practice of the Wild

There are many places on the west coasts of Ireland and Scotland that might be called 'sacred'. Ancient standing stones and Celtic crosses remind of us of the intensity of old beliefs that have faded in the modern age. Places of historical significance evoke the often-tragic dimensions of history: abandoned villages, sites of battles, massacres, clearances, the unmarked spot ten miles south of the Old Head of Kinsale where the Lusitania was torpedoed. And for many of the Celtic diaspora, the towns and villages from which their ancestors emigrated hold a particular personal poignancy. From the perspective of ecological pilgrimage, these coasts are on the 'western edge', where continental Europe reaches out to and faces the Atlantic Ocean. In Brittany they call this Finistère, in Galicia Finisterre, the end of the world, or at least the end of the 'Old World'. It is where the sailor in a small boat is confronted by the immensity of thousands of miles of ocean, the limitless sky, and the untamed force of the weather systems that batter the coast. This is a region that despite all human ingenuity remains truly wild.

When I returned to Schull a month later I met up with Suzy and Gib, students of outdoor education at Edinburgh University, Suzy from Germany, Gib from Malaysia. Neither had been sailing before, so I was a little concerned in case conditions on the Atlantic coast were too rough for them. I need not have worried: the weather was remarkably quiet, with no wind and a haze low on the surface of the sea. We spent the first night in Crookhaven and the following morning crept west along a shoreline unusually devoid of surf. The mist drew closer around us, obscuring details and enveloping anything more than half a mile away. "We might be in for a tedious time," I warned them. "Motoring all day in flat calm and very little to see." But all was new to Suzy and Gib: they had never seen the shoreline from a small boat before. Suzy gazed out into the mist, then turned to me, saying, "It reminds me of Michael Ende's *Neverending Story*. I read it as a child, and remember the 'Nothing' within which turns everything into nothingness once it touches it. It's neither a hole, nor darkness, just nothingness. How that used to scare me! It's as if I could see it from here, as if we were sailing straight into it—nothingness—but there is nothing that frightens me this time."[1]

Gib was the first to spot the splash of a couple of dolphins as they travelled past; and Suzy pointed out how the hazy sun played strange tricks on the cliffs around Mizen Head, reflecting from the sheer surfaces so that the light seemed to be running down the rock face like a waterfall.

From Mizen Head, the most southwesterly point of Ireland, I set a course across the mouths of Dunmanus and Bantry Bays toward Dursey Sound at the tip of the Beara Peninsula. The coastline gradually faded into the mist. The sea was flat, occasionally covered in tiny ripples, but most of the time like polished stone. Coral thrust her way forward, the tone of the engine never varying, the Autohelm steering a straight course, her bubbling wake stretching out behind across the flat surface of the sea.

We watched gannets circling high above the sea, flying slowly, heads angled downwards as they searched for fish. If we were lucky, we would catch sight of one at the moment it slid sideways into a dive, drew its wings back first in a delta shape then so close it entered the water with scarcely a splash. We passed clusters of guillemots, which scurried away from boat as she approached, their heads jerking anxiously from side to side. Sometimes they dived neatly out of sight one by one; sometimes took flight altogether in a flurry of excited wings. "We won't see puffins," I said authoritatively. "They are back out to sea now after the spring breeding season." But soon Gib pointed one out, then another and another.

Then came the first excitement. Again it was Gib who saw the splash and the dorsal fin of dolphins coming our way. They seemed at first to be passing us by, but then they turned and swam directly toward Coral, swimming under the hull in water so clear we could see they were big animals and could make out every detail of their bodies. But they didn't stay with us long and soon made off in long elegant leaps.

Dolphins and puffins seemed to be as much excitement as one might hope for in a day. Soon Suzy was deep in a philosophy book, Gib was on the foredeck sketching and I was catching up in my notebook, looking for ways to describe the strangeness of the misty seascape.

Then Gib called again, more excitedly this time, struggling to find the English words for what she was seeing, "Something white! Something white! Underneath!" Suzy and I hurried forward to the bows where she was leaning over the pulpit and followed her pointing finger over the side. Deep in the water, scarcely visible, the enormous shape of a whale was slowly passing under the hull: what Gib had spotted was the characteristic white bands on its pectoral fins catching the light. It moved apparently effortlessly beneath the keel and disappeared back into the deep. We looked at each other wide-eyed in amazement. But before we could catch our breath, the whale surfaced alongside Coral, no more than twenty yards away, the long slow arc of its back emerging, then sliding back under water, fountains of spray blowing from its breathing holes. Again it breached, this time surfacing headfirst so we could look it directly in the eye, see its long mouth and pale underside, the pleats running back underneath its chin that allow its throat to expand when feeding. It had a curious expression on its face, not seeming to smile like a dolphin, but rather conveying an immense calm. Then, raising its tail fins clear of the water it dived out of sight into the depth below us.

That must be it, we agreed. To expect more than three sightings would be greedy, would it not? But the whale clearly didn't think so, continuing to breach and dive in Coral's wake for several minutes before finally disappearing. It left us all with big grins on our faces. Once the excitement was over we looked it up in our reference book, and identified it as a minke whale or lesser rorqual. But the image remained stronger than the identification: we had met, even if briefly, another creature that, while immensely strange, is an intelligent, air-breathing mammal, just like us.

What more could we expect? We carried on through Dursey Sound into the Kenmare River, the visibility lifting just enough for us to see the tops of mountains beyond the coast. Then more splashes as a pod of maybe twenty small dolphins raced across our bows with a flock of guillemots hurrying in their wake. Almost exhausted with excitement and stimulus we made our way across the broad river mouth, picked up the leading lines that guided us through the rocks and into Derrynane Harbour on the coast of County Kerry, where we found a snug anchorage for the night.

After supper we sat around talking about what we had seen. "The dolphins seemed to just come up and check us out," said

Suzy, "then they travelled on, not knowing how much I was shaken by their appearance." But it was the whale that stayed in our minds. Gib smiled quietly as we talked about it, never one for many words. "It was so exciting it made my stomach hurt," said Suzy.

"One of the things we could do today," I said as we finished our breakfast next morning, "is to go out to the Skellig Rocks." It looked like it would be another calm day, and although the Irish Met Office forecast 'fog patches', visibility seemed better than the previous day.

I told them what I knew about Skellig Michael and Little Skellig, two precipitous rocks that lie out in the Atlantic about 15 miles from where we were anchored. I told them about my own visit two summers previously, how I had watched and heard tens of thousands of gannets nesting on Little Skellig, and seen the beehive huts and the old Celtic monastery perched high on Skellig Michael. Little is known about how the monks came to live on the rock, although many myths and conjectures have grown up around them. I told them the story of how, in the fifth century of the common era, a small group of monks had set off from their home monastery in a skin-covered currach, travelled down the River Shannon and out to sea. They were part of the great Irish tradition of *peregrinatio pro Dei amore*, closely linked with that of the Desert Fathers of Egypt and Syria, who went to live in the desert in order to be closer to God. After drifting for days at sea the monks were beset by fog, which suddenly cleared to reveal the two immense crags of the Skelligs rising direct from the sea. They had found their desert.[2]

For hundreds of years a small band of monks lived on the rocks. They built beehive huts for shelter, collected rainwater for drinking and seaweed to create vegetable gardens in the few sheltered spots. Most important of all, they devoted their lives to contemplation and worship. They were self-sufficient except for

the consecrated wafers required to celebrate the Eu
were delivered to them from the mainland.

The Celtic monks on Skellig Michael and the
like Saint Anthony went into the wilderness see
'living in the presence of God'. This phrase may
and archaic to modern secular ears, but I had read Douglas
Christie's scholarly argument that their contemplative disci-
plines took them between inner and outer landscapes in search
of a consciousness of the whole of creation. Through their
rejection of everyday society and their ascetic practices they were
expressing a sense of the limitless beauty and vitality of the
natural world and the deepened, even transcendent, awareness
of the self that accompanies this.[3]

There was, it seems, a powerful sense of wholeness in the
ancient contemplative traditions. This wholeness included the
monks' feeling for the living world, a simple awareness of the
beauty of the desert, an appreciation of deep silence, and wonder
at their emerging intimate reciprocity with other beings. It grew
out of their intense commitment to pay attention, and out of that
arose a sense of compassion and responsibility for their world,
broken as it was by the dominance of the Roman Empire. Those
of us embedded in contemporary culture might well benefit from
a contemplative practice through which we could comprehend
our increasingly degraded and compromised world as sacred; it
might enable us to live in a deeper and more encompassing
moral or ethical relationship with the living world; to live 'so
that we do not continue to visit our most destructive impulses
upon the natural world'.

The quality of awareness that enables us to engage with the
beauty, significance and fragility of the natural world is essentially mysterious. It requires an inner attention, with both
compassion and confrontation, to inner rigidities and distur-
bances, which the contemplatives experienced as their 'demons',
but we moderns understand as our ego attachments, our sense of

,f-importance, our fragmented selves. And it requires an outer attention, a willingness to notice everything as part of a sacred whole. All this requires disciplined practice and is profoundly challenging.

Early Christian mystics were not on a hopeless quest of mortifying the flesh in search of God but were, in a sense, proto-environmentalists, approaching their world with a subtlety and discipline from which much can be learned. Their practices finding echoes in modern environmental writers as a 'contemplative ecology', expressing our deepest feelings for the natural world as part of a spiritual longing. This is closely linked to my own sense of ecological pilgrimage as a spiritual quest.

Once we had washed up and stowed everything, we made our way out of the harbour, careful to keep the two beacons that mark the safe passage in line so as to clear the underwater hazards. The pilot book says that breakers nearly always show on Muckiv Rocks, awash to the west of the harbour entrance, marking their position. Today just tiny waves washed around its edges, not a sign of white foam. But the calm weather was misleading: as we turned west toward Bolus Head and the Skelligs beyond, we saw an ominous yellow-grey cloud of sea fog gathering round Scariff Island and drifting our way. Looking back, I saw that the entrance to Derrynane was already obscured—it would be dangerous to turn back—but ahead, in the far distance, there was a hint of a horizon. It seemed that this patch of fog might be limited to the coastline.

It wasn't. It was patchy, at times gathering right around the boat in a circle of damp greyness; at other times opening up to a hint of blue above us and a vague horizon. We motored, then sailed a light breeze, unable to make out landmarks, sailing westward on a course that should leave plenty of room to clear Bolus Head. But the fog was disorienting, it was difficult to keep the sails full, steer a steady course and keep a good lookout at the same time. With a neophyte crew I was reluctant to go below and do more careful pilotage.

In hushed silence we sailed slowly, peering through the fog and listening hard. After about half an hour we heard the splash of little waves washing on rocks and the calling of seabirds. It sounded rather close. Then a vertical cliff side emerged out of the gloom, closer than was comfortable. We had strayed off course, too near the headland. I took in the tortured strata of the limestone rock face, the water washing around the scattered boulders at the bottom of the cliff, the seabirds flying in and out of the gloom; and, after a momentary alarm, I steered Coral clear. No harm done, but a warning. At least I knew exactly where we were! It was silly to try to sail when it was impossible to steer accurately. I started the engine and set a steady course out to sea toward the Skelligs. The lower slopes of the headland were soon swallowed up in the mist, but as we motored away from land, blue sky opened above us, daylight filtered through and just the top of the cliff emerged in sunshine like a heavenly body.

The mist came and went. When the visibility opened up, we could see a circle of calm water around us, the darker blue of the sea close to Coral fading into the light blue of the sky, with no visible horizon. The sea was dotted with tiny puffins—they looked as if they were this year's chicks, just fledged. They bobbed about in the waves like little bits of fluff, struggled to take wing, but were entirely confident about diving. Two gannets seemed at first to be ignoring us, but suddenly took flight as we got close, beating a path along the water with their feet, wings powerfully lifting their bodies clear. They are very big birds when you see them up close. A small fishing boat came into view about half a mile away, a bright red hull almost glowing against the featureless blue, seeming to float in a space between the gently undulating sea and the featureless sky. As we passed it, the two men on board paused from attending to their lobster pots to raise hands in solemn greeting.

disoriented - cannot 'capture' the moment, only 'live it,' experience it -

'awestruck' is a more fitting response)

* pg 89

The mist closed about us again, but then a stronger shape began to emerge: a hint, a ghostly outline, then a firm presence. A pyramid of rock rose in front of us, its base hidden in the murk, so that it appeared suspended above the surface of the sea: Little Skellig, with its colony of gannets. In a moment of excitement, Gib and Suzy hurried forward with their cameras to get a better view, but the rock immediately disappeared as the fog closed back around us. Disoriented, I took Coral forward very slowly, caught a first whiff of bird shit, then the whole rock face opened less than twenty yards in front of us. The mist swirling around it, gannets in the water all around us, gannets on every available ledge of rock, the hubbub of their harsh, grating call filling our ears.

I turned off the engine. Coral rocked almost imperceptibly on the strangely calm water; we were just a few yards from the rock but I knew there was an immense depth beneath us. We stood on the deck and silently took it all in: this huge lump of rock, massively solid yet full of fissures and ledges and crags and gargoyles, rising sharply from the sea, covered in gannet droppings as if carelessly whitewashed; the smell of rotten fish and the sound of the birds; the pattern of dots they formed sitting on their nests; the shadows of those flying past fleeting across the sea.

Further west we caught a glimpse of Skellig Michael, a second ghostly shape lurking in the mist. Leaving the gannets to their own business, we motored the half-mile or so toward it. Again it came on us abruptly. First we saw the shapes of the tourist boats that had brought visitors from the mainland clustered around the foot; then the upward sweep of rock; and through the mist clinging in the crevices, we could just make out the beehive huts constructed by the monks hundreds of years ago. Slowly we circled round. Skellig Michael is bigger by far than Little Skellig, rising so high out of the water that we had to crane our necks to see the top. Suzy and Gib were silenced, awestruck it seemed, by its mysterious grandeur. I was content to make a quiet circum-navigation, enjoying the way the day had unfolded, feeling a bit like the archetypal ferryman who had brought visitors to this sacred spot. How much better could this day's pilgrimage have been, I wondered, with the brush with danger, the slow passage across a boundless sea and the rocks appearing so mysteriously out of the mist?

We rounded the western end of the rock and turned back toward the mainland. As we passed the cliffs on the northern side, we could see the old landing place, the steps coming down to the water's edge, the path that follows a steep angle up from the sea then turns sharply to continue up the higher cliff toward the huts. We imagined how this was all cut by monks with simple hand tools, how they had laboriously carried supplies up the cliff from their boats in their robes and sandals.

Then the sun finally broke through, the mist evaporated and along with it some of the mystery of the rocks. In the bright daylight we quite suddenly dropped our quiet solemnity. We even got a bit hysterical. Suzy, who had enjoyed diving from Coral's side every morning, wondered whether she could swim ashore, climb the path and greet the tourists at the top in her bikini. Thankfully she wasn't too serious.

But she was serious later, as we sailed back toward the mainland, suddenly asking us, "What do you take away from an experience like that?" We tried to answer her but didn't get very far, even when we came back to her question after supper that evening. Gib said, "I felt we had entered another world, the gannets' world, not our world." Suzy agreed. "Little Skellig was surreal almost, totally unexpected: the sounds, colours, movements, shapes and shades. It was so unknown, such a surprise, so unfamiliar, it took me into worlds I didn't imagine existed," she said. We all agreed that the things we had seen in the past two days—the dolphins leaping, the whale emerging through the surface of the sea, the puffins bobbing around, the gannets clustering around Little Skellig and the majesty of Skellig Michael—were impressed strongly on our minds. They were images we could recall easily and vividly, even if we had difficulty finding words to describe them.

For my part, I found this second encounter with the Skellig Rocks less dramatic than my first, two years ago. Then I was dumbfounded and awestruck. This time, seeing the rocks emerging and retreating in fog, just as we had imagined the monks had seen them all those centuries ago, made me more thoughtful. It reminded me of my visit many years ago to the Grand Canyon. It was January, snow was on the ground and the canyon was full to the brim of fog. My American host was disappointed that I wasn't able to 'see it'; and yet I felt I *had* seen it with an extraordinary grandness. Now I had seen the Skelligs similarly appearing then disappearing. Somehow fog turns one's perceptions upside down or inside out: you have a hint, a glimpse of something special, only to have it almost immediately obscured. This seems to be an appropriate way of understanding spiritual experience. Grasp at it, try to hold on, and it is gone.

Both our encounter with the whale and our experience of the Skellig Rocks in the fog seem to be to have been sacred moments. But I also remember Gary Snyder's warning that there is no rush to call things sacred, we should allow time for them to speak to us. And what do we mean to convey by words like 'sacred' and 'holy' in the context of an ecological pilgrimage?

Western theologians such as Rudolf Otto and Mircea Eliade make a strong distinction between the 'sacred', which refers to a transcendent realm of gods or God; and the 'profane', the everyday, that which is of this world, 'mundane'. In this view, meaning, order and value all derive from the sacred. Sacred places are those where the transcendent qualities of the sacred pour through into the mundane. Such places make available experiences that are 'numinous': encounters with the Divine, with the wholly Other, that are simultaneously overwhelming, awesomely fearful yet enthralling and captivating. Many religious pilgrimages are devoted to reaching for this kind of experience that Otto called *mysterium tremendum et fascinans*.[4]

This kind of dualist view of the 'sacred' is unsatisfactory and misleading: it splits heaven from Earth (to say nothing about hell) so that all that is worthwhile derives from a transcendent realm. In the extreme, life on Earth is seen as fallen and sinful. But from an ecological perspective, Earth is seen as part of an evolving universe. Some might take a reductively materialist view that there is nothing but matter and energy. But we may also hold that there is a divine or spiritual power that is not outside and separate but immanent in the whole: as the poet Wendell Berry puts it, 'there are no unsacred places; I there are only sacred places I and desecrated places'.[5] The universe, and everything that is in it, has both material and spiritual dimensions and is thus both self-creating and self-transcending. In philosophical terms this is a panpsychic view; in religious terms a pantheist view; both views hold that mind/spirit/psyche is immanent in creation, at one with and interpenetrating the material.[6]

This perspective has much in common with the Buddhist view that all things have Buddha nature. Similarly, the Taoist view is of the cosmos as a 'boundless generative organism': the 'ten thousand things' of the world, in constant transformation, arise from and fall back into the source of being. Everything, both material and spiritual, derives from an evolving Earth within an evolving universe of which we humans, and the whole community of life on Earth, are a part.[7]

This view, that everything partakes of the sacred, raises the question, 'So what, then, is particularly sacred about this place or that?'

The writer Barry Lopez has written extensively about the indigenous people and natural world of North America. He tells us that his work is a 'quest for the divine'. By this he doesn't solely mean the 'presence of God' (although he doesn't actually rule that out), he means a quest for the numinous dimension of ordinary life—and immediately goes on to say that this is not ordinary at all! For as soon as we pay attention, really pay attention with what might be called a 'moral gaze', everything becomes rarefied, special, sacred. All distinctions between the mundane and the sacred collapse. When we pause long enough to notice, we are in a particularly intimate relation to the whole of creation.[8]

I think the theologians are right in that there are places, like the Skellig Rocks, where the experience of the sacred, even a sense of *mysterium tremendum et fascinans*, opens into the everyday. But this is not a pouring through from a transcendent realm; it is an opening to the experience of the specialness of ordinary world, to our intimacy with the whole. As Gary Snyder puts it, the sacred is that which takes you out of your little self into the wider whole.[9]

Most places we think of as sacred have been so defined by human culture and history. They are sacred because communities have enclosed them and marked them as special with a megalith, a stone circle, or a building dedicated to a deity or saint. Such a place accumulates a quality of holiness as generations of worshippers gather in prayer or celebration or mourning, and this quality may persist for future visitors even when the original founding beliefs no longer hold their convening power.

But it is not just humans who mark out the sacred: the pilgrimage routes and gathering places of species that migrate across the planet, the spawning grounds of great shoals of fish, the delicate spots where wrens build their nests—all these have qualities of the sacred. Places come to be seen as sacred because of their natural beauty or grandeur: dramatic landscapes, water-falls, quiet forest groves. They convey a grandeur or peace that passes all human understanding, to borrow words from the

Christian blessing. Of course, some of these are also marked by humans to emphasize their natural features. Philip Marsden, in his exploration of Bodmin Moor in Cornwall, describes how the Neolithic inhabitants moved stones to draw attention to ritual features in the landscape. In particular he shows how stones were placed at the top of Garrow Tor like 'the aisle of a great open air cathedral', deliberately aligned to provide dramatic views of Rough Tor, over which the Pole Star stands. This 'sacralized' or 'ritual' landscape holds its power to the present time.[10]

A third kind of sacred place is made so by history or legend: the cave in which a saint is said to have lived, the place where the Buddha attained enlightenment, where Christ was crucified, where the Lakota Sioux met the US Cavalry at Little Bighorn. Such places can accumulate aura to them that can be felt even by those not familiar with the history. And finally, there are places that are sacred to individuals and families: places of birth, death, commitment or parting, that stand for crucial moments in our personal history.[11]

The places in the world we identify as sacred have been marked out as such; they are in some senses set apart from the ordinary, and yet in another sense they remain ordinary. As geologian Thomas Berry puts it, we are part of the sacred dream of the whole Earth: 'In the beginning was the dream. Through the dream all things were made, and without the dream nothing was made that was made'.[12]

Chapter Seven

Pilgrimage as Homage

And then Serafina understood something for which the witches had no word: it was the idea of pilgrimage. She understood why these beings would wait for thousands of years and travel vast distances in order to be close to something important, and how they would feel differently for the rest of time, having been briefly in its presence.
Philip Pullman
The Subtle Knife

High pressure with light winds continued to dominate the weather for the rest of the week that Suzy and Gib were with me. As we travelled north from the Skellig Rocks to the Blasket Islands the sea remained uncharacteristically calm. Strong winds kick up heavy seas in the tidal streams between the islands, making the passages perilous. The islanders would have worked the seas in all conditions—Great Blasket was inhabited up until the 1950s—but this was a good time to explore the islands with neophyte sailors, and to approach the outer islands that are often inaccessible. We decided not to land at the ruined village on Great Blasket, which was busy with tourists, but take the opportunity to visit Inishvickillane, the most westerly island in Ireland ever to be inhabited—and said by some to be the home of fairies.

In oily calm seas we motored westward down the length of Great Blasket, passing through flocks of cormorants and guillemots sitting on the water and seeing more and more baby puffins scurrying around. As we got closer to Inishvickillane we could see the little bay on the northeast corner that serves as a fair-weather anchorage, no more than an indentation in the coastline, scarcely sheltered. I called on Suzy and Gib to get ready to anchor—this was one part of sailing they had learned—but then we saw that a large mooring buoy had been installed by the landing place. Should we borrow the buoy or drop the anchor? We took the buoy, pleased to avoid the trouble of anchoring in deep water while at the same time mildly put out that in this place on the edge of the Atlantic these modern conveniences had been installed.

Once safely moored we just stood in the sunshine and gazed at the shore. It really did feel as if we had arrived at a magical deserted island. On this sheltered eastern side waves of grass rolled down the cliff side, dotted about with bright yellow flowers and clusters of purple thrift. Puffins, guillemots and gulls flew in and out continuously, bringing food to their chicks; from time to time the air was filled with a gentle cooing, an intimate conversation between adult and young. We paddled ashore in the dinghy and landed on the stony beach, to look back at Coral lying comfortably to the buoy.

Suzy and Gib scrambled up the cliff path to the top to look out over the Atlantic, calling back to confirm what the pilot book clearly stated: the path is dangerous and should not be attempted. I had anyway decided it was too awkward for an older man, so stayed on the beach and watched the puffins flying in and out of their burrows with small fish in their mouths. I was pleased when Gib and Suzy were safely back on the beach. They told me what they had seen: the precipitous drop on the western side into the Atlantic; and the view over the whole of the Blasket archipelago: Inishnabro just across the narrow passage to the north; Tearaght way out in the west; the long hump of Great Blasket; and the distant mainland. No fairies, though—maybe we didn't believe in them enough. Before leaving we sat quietly on the beach, each of us in our own thoughts, playing with the pebbles, looking back to the mainland, and watching the birds. Two large seals swam into the bay, and stayed with their heads out of the water, seeming to watch us watching them, before swimming away.

These quiet days prompted another response to the question Suzy had asked earlier after our visit to Skellig Michael: what do we take away from experiences like this? Maybe we come to these places with a sense of reverence and to pay homage, we thought. And maybe we should not be frightened to use such words. We come to acknowledge the land and the sea, the animals who live here and the history of the peoples, for their own sake, not to make our own sense of it, not to have our own 'spiritual' experiences (although when these come we may embrace them). Being here, through our appreciation, and also our tiredness and discomfort, through the effort of coming; that, maybe, is enough.

Homage is an act of honouring. While the word has its origins in feudal relations between lord and vassal, it has in modern times taken on a wider meaning. In an act of homage we do something special, often ceremonial, to demonstrate our respect. We buy flowers for our lover, contribute to a *Festschrift* for a teacher, or maybe write a poem following the form of a great master. To remember that 'April is the cruellest month' is to gesture in homage to one of our great twentieth-century poets.

In the courts of European monarchs, protocol insisted that one bowed or curtsied to the royalty, an action that appears archaic, although it persists to this day. In Catholic, Orthodox and high Episcopalian churches, the faithful bow to the altar and make the sign of the cross—although such ceremonial practices were frowned upon as near idolatry in my Nonconformist upbringing. Acts formally demonstrating respect continue in secular life although are less common than they were: Gentlemen no longer raise their hat to a lady when passing in the street; in England we now rarely stand for the National Anthem. However, the symbolic power of acts of homage remains, as does transgressing them: evidenced by the outrage in the USA when American football player Colin Kaepernick refused to stand for the national anthem in a silent protest about the treatment of people of colour.[1]

I was challenged to reconsider my understanding of homage on the Chan Buddhist retreat when I was first invited to prostrate myself to the Buddha. I had got used to the simple gesture of placing hands together and bowing on entering the meditation hall, of bowing similarly to honour the Master and the other participants on the retreat. This was a simple symbol of respect and equality. But to follow the gesture on and down into the full-length prostration seemed to me to be an act of subservience. My Nonconformist mind rebelled. However, in time and with practice, I learned the value of this as a ceremonial act, the value of what Buddhists call 'taking refuge' in the Buddha, the Dharma and the Sangha, allowing myself to be held by his example and the teachings. Not least, I learned to let go of a little of my self-importance. I was even more resistant at a later retreat when I was invited to prostrate myself to an image of people who I considered my 'enemies', who had harmed me in some way. But again, I found that through prostration my anger could be absorbed in a larger whole, and I could acknowledge and be thankful for what I was learning from the conflict.

In societies rooted in Hindu, Buddhist and Taoist philosophy the bow, with hands placed together, can be seen as an expression of reverence quite different from the hierarchical implication of the Western tradition. Classical Chinese scholar David Hinton describes this bow as an essentially silent gesture, an 'elemental movement' that 'can only be called a dance', because it 'so perfectly expresses a spiritual gesture offering the centre of identity to something beyond'. In our everyday life the sense of self is insistent, rarely opening to the world beyond it. Consciousness mirrors the outside world, but is never part of it. The ritual gesture of the bow is a way of cultivating an opening, dropping the self-centred stance and weaving together inside and outside. As I learned from my prostrations, when I bow, I acknowledge I am part of a wider whole.[2]

Hinton's book *Hunger Mountain* is a meditation on a series of walks up the mountain close to his home, drawing on classical Taoist and Chan Buddhist poetry, philosophy and calligraphy. He tells us that 'Things are themselves only as they belong to something more than themselves: I to we, we to Earth, Earth to planets and stars...' This he relates to the Chinese graph for *sincerity*, which implies that our inner thoughts are the same as our outer thoughts and spoken words. But in a more fundamental sense, sincerity is the 'elemental structure of our Cosmos', where the 'ten thousand things are in constant transformation, appearing and disappearing perennially through one another as cycles of birth and death unfurl their generations: inside becoming outside, outside inside'.

Hinton explains that in ancient Chinese thought this is 'the deepest form of belonging', for 'Cosmos, consciousness, and language are woven together in a single unified fabric'. Meditation practice reveals that the human mind is not a 'spirit centre', not a centre of thought and intention, but an 'opening of consciousness that watches thought coming and going'. As we move deeper into meditative practice so that the 'restless train of thought falls silent' and an empty mind can attend to the world with 'mirrorlike clarity... leaving its ten thousand things utterly simple, utterly themselves, and utterly sufficient'.

So in this tradition, the ritual gesture of the bow is not a gesture of subservience, but a physical expression of an emptying of self to the wider whole, and so becomes the underlying structure for all spiritual and artistic practices. Meditation, calligraphy, poetry, landscape painting are all gestures that open the centre to the ten thousand things beyond. The traditional Taoist practice of living as a recluse among the mountains can be seen as making life itself a bow, in the sense of an ongoing opening to the wider whole.

There are parallels with this sense of the bow in Western traditions. Reflecting on his book *Waterlog*, Roger Deakin suggests that in his practice of wild swimming he was 'taking part in the existence of things'. This phrase is taken from the poet Keats: in his letter to Benjamin Bailey, he makes his celebrated assertion, 'I am certain of nothing but of the holiness of the Heart's affections and the truth of Imagination'; Keats continues, 'if a Sparrow come before my Window, I take part in its existence and pick about the Gravel'.[3]

In contrast to the radical absence of self that Hinton expresses, Keats retains the Western view that there exists a soul, or 'spirit centre', that can be given up. Nevertheless, it seems that the 'absence of identity' was central to Keats' view of himself: as Andrew Motion puts it, 'he described a state of creation which allows the lack of a fixed identity to become a means of entering the world'. Maybe the phrase 'taking part in the existence of things' expresses a sense of homage as a radical opening to other in a way that is easier for the Western sensibility.

Jonathan Bate, in *The Song of the Earth*, his 'ecological reading' of English literature, explores Keats' celebrated poem *Ode to Autumn*. This poem, evoking links and reciprocal relations within nature and between humans and nature, Bate suggests, 'comes to resemble a well-regulated ecosystem'. It seeks not the aesthetic transcendence of some of Keats' earlier poems, but rather 'an image of ecological wholeness' and 'a sense of being-at-home-in-the-world': it is not written from the perspective of the external observer but as if from within. As with the Taoist bow, the centre is opened to the ten thousand things. Hinton reminds us that 'we need to keep bowing, to keep reweaving that center back into the generative silence of landscape and Cosmos'. This for me is the essence of homage.[4]

This insight—that pilgrimage could be seen as homage to the world—arose in my conversations with Suzy and Gib following our visit to Inishvickillane. My reading and reflections through the following winter deepened this insight: I began to understand my pilgrimage as a prolonged bow that endeavoured to empty myself of everyday distractions and open myself to the wider whole (an endeavour which was only on occasion successful). As Keats points out to us, the ordinariness of the sparrow can call for an act of homage just as much as the magnificent white-tailed eagles I was to see later in my voyages.

There was that wet and windy day in Bertraghboy Bay, Connemara. I was on my own, Suzy and Gib having left for home a week or more earlier. It had been raining since I woke up. The pattering of rain on the deck just above my head was punctuated by the abrupt plop of larger drops falling from the furled mainsail. The noise of the wind in the rigging rose and fell as squalls came and went. In the stronger gusts the pattering on the deck grew into a harsh rattle, as if a handful of gravel was being cast across the deck; the anchor chain clanked in the stemhead as Coral swung round. Looking out, I could see water pouring down the cabin windows and collecting in little pools before running along the sidedecks and streaming away through the scupper drains.

The previous day had been long and tiring, spent mainly on my feet in the cockpit as I sailed up the coast. I had arrived late at Roundstone only to discover the anchorage was uncomfortable in the freshening southerly wind. So, rather late in the evening, I had brought Coral round to better shelter in Bertraghboy Bay. I was resting: I didn't have anything to do and I didn't want to do anything. I was just hanging out in the cabin, drinking tea, munching biscuits, doing odd jobs, listening to the rain and reading Tim Robinson's fascinating book, *Connemara: A Little Gaelic Kingdom*.[5]

From time to time I stood at the bottom of the companionway and stared into the circumference of wet bleakness. In the cockpit, the rain was gradually filling the washing-up bowl I had left out with last night's dirty dishes. The ensign flapped soggily from the backstay. Raindrops hung bright from the safety rails, seeming to reflect the whole world, then dropped to the deck. Round Coral the dark greeny-blue of the bay was dappled with the circular splash-marks of raindrops. High grey cloud covered the sky, heavier rainclouds blowing across below. When the rain slackened, the far shore appeared as a dark, scarcely-green curve between water and sky, but the Connemara Mountains beyond remained hidden. But soon squalls returned and all I could make out was the nearby fish farm, its black framework skeletal against the water.

All morning the rain persisted. In the afternoon the wind blew up to near-gale force and veered westerly. It howled through the rigging and set the halliards drumming against the mast. The sky lightened in the south and west with thinner cloud and streaks of blue. I took this as signs of the cold front coming through. I watched the clouds racing across the sky, expecting the wind soon to blow itself out. But no: instead I saw that Coral was slowly drifting across the bay and realized that with the wind shift the anchor was no longer holding firm. I got to work on the windlass, hauling up the chain and anchor made heavy by mud and weed dredged up from the seabed. I took the opportunity to shift Coral across the bay to a spot on the northern shore that was more sheltered now the wind was in the west. After carefully setting the anchor and making sure all was secure, I retired, wet and windblown, to the cabin.

Around teatime the wind finally eased and then dropped to practically nothing. Through the early evening the sky cleared and a deep sense of calm settled across the bay. I sat outside with my supper looking at the mountains, purple-grey in the evening light. A straight line of cloud cut across the taller peaks and rose above them in curly cumulus, grey underneath and white above. Between the mountains and me lay the poor, boulder-strewn farmland of Connemara. The low evening sun caught on some facets of the mountains while leaving others lurking darkly in shadow. But to my right the cone of Cashel Hill remained in full sunshine, grass green with grey outcrops of granite welling out from underneath. The world around me was bright, with different shades of green and complex layers of curves upon curve in the hills, and an odd little bunch of trees clustered round a house.

As I finished my supper, I realized how the breathtaking beauty of my surroundings—the clear air, the quiet rippling of the bay interspersed with the penetrating shrieks of terns fishing nearby, the expansive view of water and mountains—had gradually permeated my awareness. It was high water of a big spring tide and the bay was full to the brim, lapping at the grassland all the way round. It was as if the fullness of the tide had filled me with a sense of the presence of the world around me.

I sat there thinking, "Maybe this is the pilgrimage. Maybe the point of coming this long way was to wait through the rain and wind all day and now to sit here looking at the mountains of Connemara in this quietness, watching the way the clouds hang around the tops of the mountains."

Moments of grace such as this cannot be willed, they arrive unbidden and arrest one's attention. But of course, that whole long, slow day watching the weather had created the conditions in which that moment could occur. My restless train of thought fell silent; everything was sufficient for the moment; and for a few moments I too was taking part in the existence of things.

Chapter Eight

Tourist or Pilgrim?

... the tourist is a conscious and systematic seeker of experience, of a new and different experience, of the experience of difference and novelty — as the joys of the familiar wear off and cease to allure. The tourists want to immerse themselves in a strange and bizarre element... they choose the elements to jump into according to how strange, but also how innocuous, they are; you recognize the favourite tourist haunts by the blatant, ostentatious (if painstakingly groomed) oddity, but also by the profusion of safety cushions and well marked escape routes. In the tourist's world, the strange is tame, domesticated, and no longer frightens; shocks come in a package deal with safety.

Zygmunt Bauman
"From Pilgrim to Tourist—or a Short History of Identity"

Tourist or pilgrim? These questions arose as soon as we arrived in Ireland. Once Steve and I had sailed Coral across the Celtic Sea to Baltimore, the weather set against us again, blowing a stream of arctic air down the west coast of Ireland. The days were sunny, but cold and windy. The northerly winds meant it was not possible to continue the voyage to Galway as I had planned. Since this was Steve's first time on the southwest coast of Ireland, he naturally wanted to see as much as possible. This seemed only fair, especially after all his hard work pushing Coral to windward, although it meant taking on the perspective of a tourist and sightseer rather than a traveller and pilgrim.

Once rested, we sailed down Long Island Sound to Crookhaven, a deep and narrow east-facing bay a few miles from Mizen Head. In the not-so-distant past, Crookhaven was an important refuge for sailing boats waiting for favourable winds across the Atlantic or up the Bristol Channel, and myth has it that you could at times step from boat to boat across the bay without getting your feet wet. I first visited with my family on Corulus, a 28-foot Twister, the smaller sister to Coral. It must have been 25 years ago at least, and then the bay was empty apart from a few boats at anchor. Now it is packed with empty mooring buoys, so finding a place where we could anchor was really difficult. As the young man behind the bar in O'Sullivan's pub told us, many of them had been laid before the financial crash, when there was money around in Ireland, and most of them are no longer used.

After a walk to Galley Cove and a couple of pints of Beamish stout in O'Sullivan's bar—where we were assured it is so much better than Guinness—we watched the sun go down. The steep sides of the bay were soon enveloped in deep shadow, while at the western end the last of the sun caught on the stone walls around a green field and the white gable end of a farmhouse. The evening shadow crept over the green by the minute, and when all was completely wrapped in darkness the high clouds turned pink and purple, filling the sky and reflecting in the water.

The following day we thrashed against the wind round Mizen Head, the most southwesterly corner of the whole of the British Isles, into Dunmanus Bay, the smallest and most underdeveloped of the five narrow bays that form the coast of southwest Ireland. Roaringwater Bay, Dunmanus Bay, Bantry Bay, Kenmare River, Dingle Bay are all flooded valleys formed from the upheavals in the limestone rocks; between them are narrow peninsulas pointing like outstretched fingers out into the Atlantic. Dunmanus Bay is particularly long and narrow, with stone-walled fields and scattered white houses rising up from the rocks along the water's edge. An abrupt line above the fields marks the point where cultivation ends and the rough hillside starts. As we sailed into the bay we watched the gannets and guillemots, and wondered yet again how to tell the difference between cormorants and shags. Steve was just going below to get the bird book when I caught sight of a familiar shape. "Look there!" I called to him, pointing at the dolphin that was leaping through the water toward us. Soon a group of them was following us, some fifteen or so playing around in the wake and the bow wave. It was the first time Steve had seen dolphins in the wild. He stood gazing at them, open mouthed and enchanted, until they had enough of us and disappeared as quickly as they came.

After popping into Dunmanus Harbour to pay our respects to the ancient castle tower and the spot where I anchored on my previous voyage, and piloting our way past the rocks around Carbery Island, we dropped our anchor in Kitchen Cove, reasonably well out of the harsh winds, and basked for a while in the sun. That evening before supper we went ashore and enjoyed a couple of pints (Murphy's this time) chatting to the mainly English people outside the pub about sailing, their holiday cottages, the weather and how quickly and cheaply they could fly over here from London. In complete contrast, as we climbed back into the dinghy to return to Coral, we exchanged greetings with a local man working on his fishing boat. "Lovely place," we said politely, and got a more enthusiastic response than we expected. "I've been in London and I've been in New York, working on the buildings. Now I am happy to be back here," he flung his arm in an encompassing gesture to the water and the surrounding hills. Everyone seemed to be in love with the place.

"I feel I am on holiday now," I said to Steve. "Rather than on a deep ecology pilgrimage."

"But there is still deep ecology here," he replied. "Look at the way all these people love this place. They wouldn't talk in your terms, but the feeling is still there deep down."

I partly agreed with him. But only partly. I felt it important to notice how the line between everyday appreciation and the kind of pilgrimage I was attempting is essentially very narrow. When I first came to Dunmanus Bay on my own two years ago and anchored in Dunmanus Harbour, I saw and wrote about only the wild and ancient side of the bay. On this visit we had come only a few miles further inland to Kitchen Cove and the tiny settlement of Ahakista, but here we were much more in touch with the 'civilization', only a few miles from Bantry Town itself. This delightful little cove has been sought after as a vacation spot for many years, as is evidenced not only by the English visitors at the pub but by the Victorian and Edwardian piles scattered amongst the wooded hills (the largest and most elegant of which is now owned by the entertainer Graham Norton). Two years ago I didn't see how the bay is an important pathway between the wild and the tamed, far more so than I had originally imagined.

Steve cooked pasta for supper. Before we went to bed we enjoyed what was possibly the most important discovery of this trip so far: a dessert made from dried apricots soaked in a spoonful of Calvados (all the best yachts have a bottle on board) with yogurt and a little honey. The line between the wild and the civilized really is very thin.

Several weeks later, now on my own, I made the long passage north from Dingle to Inishmore, the largest of the Aran Islands in County Galway. Through the long hot day, even though I was well off the coast, there was plenty to look at. There were puffins, guillemots, razorbills and shearwater, mainly resting on the quiet sea. As I passed the Shannon estuary, with the lighthouse on Loop Head on the horizon, the resident dolphin pod paid a brief visit, but I think they were too busy hunting fish to bother with me. I thought I glimpsed a whale breaching, but then it might have been a very large dolphin. And I passed a sunfish, flopping around on the surface of the water as they do, in what is known as surface basking behaviour: the sunfish swims on its side, presenting its largest profile to the sun, as a way of warming up in the sun after a deep dive into cold water.

In the afternoon, as the mainland warmed in the sun, a sea

breeze set in from the west and we made good speed. Just as I was getting truly tired, the Aran Islands appeared over the horizon: the long line of Inishmore to the west, and the rounder bumps of Inishmaan and Inisheer to the east. Coral surged through the water as the day drew to a close, the lowering sun casting golden light on the sails so the shadow of the rigging danced across the huge expanse of the No.1 genoa I had set. It was very late by the time I took her round the lighthouse on Straw Island, past the green buoy marking the end of the spit, and picked up a visitors' buoy off the end of the pier.

I had anticipated this visit to the Aran Islands for a long time and prepared by reading books on the geology and history of the islands. In particular, I had studied Tim Robinson's two detailed accounts of the island: in *Stones of Aran: Pilgrimage*, he walks the whole coastline, looking into the geology and history of every significant rock, recovering the old Gaelic names and the stories of the landscape; in *Stones of Aran: Labyrinth* he undertakes a similar detailed exploration of the interior.[1] From his books I understood that it would be inappropriate to approach the islands with an attitude of 'Rousseauistic nostalgia'. Even though he describes the island as one of the last precarious footholds of the Irish language on the modern world, the old — and precarious — life on the island based on farming, fishing and the collecting and burning of seaweed to make kelp ash has passed; the ever-increasing numbers of tourists, mainly day-trippers, has brought a degree of prosperity. Of course I expected development, modern facilities, the coming and going of ferries. But I was not prepared for the impact of the recent engineering works: the new sea wall that enclosed the harbour, a half-kilometre sweep of piled-up boulders capped with concrete; the huge car park lit by clusters of brilliant sodium lights, so bright they hurt my eyes at night and sent an orange glow into the sky.

Robinson's description of the harbour at Cill Rónáin (Kilronan as Anglicized in the sailing directions) is typically thorough. He starts with the oldest, the turf quay in the corner of the bay, now no more than a stub. The new quay was built in stages: the first hundred and fifty yards built in the 1850s from three- and four-foot cuboids of limestone, split and dressed by hand; the second section added in the 1900s of concrete with iron bollards, allowing bigger fishing boats to land their catch and a thrice-weekly steamer from Galway. In the 1980s a further extension was built of prefabricated concrete boxes sunk to the seabed. These developments accommodated the increasing size of ferries and fishing boats, but never provided a truly secure harbour.[1]

The new sea wall and harbour developments, undertaken in the early years of the present century, were an enormous under-taking involving the removal of thousands of tons of material and costing millions of euros. It was voted 'Best Engineering Project of 2012', acclaimed as providing shelter from ocean waves, of huge benefit to the local community and sustaining the strong local heritage and Irish culture unique to the island.

I was shocked by its ugliness. I could appreciate the shelter provided by the new sea wall which allowed me to leave Coral safely on a mooring buoy: the smaller two islands have no safe anchorages where a yacht can be left even for a short while. But did such a small island really need facilities for a roll-on roll-off ferry and the associated huge car park and lighting? Would it not be better to keep cars away from these narrow roads? And who was really benefiting from the millions of public expenditure? There is relatively little overnight accommodation on the island, and most of the visitors seemed to be day-trippers, so spending relatively little during their visit. Somewhere I read that the main economic beneficiaries of the huge public investment are the ferry companies, who bring up to 2,500 visitors a day in and out during the peak season.

But who was I, an urban Englishman, to criticize? I felt very cautious about asking local people to comment for fear of sounding judgmental. Eventually I got chatting to the skipper of the yacht on the next mooring buoy who told me he sailed over to the island regularly from Galway. When I plucked up courage to ask what people thought of the development, he gazed over at the sparkling new concrete and after a pause replied, "Och, we did some crazy things during the Tiger Years," and that was as far as I got.

I spent most of my first day at Inishmore resting after my long sail. I wandered around the town for an hour or so, finding it as unattractive as tourist hubs everywhere—and for that matter many popular pilgrimage destinations, full of souvenir shops and fast food outlets. I watched visitors stream ashore from the ferries and set out for the sights in minibuses, horse-drawn buggies and on bicycles. I realized that if I were to get a sense of the island and visit any of the famous sights before the crowds, I would need to be up and about early. So the following morning I was at the bike hire shop as it opened, taking charge of a solid machine with 21 gears, and set off along the northern coast.

The limestone rocks that make up Inishmore were laid down in layers of sediment 320 million years ago in the depths of a tropical sea; they form part of the limestone 'pavement' that extends across from the Burren in County Clare on the mainland. On Inishmore the strata are tipped up, sloping from sheer cliffs on the southern coast to sea level on the northern side. As water enters weaknesses in the rock it gradually dissolves the limestone, creating vertical fissures in the pavement. The whole island is in a slow process of erosion.

I cycled along the northern shore, where that pavement slips into the sea at a shallow angle. In past times seaweed was collected here, with backbreaking labour, by women, men and children and burned in the kilns to reduce it to kelp. The kelp was then shipped to the mainland and sold for a heartbreaking pittance. Ruins of the kilns still dot the coast as a melancholy reminder of hard times past. Then I turned toward the 'must see' sight, Dun Aonghasa, a Bronze or Iron Age fort perched on the southern cliff top toward the western end of the island. The visitor centre was, as I hoped, still empty. I locked up my bicycle and trekked up the path—the day already hot and promising to be far hotter. The Dun consists of four huge semicircular walls that stretch across the top of hill to enclose a promontory at the cliff top. It is of similar dominant scale to the sea wall I had been objecting to, but of natural stone rather than raw concrete. Close up, I became fascinated by the intricacy of the stonework: no mortar was used, the huge stones laid together so closely that they mimicked the natural fragmentation of the limestone along its fault lines. I placed my hand on one of the blocks, imagining that this stone had been handled and put in place by another person some 3,500 years ago.

I entered through the remarkably square doorway in the outer wall and walked through to the inner enclosure. For a moment I thought I was the first to arrive at the Dun that morning, but no, a woman was sitting on her own in the shade of the walls. She looked very content and self-contained, so we exchanged scarcely perceptible nods of greeting and then ignored each other. In the enclosed space within the inner wall there was scarcely a sound, just a hint of the light surf at the bottom of the cliff (nowhere on Inishmore seems to be away from the sound of the sea, even in calm weather) and the scratching of my pencil in my notebook.

I sat in the shade of the wall to cool down and catch my breath after the hot climb, feeling rather smug about having arrived before the crowds. But that smugness gave rise again to that question that kept recurring: where is the dividing line between tourist and pilgrim? I realized it was so easy to forget the purpose of my journey, my quest to open myself to the world around me, in the heat and tiredness, the tedium and the loneliness of my journey. Inishmore and the Dun broke this pattern, providing me with a focus and a place to visit. Did that make me a tourist? Had I come here simply out of curiosity? Partly, but not entirely. As I sat for a while in the shade, watching the grass blow gently in the wind, and listening to the never-ending sound of breaking surf, as two crows staked out their territory, I felt more connected to the presence of this ancient place.

The limestone pavement on which the fort is built reaches out to sea and sky then ends abruptly. There is a sharp edge at which the cliff plunges straight down into the Atlantic. Actually it is not straight down, for the top of the cliff overhangs slightly. It is thought that the Dun was originally an oval shape, but that parts of the cliff and fort collapsed into the sea since it was built. I walked cautiously toward the edge and peered down at the water, feeling my body contort itself in spontaneous anxiety and the empty sickness of vertigo, so that while my head craned forward my bottom stuck out landwards in futile counter-balance. My body simply refused to let me approach closer while upright, so I lay full length on the rock and wormed my way forward till my head was over the edge. With a strange ambivalence, feeling both vertigo and exhilaration, I looked down hundreds of feet to the glittering surface of the sea. Even then I couldn't allow my shoulders over the edge. To my left I could see the ledges of limestone pavement around Poll na bPeist, the rectangular hole in the rock known as the Worm Hole. The cliffs there are a mere ninety feet; those at the Dun three times that height. As Tim Robinson puts it, 'the dramatic change in scale projects one's gaze into legendary perspectives'. It is indeed difficult to realize that ancient humans, not giants, built this extraordinary structure.

Then the stream of visitors began. A young man came through the stone doorway and immediately blew his nose, abruptly breaking the silence. The loud snort startled me out of my reverie. Gradually more and more people came, filling the place with their conversation and their curiosity. I slipped away, pleased—or was I smug?—to have got there early. As I walked back down the path I was going against an increasing stream of visitors struggling up the hill as I had done earlier.

In the intense heat of the afternoon it felt more like Provence than a northern Atlantic island. At serious risk of sunstroke, I cycled down the side roads, through countryside where stone walls criss-cross the limestone pavement, seeming to divide the land into near-barren fields. I met an old gentleman sitting outside his cottage who pointed out the way, "To the Worrrrm Hole," with such exaggerated rolling of the "r" that one might imagine he was acting (and overacting) the part of a Gaelic-speaking local. I left my bike by the side of the road and followed the arrows painted for the benefit of visitors, which led me over the piles of huge rocks that constitute the 'storm beach', where the sea in its wilder moods tosses huge boulders on to the cliff tops. Once over the storm beach I scrambled down to the flat pavement that steps abruptly a few metres down into the sea.

I found the Worm Hole itself extraordinary. Robinson describes it well: 'An exactly rectangular block of stone has somehow been excerpted from the floor of the bay in the cliffs… and the sea fills the void from below… It looks like a grim and sinister swimming pool, the work of some morose civil engineer'. But increasingly I felt I was looking at sights as a tourist—consuming them as it were, ticking them off a 'to do' list—rather than dwelling with them in as a pilgrim might.

Walking back I stayed further inland, stepping across the vast flat stones and negotiating the fissures between them, some of which run in straight parallel lines for some twenty or thirty yards, creating micro-climates in the cracks, where delicate flowers bloom under the protection of the miniature crags. The limestone is weathered into fantastic shapes, some rounded, some with strangely curved sharp edges. The stones ring out when they are struck. Mostly this was easier walking than across the storm beach, although I did once tread on a grassy spot that hid a small crevasse. As my foot sank between two rocks I wondered if I would hear the snap of broken bone, but as I was moving cautiously no harm was done at all.

By now I had been in the intense sun for most the day, and I struggled to cycle back to the harbour, taking every opportunity to shelter in the few patches of shade along the way. My bottle of orange squash was tepid and unpleasant (and nearly all gone), so I was delighted to eventually become a full-blown tourist and join the throng at Joe Watty's bar for a pint of iced water (essential) and a Corona beer (delightful).

I had no desire to stay any longer in the tourist hot spot of Cill Rónáin. The 'western edge' was not here, but along the cliffs of the southern coast. I took Coral back through Gregory Sound and turned west. I was headed again in the direction of the Worm Hole and Dun Aonghasa, but this time at sea level. The weather remained quiet enough for me to safely sail round Inishmore close to the shoreline before I continued north to Connemara.

From the cockpit I could clearly see the lines of limestone strata, laid down millions of years ago, topped by the storm beaches like the one I had clambered the previous day. Now I was looking up from below at the piles of enormous boulders heaped, not just above the high tideline of a beach, but at the top of cliffs that my chart told me were thirty to eighty feet high. I had read in Tim Robinson's account of the storm beach 'composed of vast numbers of blocks it would take many men to move, and furthermore separated from the cliff's edge by a clear space of ten or twenty feet'. I had at first imagined that the boulders were thrown up from the bottom of the sea; but they are actually ripped off the edge of the cliff and moved inland by degrees by giant waves that overtop the cliffs.

Where the coast was lower I could see past the storm beach to the fields beyond, so covered with fragments of rock I could not imagine it was worth the labour of collecting stones to wall them off. Further along the coast the cliffs rose dramatically to a height that even the biggest waves could not top. But here the pounding seas erode the softer parts of the lower levels so the heights overhang the water's edge, in some places quite markedly.

Eventually I reached Dun, where from the sea the cliff, grimly grey with discoloured streaks from seeping water, appears as thick strata of rock separated by deep horizontal fissures. Looking more closely, I could see that the whole rock face is divided both horizontally and vertically, giving the appearance of an enormous version of the walls of the Dun itself. At the top of the cliff I could only just make out the walls that had seemed so enormous close to, and next to them the minute figures of people standing where I had stood the previous day.

Leaving the Dun behind me, I continued on down the coast and turned north through the sound between Brannock Island and the end of the Inishmore. Some fifteen miles ahead of me lay the coast of Connemara and Kilkieran Bay, my next destination.

I sailed north with a strangely heavy heart, disappointed with my visit. Inishmore is a remarkable place. First for its lessons in geology: it is one thing to read about how erosion creates limestone pavements, quite another to actually walk over them. Second, for its lessons in history: while this is not my part of the world, I know it has been deeply influenced and impoverished both by its own conflicts and by those imported from England. For me, however, these qualities were overwhelmed by the visitor culture: not so much by the curiosity of the people who visit, but by the infrastructure that is required to cater for them and to profit from them. The tourist business requires that large numbers of visitors move through the sites fairly quickly and are returned to the tourist hub where they can spend their money.

It is all too easy to make a crude distinction between tourist and pilgrim. We are all both. The line between is a subtle one that I found myself continually crossing and recrossing, never entirely sure which side I was on. Indeed, nature writer Paul

Evans refers to people like me who go in search of wild places as 'wilderness tourists'.[2] Religious pilgrims who go to sacred places in search of a holy realm will often take time out for sightseeing; and tourists visiting the same places may find themselves affected more profoundly than they had bargained for. The tourist may see a haughty arrogance in the pilgrims' claim to a higher purpose; and the pilgrims may look down on the superficiality they see in the tourists.

Although definitions and distinctions are slippery, I do think the difference is worth holding in mind. The first time I visited Dunmanus Bay I anchored in the remote little harbour dominated by the tower of the castle with scarcely another person in sight. How different it had seemed on my second visit, when Steve and I had sailed further up the bay and discovered the pub full of English expats who were visiting their holiday cottages. Similarly when I first sailed to Great Blasket on a cold April morning it seemed wild and unapproachable. Two years later in June the sun was out, visitors were being ferried out from the mainland, the beach busy with families enjoying a day by the sea. The mysterious specialness I had conjured up for myself was nowhere to be found. The Skellig Rocks, in contrast, seem to be too remote and inaccessible to be overwhelmed as tourist destinations—although since my visit they have been used as the location for the filming of scenes from the recent *Star Wars* film amid complaints from conservationists that the number of visitors and helicopter flights threaten the World Heritage Site and disturb the wildlife. On Inishmore I found the babble of the human overwhelmed the presence of the land, and to some extent I allowed myself to get caught up in consuming the sights rather than dwelling with experience.

I suspect that deepened encounters with the more-than-human world, moments of grace, are less likely at these 'destinations', except maybe out of season. Such destinations are in large part constructed to cater for the tourist experience, the novelty, even oddity, of the sights balanced with plenty of safety cushions and escape routes. For a deeper encounter one needs to find one's own special times and places, maybe in the local woods, maybe 'the primrose at the river's brim': places that carry qualities these major destinations may have lost. Mark Cocker writes of discovering and rediscovering such places as he visits the rook roosts around his home, 'the odd sort of pleasure in greeting once more the smashed horse-chestnut stumps... I rootle around in one old lean-to barn for the winter's crop of owl pellets... I love the idea that in all the world no one else has seen and smelt and relished the details of this unwatched, unconscious place'.[3]

My equivalents to Cocker's 'unconscious places' are those anchorages where I have spent a quiet night. In the falling darkness I maybe look across the water to the bright lights of a ferry port and the feeble glow from windows rising dimly up the hills behind. Other than that, no lights are visible: the shore of the bay remains in deep darkness. I light the Tilley lamp inside Coral's cabin, and as the pressured paraffin flares the mantle into dazzling bright, the darkness around me seems to gather closer and deepen. Where previously a vague grey light seeped through the cabin windows, they became shiny black mirrors reflecting the interior back onto itself, suggesting an emptiness outside. I find myself contentedly alone, hours from other human beings. No one knows where I am.

Chapter Nine

Finding the Way

The endless path
Drops over rocks to the sea.
On the cliff top, the sign less signpost
Points over the ocean
John Crook
The Koans of Layman John

As Coral emerged from Brannock East Sound at the northern end of Inishmore, the easterly wind caught her sails, heeled her over, and set her bouncing off over the short sharp waves. It was an overcast day with the sun just seeping through a thin ceiling of cloud. The Connemara coast was visible in the distance as a line of darker grey between pale sky and steely sea. I could easily make out the old watch tower on Golam Head, a stubby pencil line sticking into the sky, which is the key marker for pilotage on this coast. Once clear of the sound and in deeper water, the waves became longer and Coral's motion easier. I brought her round on to a close reach, heading away from the fragmented limestone of Inishmore to find a new anchorage on the mainland.

The rocks of southern Connemara are granite, igneous rocks, cooked in the belly of Earth, extruded in nine or more batholiths around 400 million years ago, then worn down by glacial action. Granite is hard and crystalline, so different from the friable limestone of Inishmore where contemporary, as well as archaic, weathering is evident. But not all granite is the same, as even a quick look at the chart of Connemara will suggest. The coast from Galway follows an almost straight westward line for twenty miles, with only a few small inlets, until it reaches Cashla Bay, the first serious shelter west of Galway and the main ferry port for the Aran Islands. From Cashla Bay west to just beyond Roundstone the coastline is fragmented, indented with large and small bays, scattered with islands and rocky outcrops of all shapes and sizes. These reach over five miles offshore in a maze of rocks and shoals that at first glance looks impossible to navigate. Beyond Roundstone the granite stops and older volcanic and igneous rocks run out into the Atlantic at Slyne Head.

A significant fault line in the granite runs inland from the region of Cashla Bay. To the east, the granite is composed of large crystals, formed deep in the slowly cooling interior and so more resistant to weathering. To the west, the granite cooled more quickly, the crystals are smaller, the rocks riven with cracks, all of which opens this stretch to erosion, as is evident in the tormented, fractal nature of the coastline.[1]

When I first unfolded a chart of this coastline and saw the mass of pale blue that marks shoal water and the Admiralty glyphs for hazards, both awash and underwater, I thought to myself, "How on Earth do I find my way through that lot?" I read the sailing directions, which told me, 'The coast of Connemara is rock-studded, challenging and unforgiving in pilotage'. So, as Coral sailed the short passage from Aran, I checked the chart again and again to make sure I was on a safe passage. The chart shows deep water around Golam Head, but Fairservice Rock lurks underwater just offshore a little to the west of my course. I went below to the chart table to do some formal pilotage. The waypoint I had set off the Head was bearing 29° magnetic, according to the GPS. I set the protractor and drew a line on the chart: I would pass well to the east of the hazard. Feeling more relaxed, I looked toward the cluster of visible rocks around the entrance of Kilkieran Bay. The nearest one must be Seal Rock, I decided, although it looked bigger than I expected. Behind it lay a cluster that, from my reading of the chart, must include Eagle Rock and two smaller companions, but from this angle they all merged into one dark jagged line along the surface of the water. I stood in the cockpit shuffling between chart, pilot book and binoculars, trying to sort which rock was which. Slowly, as we approached Golam and the perspective changed, the nearer rocks moved across my field of vision in front of their more distant neighbours. I began to distinguish their shapes and relative positions. I also began to understand the transit lines that are marked on the chart, which show the safe passages between the hazards.[2]

Finding my way in Connemara was all about transits, lining up two landmarks that show a safe passage between rocks and steering the boat along the virtual line they mark. Usually there are several such transits that work together to confirm safe passage. The reference points may be specially erected navigation marks, such as lighthouses or beacons; other prominent constructions such as water towers; or natural features, such as a clearly identifiable rock or the end of a headland. In the days of sail, ship's masters were often accomplished artists, sketching the shores with ink and watercolour to show the transits; some old Admiralty charts included illustrative etchings down the side. Modern sailing directions have colour photographs, which are often less helpful than sketches. But many transit lines only exist in the heads of the sailors who are familiar with the waters; visitors have to find, and invent, them for themselves.

Transit lines look clear on a paper chart but are often difficult to decipher in practice: 'Golam Head well open N of Redflag Island' leads all the way west by north through the Inner Passage up toward Roundstone; Carricknamackan, the low grey line in the middle distance lines up with the south edge of Eagle Rock to clear the dangers going eastward toward Cashla. I had done my homework, studied the charts and pored over the pilot book many times before leaving home. It was not until I studied the rocks, learned their outlines, watched how they merged with each other and separated according to the direction of my view that I was able to remember the names and understand the transits.

Where no suitable transits exist, one establishes 'position lines' by taking bearings with a hand compass from landmarks and plotting them on the chart. Two position lines show the ship's position where they cross; three lines are much better; a pilot may also use the depth sounder to provide additional information. But this takes longer than sighting along a transit line and so is less helpful when close to hazards. There is always a degree of error that must be accounted for—more so with position lines than transits—and of course both may be impossible to follow in poor visibility.

My first task was to find a safe anchorage in Kilkieran Bay, somewhere remote and quiet after the busyness of Cill Rónáin on Inishmore. Once I was closer to land and clear of the offshore hazards, I brought Coral round to port to clear Golam Head and studied the eastern coastline of the bay. Immediately north of the Head I could see the seaweed-covered rock in the middle of the entrance to Golam Harbour. Beyond that the chart shows the islands of Freaghillaunmore and Freaghillaaunbeg. Not only did the names tie up my tongue and run together in my head, it was almost impossible to distinguish one island from the next until the narrow channel between them opened as I passed. They were both low-lying, with scattered boulders along the shoreline and outcrops of granite separated by low scrub. Here and there a roofless ruin stood between tumbledown stone walls following a winding path from the water's edge to the low ridge above.

The long Gaelic names I found difficult to remember, let alone pronounce. This area of Connemara is *An Gaeltacht*, a Gaelic speaking region. But the names on the Admiralty Charts are not in the original Gaelic, nor are they translations: the naval surveyors who mapped these waters in the nineteenth century created Anglicized versions of the Gaelic. Golam Head in Gaelic is Ceann Gólaim; Kilkieran, Cill Chiaráin; Lettermore, Leitr Mealláin; Freaghillaunmore, Fraoch Oileán Mór; and so on. As Tim Robinson points out, 'some of the rocks have acquired strange English names, through over-literal translation of the prosaic Irish'. For example further up the coast are rocks named Wild Bellows and Sunk Bellows on the chart. Robinson tells us that the word *bolg* in Gaelic can mean a swelling such as a shoal, as well as bellows; and that *báite* means merely submerged as well as sunken or drowned.

I sailed on gently into the bay, continuing to puzzle over the chart and pilot book while keeping a careful eye on the depth sounder. Then, as so often, everything fell into place: the headland Coral was approaching emerged as Dinish Point, she was sailing straight for the shoals off its southwest corner. I eased Coral out toward the middle of the bay, looking out for the two low hills on Lettermore Island—Lettercallow and Lettermore—that with Dinish Point provide alternative transits to clear the shoals. Gradually the features of the bay became clear.

Once past Dinish Point and the fish farm nestled on its northern shore, I could turn into the sheltered waters of Casheen Bay. The two islands ahead—Illauneeragh and Inishbarra—merged together, more boulders and low scrub. In the far purple distance loomed the Maamturk Mountains and the Twelve Pins; along the waterline little coves shone with beaches of bright, almost white sand. I felt with a twinge of alarm that while I was gazing at the scenery the depth sounder, which had been showing over thirty feet of water, suddenly showed fifteen, then ten. I edged Coral away from the islands into deeper water, belatedly noticing the shoal spit marked on the chart. I might have stopped there, next to these lovely beaches, but continued on, skirting the second fish farm, to the end of the bay where I could anchor in deep water sheltered from all directions. The water was clear and motionless, patches of weed floating on the surface. The anchor quickly found a firm hold and once I turned off the engine I was enveloped by a penetrating silence.

I spent the following morning learning my way around Kilkieran Bay. Some of the transits identified in the pilot book were easy to identify, others quite obscure. There is a transit line to clear Fock rocks, which lurk below high water in the middle of the bay. The pilot book instructed me to line the bump on Green Island with the chapel—'a grey, slated building'—on distant Lettermullen. I found the former, but even after long staring through binoculars could not clearly identify the latter against the morning sun. Searching for the chapel I disoriented myself; when I put down my binoculars I felt completely lost. Nothing made sense any more: all the features were flattened out. Where had Dinish Point gone? Was that Ardmore Point in front of me? It was too foreshortened to be sure. I had a moment of anxiety while I checked and rechecked, before everything fell into place again. And so it went on. I spent another hour or so pottering around the bay, checking landmarks and transits. Then I set a course out past Golam Head again, feeling satisfied that I had made a first pass at understanding its layout and the main pilotage marks.

These inshore transits and their markers are the marine equivalent of local footpaths. Those identified in the pilot book are the obvious ones: local sailors, both professional and leisure, will be aware of many more, both consciously and unconsciously, with different transits for different visibility conditions and states of tide. They will know how to avoid the isolated Outer Hard Rock off Ardmore in the same easy, half-aware and half-automatic, way I know where to change lanes driving down Wellsway into Bath.

In Kilkieran Bay the only man-made object that serves as a marker is Golam Tower; except for the invisible chapel, all the others are natural features which might be more or less visible according to the angle of the sun, the height of the tide, the presence of mist, and so on. In Brittany, which is more densely populated, natural features remain important, as do lighthouses, beacons and other nautical installations. But often, even in the small Breton ports, it is the church spire that provides the landward marker for significant transits and provided a guide for sailors well before the modern navigation marks were installed. Jesus' promise, "I am the Way..." seems to have been adopted literally. It seems very likely that church towers and spires were built so as to provide guides for mariners; and that Christian buildings were erected on even older sites that had both practical and spiritual significance.[3]

A few days after arriving at Kilkieran Bay I took the Inner Passage between the hazards close to the mainland shore and the rocks and reefs further offshore up to Roundstone. This longer passage is marked by a main transit line, described in the pilot book as 'Golam Head well open north of Redflag, 125°'; a number of other transits are offered to check one's position along the way, and one is advised to check off the islands and rocks to each side of the passage as they are passed.

These longer passages were in common and essential use not so long ago by the sailing boats that supplied the communities all along the coast of Connemara. Robinson claims that over 400 or them—big-decked Galway hookers up to forty feet long and smaller open boats—were active in the 1830s, and they continued to sail commercially well into the twentieth century. With their gaff rigs and tan sails they still can be seen, maintained by enthusiasts and raced at regattas along the coast.

Longer still are the passages down the whole of the Atlantic seaboard from Iceland and Scandinavia, encompassing the coasts of Scotland, Ireland, Wales and the English West Country, through Brittany, Portugal and Spain to the entrance to the Mediterranean. As Barry Cunliffe traces in his book, *Facing the Ocean*, these seaways have brought together the communities along this coast in trade and cultural exchange for approaching ten thousand years, from a time when transport by land across the continent was far more difficult. The course I sailed earlier in the year from the Scilly Isles to Baltimore would have been part of one of these seaways. Robert Macfarlane points out that these seaways are as significant as the ancient tracks on land. Moreover, there is the same relationship between the immediately local, the middle and long-distance paths at sea as on land. Following these transits is another example of following what Macfarlane calls the Old Ways.[4]

And how quickly one becomes accustomed to the landmarks! Of course, in the two weeks I explored the Connemara coast I didn't gain the familiarity of a local. But I soon felt at ease with the main landmarks and their relationship. As I looked down from St Macdara's Island along the transit to Golam Head, I had a good idea of the location of the hazards inshore and offshore along the way. When I returned to Kilkieran Bay with wind against me, I had to tack either side of the transit line, approaching close to the hazards on either side. As I did so, the relationships between the different islands and headlands changed and so reoriented me along the way. By the third time of taking the passage I knew where I had to tack to avoid the Carrickaview breaker without consulting chart or GPS. I made mistakes, but I was sufficiently cautious that these mistakes were not dangerous, but rather provided me with new understanding.

Of course the charts, pilot books and GPS were essential. The first two allowed me some tiny insight into the collective knowledge of this coast gained by sailors and chart-makers over centuries. The last gave access to (almost) pinpoint positioning in latitude and longitude, and a way of double-checking against the physical observation. GPS, with its translation of physical space into coordinates and waypoints, is a wonderful aid, but I often felt it created an abstraction that disengaged me from the reality of the coast around. In contrast, eyeballing pilotage brought me into more direct encounter with the physical world and through it I have begun to know and be in relationship with the coast of Connemara. Even as I sit at my desk writing two years later I can call to mind the bleak cylinder of Golam Tower, how Redflag Rock looks just open to the south, the patch of sand that shows on Inishmuskerry as one sails past, the extensive surf on Tonyeal Rocks near St Macdara's Island. Understanding and working with these landmarks and transits brought me into a sense of presence with the seascape. I felt I knew the place in a more complete way, and were I to return the detailed memories would come flooding back.

Another traditional form of pilotage is known as dead reckoning. Here, one starts from a known position and plots direction and distance travelled on the chart every hour, taking into account the effect of tidal streams, leeway, and other variables. It is more often used for crossing open sea than for coastal passages. The term 'dead reckoning' is said to be derived from 'ded' or 'deduced' reckoning, which suggests 'to trace from the beginning'. However, the common term 'dead reckoning' seems to me to acknowledge that this is not simply rational/empirical process but a skill with an intuitive dimension.

Radar, global positioning, and other electronic aids have taken a lot of the uncertainty out of navigation and pilotage. A passage can be planned with much more assurance that one will arrive where one intended to. But all forms of navigation can give us a dangerous sense that we know exactly where we are. Charts may get soaked or blown overboard, buoys may move position, perches (poles fixed to rocks to show their position) get blown away in storms. We may confuse the transit lines or make mistakes on our arithmetic. Dead reckoning is subject to cumulative errors arising from the quality of the information available and the judgements of the navigator, who should always explicitly acknowledge the uncertainty of a plotted position. Electronic aids may malfunction, and uncertainties are still built in: the GPS and the chart are often based on different 'datum'; the surveys on which the information is based can be decades old, especially in Western Ireland and Scotland. There is always a degree of uncertainty built in to the information and its interpretation. Pilotage is a continual process of inquiry, interrogating both information and its interpretation, and continually seeking more data and alternative interpretations. Especially when one's position is uncertain, it is all too easy to interpret the evidence to confirm where one thinks one is. Certainty is the greatest enemy of safety: the map is not the territory, the information available is as good as the mapmaker and the choices as good as the navigator.

It seems evident to me that there is a link of some kind between these accounts: finding my way in the literal sense of navigation and pilotage, finding one's way as a pilgrim, and finding our way as a human community through climate change and the environmental crisis. Pilgrimage involves physical movement through symbolically charged landscapes. More generally, the metaphor of the journey or the path is often used in relation to human endeavour: Jesus' promise that "I am the Way..." may be literally as well as metaphorically built into some transit lines, where one of the landmarks is a church spire. More enigmatically the Tao Te Ching, depending on the translation, tells us not to confuse the way we can speak about with the real or eternal Way—which in various translations tells us that the Way you can go, or the Way that can be spoken, isn't the real way. Eliot reminds us, 'We shall not cease from exploration...'[5]

Many pilgrimage routes are established and well marked. They provide a form of certainty and a container that allows deep contemplation. But all pilgrimages include a greater or lesser degree of disorientation: unfamiliar sites, the stress of travelling, footsore weariness, concern about where one may eat and sleep, the danger of thieves and even violence. Other forms of pilgrimage, however, involve wandering with no fixed goals and no permanent means of sustenance.

The lessons from navigation and pilotage teach us that it is a mistake to be too sure of where you think you are and where you are going. The many voices offering ways through the environmental crisis—and equally those who deny that there is such a crisis—often appear strangely sure of themselves. One has to shout loudly and have clear proposals in order to be heard above the din of competing priorities or alternative suggestions. The media are full of arguments for and against use of fossil fuels, nuclear power, wind power; for some, the preservation of the countryside is most important, for others it is human poverty, for others the protection of species; some are committed to a vegetarian or vegan diet, others willing to be moderate carnivores. Maybe the largest, and most dangerous, certainty is the political commitment to a rise in global temperatures of no more than 2°C. This is an arbitrary and impossibly exact figure that provides a sense of certainty where none exists; our political system contributes to the crisis by developing policy and action out of fragmented and decontextualized information.

The environmental crisis tells us that we as a civilization, maybe as a species, have lost our way. If we are to navigate to some kind of safety, we need not to be too sure of ourselves, lest we interpret the information to conform to our prejudices. We must look for the whole of the evidence and its context; draw on all the information we have, all the different perspectives, in a brave and unrelenting process of inquiry.[6]

Chapter Ten

Sacred Places: Macdara's Island

A sailing vessel came into Oileán Mhic Dara. It was driven by bad weather. She spent a couple of nights there and the crew killed the bull that was on the island and the ram that was with the sheep. When she sailed out in the evening she found herself anchored in the same place the next morning. This happened three times. The crew said to themselves that the island must belong to some saint and that it wasn't right for them to kill the beast and that they should show some honour to the saint. So they built a church in his honour and St Mac Dara's church is there ever since.

As told by Tim Robinson

Connemara: A Little Gaelic Kingdom

The Inner Passage runs between the off-lying rocks and the chain of little islands along the southern coast of Connemara. It is not a particularly difficult passage, nevertheless on this first time through I was keyed up, on high alert. That phrase in the sailing directions kept running through my mind, describing these waters as 'strewn with rocks'. So I held carefully to the transit line—'Golam Head well open N of Redflag Island'—that marks the safe passage, and ticked off the islands as I passed: Birmore with its shingle patches; Inishmuskerry and its sandy beaches; little Duck Island, only a bit more than a rock; Carrickaview, always awash and covered in breakers; and Mason Island with ruined houses that stand bleak against the skyline. I kept on my feet the whole way through so I could keep a good lookout, even though, with the onshore wind blowing up moderate waves, Coral was rolling uncomfortably. Once past Carrickaview breakers I relaxed a little, and saw I could either carry on and take the weather passage around Macdara's Island, or divert through Macdara Sound into narrower but more sheltered waters. The waves were breaking on the exposed seaward shore of Macdara. As the narrow sound between Mason and Macdara islands opened up, breakers on each side, I could see through to quieter water. I put the tiller to windward and sailed Coral into shelter.

Immediately through the narrow sound there lay a pretty little bay to port. Scarcely a bay really, just a shallow bight sheltered by the reef between St Macdara's and its off-lier, which itself is no more than a pile of big stones with a thatch of grass on top. Come high spring tide in a few hours, the waves would break across the reef and the shelter gone, but for the moment it was perfect. I took Coral cautiously into the bay and dropped the anchor.

As I paused to get my breath the sun came out. The earlier rain had cleared the air, so in the bright light the island came into sharp focus. On the shoreline, granite boulders framed a tiny white beach. Above, grassy slopes cropped by sheep led up to a small stone building partly sheltered in a shallow hollow. This was the chapel mentioned by Robinson. The whole building appeared quite plain. Most notable was the roof, its stone tiles covered in golden yellow lichen, rising sharply to a high apex with a rather extravagant decoration at the top of each gable.

The little bay and the chapel seemed to dance in the brilliant light shimmering off the surface of the water. In the opposite direction, north to the mainland, the view was more sombre. A metallic sea reached toward the low coastline, beyond which rose the Twelve Bens of central Connemara. They seemed to march, smoky blue, along the line of the horizon, low stratus clouds marking a dark line across the peaks, lighter cumulus piling up above with shafts of sunlight shining through.

Terns, delicate little creatures, were fishing all around Coral, twittering away as they did so. Sometimes known as sea swallows, theirs is an acrobatic flight. They flutter on long, pointed wings, darting this way then that, a little glide down to the water as if to get a better view, then a sharp rise to almost stall in the air. When they see fish they cluster above the surface and half dive, half flop into the water—they don't go deep like gannets—to make a catch.

After lunch I hurried to put on waterproofs and boots, inflate the dinghy, lower the outboard into place, and climb in with my camera. But the outboard wouldn't start, a recurrence of the old problem still not resolved. By the time I got it going the tide was nearly at the top of the reef and heavy rainclouds were blowing in from the south again. Soon the rain was hammering on the spray hood. Landing would have to wait for another day. Or maybe again, just to be here was enough. What a place to stop for lunch!

A few days later the tide and winds were right to return and make a landing: low tide would be early afternoon and the winds were forecast to be light from the south. I motored out from Roundstone, noting the landmarks as I passed, feeling I was getting the hang of the local pilotage. As I approached the island I could just make out a small boat among the rocks in the bay. Not other visitors, I hoped: I wanted the island to myself! As I got close I could see it was a local boat, with two men checking their lobster pots. These traditional open fishing boats are of substantial build, wide of beam with a pronounced sheer in the bows. They retain the long wooden oars flattened at the end into a narrow blade, with old-fashioned thole pins in place of rowlocks, but most of the time rely on an outboard engine. Once the men had finished in the little bay off the chapel, they carried on along the north coast of the island, pulling up lobster pots as they went.

The ebb tide had just started. The little bay was still quite full, but waves were no longer breaking over the reef. I set Coral to anchor carefully some way offshore, so that as the tide dropped she would have plenty of water. Anchoring takes quite a lot of running back and forth from the bows to the cockpit: forward to drop the anchor, aft to put the engine in reverse, forward again to pay out more chain and check the holding, and so on. I wanted to be quite happy the anchor was holding well, since I was planning to leave Coral on her own for a while.

Putting camera, notebook and pencil, and a box for collecting wildflowers in my waterproof bag, I took the dinghy ashore. Through the sparkling clear water I looked down at the forest of brown seaweed waving in the current. Nearer the sandy shore the weed stopped and the bottom was strewn with coloured pebbles: browns and greys and reds, coarse and fine textures, all refracted through the glittering web of sunlight on the surface. At the water's edge, where the little waves wetted them, the pebbles gleamed in the sunshine; further up the beach they were dry and comparatively dull. Massive chunks of granite emerged out of the sand, criss-crossed with cracks in which bladder wrack was doing its best to keep a roothold. On the grass above the beach stood a small and very weathered Celtic cross; behind that the chapel itself, lichen-yellowed roof reaching into the blue sky, with fair weather clouds blowing in from the sea beyond.

It is not possible to write about Connemara without feeling the shadow of Tim Robinson, whose trilogy of books explore history, language and landscape in the most extraordinary detail. His account of the chapel in *Connemara: A Little Gaelic Kingdom* notes the enormous granite blocks, the high-pitched roof with its elaborate finials, and writes that 'it shows no deference to the power of gales beyond the slight concession of locating itself in a shallow dip in the eastern flank of the island, where it is spared the worst of the westerlies'. Robinson dates the chapel to the twelfth century, not, as the pilot book suggests, to the fifth; but he does accept the possibility that there was an older, wooden building on this site, noting details in its construction that suggest that the stone reconstruction follows quite faithfully an older wooden original. The chapel was restored in 1976 by the Office of Public Works.[1]

There are many accounts of St Macdara being associated with stormy weather: it is said that, when passing through his sound, sailors are required to 'bow down their sails three times, in reverence to the saint'. The punishment for not doing so was to be 'tossed by sea and storme'. I, of course, being ignorant of this had failed to follow this custom when I first went through the sound, so on landing I was careful to apologize to the saint and bow to the chapel in contrition, partly, but only partly, tongue in cheek.[2]

So who was this St Macdara? Robinson's careful inquiry suggests that his first name Síonach and its variations Sinach, Sionach, or Siothnach, is associated with wind and stormy weather. Síonach Macdara, then, is the stormy one. Robinson comes to the conclusion that when Christianity first arrived in Ireland, many of the old pagan gods had to go underground or hide among the peasantry as fairies. But some, more daringly maybe, became saints. Since there seems to be no record of a religious foundation of any kind on Macdara's island, Robinson suggests that Síonach Macdara is far older than even the original chapel: 'he is a regional Celtic god of the winds in Christianized guise'.

This idea greatly appeals to me, for 'on the western edge' in its fullest meaning refers to not just the geographical edge of the British Islands but also to the 'edge' of European civilization. The far west of Ireland has historically held on to ways of understanding our world that have been overwhelmed by other forces on the mainland (developing a form of Christianity that remained close to the old ways, preserving scholarship and writing during the Dark Ages being among them). The story of Síonach Macdara shows how different strands of understanding our world can be twined together.[3]

I walked up the slope toward the chapel. While it looks well in its setting from a distance, close up it is evidently so heavily restored that any feeling of antiquity requires considerable imagination. A description written in 1898 reported that: 'No mortar is visible in the walls of the church; huge and well cut granite quoins are used, the joints being well filled with spawls, or small broken stones'. The modern restoration has used mortar to point in the stones, which is out of keeping, although if it had not been thoroughly restored the stormy Atlantic would soon have demolished it into a pile of granite, as it has the other buildings hinted at in the surroundings. Most disappointing is that the entrance is barred by a heavy iron grate and padlock, to which has been welded a Christian cross. There is something oddly contradictory in the symbols offered here! The interior is in any case completely plain, with the floor covered in what looks like roadstone.[4]

So, preferring to enjoy the chapel in its context rather than close up, I wandered around the island, finding my way along sheep's paths through boggy places where earlier in the year wild iris had bloomed, and clambering over granite outcrops polished smooth by glaciers (geologically the whole island is a granite dome ground down by ice). The grass below the chapel was studded with hawkweed, which from a distance brought to mind a scattering of golden coins shining in the bright sun. Looking closer I found a wide variety of wild flowers, and collected samples intending to identify them back on board Coral (my inadequacy as a botanist was revealed: I was completely unsuccessful in finding out what any of them were, but I carefully put them in my flower press in the hope that someone might help me when I got home). Among the flowers, indeed all over the sheltered side of the island, butterflies were flitting about. One was a dusky mid-brown, with a small spot toward the outer end of each wing, a meadow brown, I think; another was white, with orange colouring at the end of its wings, which never settled long enough for me to get a good look.

I looked back to where Coral was riding to her anchor in the bay, with the reefs off Mason Island behind. She was quite safe. I made sure the dinghy was hauled above the high water line and set out around the south side of the island, where shelving granite slopes down into the Atlantic. I walked above the line of the storm beach and was soon followed and harassed by oyster-catchers, who clearly didn't like me being there. They circled low over my head, flew off in wide sweeps and then dived back toward me, keeping their high-pitched cry going all the while. As they passed near me I could see their black and white feathers, and their long orange beaks wide open as they shrieked at me. I took care not to go near anything that looked like a nest, and after a while the birds gave up on me and flew off on more important business. Meanwhile two young gulls, still in speckled juvenile feathers, seemed to lurk on an outcrop higher up the slope; and an enormous black-backed gull sternly stood sentinel on the boulder that marks the highest place on the island.

I walked right round the island until, back on the northern side, I came to an upright stone on a high point just above the chapel, overlooking the bay, maintained in place by a cairn of small boulders. Weather worn, it was scored with lines that might or might not be traces of a Celtic cross. On one side of the cairn was a plastic fishing float with the loop for making fast a line pointing upwards. It was clearly placed there intentionally, firmly supported in position as part of the cairn. Was this some modern day offering to the ancient storm god in the guise of a Christian saint, a supplication to keep fishermen safe and their lobster pots full? If so, it felt to me entirely understandable and appropriate. If the old gods are still with us, maybe they will lead us back to a respect for the land and sea of which we are a part.

I sat under this maybe-cross, remembering my intention to meditate formally on landscape. After taking a while to slow my breathing and allow my thinking mind to calm down somewhat,

I opened my eyes to the scene in front of me. Could I intuit its form, its storm-battered quality? Could I feel the rhythm of the tides that cover and uncover the reefs? Could I sense the form of diverse habitats occupied by different kinds of beings? And what of the whole of southern Connemara that lay out in front of me across the bay? Could I comprehend the structure of its granite coast, its boggy flatness and the ranges of mountains that rise up in the distance?

There was far too much thinking going on to call this meditation; whatever, this is what I wrote in my notebook:

> still the grass in front of me is blowing in the wind
> still the waves breaking on the rocks
> still the oystercatchers flying by with their high pitched call
> still the butterflies flittering away
> and still...

Back at the beach, I selected a pebble to take home, to go with those I have collected from other granite islands I have sailed to—St Agnes in the Scillies, Ouessant in Brittany. Now the tide was low, more of the seaweed was floating to the surface and the waving jungle of browns and greens and reds, shiny with wetness, seemed thicker and more tangled. I pushed the dinghy into the water and paddled offshore so as not to get the outboard's propeller caught in weed. As I did so, a gaff-rigged cutter with a black hull, long bowsprit and tan sails full in the breeze drew into the bay. The tiny figure at the helm put the tiller over; as she tacked around another tiny figure hauled on the mainsheet. Her brown sails shook in the wind as she went about, then filled again in a powerful sunlit curve and she headed off westward toward Deer Island.

I had wondered if I would land on Macdara's island a second time after lunch, but it seemed that Síonach—or Sinach or Sionach or Siothnach—had brought me fair winds. The cutter sailing off so bravely showed me it would be a real sin to ignore the gift, so I hauled up the anchor and set off for a pleasant afternoon sail around the islands.

Chapter Eleven

Danger and Difficulties

For those who would seek directly, by entering the primary temple,
the wilderness can be a ferocious teacher, rapidly stripping down the
inexperienced or the careless. It is easy to make mistakes that will
bring one to an extremity.
Gary Snyder
The Practice of the Wild

After exploring Connemara, I took Coral round Slyne Head to Clifden at the far western end of the peninsular and left her there for a few weeks. I then joined up with a new crew for the third leg around the west of Ireland and on to Scotland. Susi and Dave were, like Suzy and Gib, students of outdoor education, used to adventures in the wild, but with little sailing experience. After a couple of days settling in, sailing in stiff winds around Clifden Bay to help them find their sea legs, we set off northwards past Inishbofin, Clare Island, Achill Head to Blacksod Bay. We had two good days of fast sailing in moderate westerly winds. Coral was happy with all plain sail set, plunging over the seas, throwing up water from her bows; and the crew seemed happy too, chatting and dozing as they got used to the long days in the cockpit. Past Inishbofin we were too far offshore to see much of the coast until we reached Achill Head, which reaches out into the Atlantic in a thin sliver of rock, rising in steep cliffs nearly 700 metres straight from the sea. We kept well offshore, but could nevertheless see how the south-facing side is folded into a series of ridges and appears lush with vegetation, while the north is bare rock with evidence of landslips. There is a fair weather anchorage close to the point, not appropriate in today's fresh winds. What we saw from a distance was spectacular enough, with the head one moment bright in sunshine, the next disappearing in cloud and mist.

Blacksod Bay is well sheltered from the Atlantic by the low Mullet Peninsular; we were glad of this since gale force winds kept us there for two days. On the third day the weather, while still fresh, had moderated enough for us to set out around Erris Head, where the coast takes a turn to the northeast. For the first couple of hours we tacked out of the bay directly into the Atlantic swell. Wave after wave rolled toward us, each one a hillside of water with wavelets rippling down its steep face. Well reefed down, Coral made good progress, climbing each wave in turn, seeming to pause on the crest before plunging down the other side, white water streaming around her. With Coral heeled well over and Aries holding an exact course on the wind, the three of us sat snugly side by side on the windward seat of the cockpit, our seaboots firmly wedged on the lee side, looking down past our feet at water swirling along the lee rail. This was tough sailing, but it was also deeply pleasurable: we laughed together at the size of each wave as it rolled toward us; and exclaimed how the sun, as it peeked through the clouds, picked out the streams tumbling down in sparkling ribbons from the summit of Slievemore on Achill Island. Our third long tack took us past Turduvillaun, the last of the rocky islands at the southern end of the Mullet Peninsula. This was the first time Susi and Dave had seen heavy seas crashing on the shore from a boat, and they watched in some awe as the swell rolled up the rock face and broke over it. Sheets of broken water, dazzling white, rose high in the air, then streamed down the rock face in sparkling waterfalls, soon inundated by the arrival of the next wave.

Once round the headland we were able to bear away northwards up the channel between the Inishkea Islands and the mainland. Now, with the wind on the beam and the islands sheltering the sound from the extremes of the swell, Coral, even with her mainsail reefed down and flattened, raced along on an even keel. We relaxed, wondered if it was time for coffee and realized it was already lunchtime. Cup-a-soup and warm pitta bread were more than enough to keep us going, and our spirits remained high as we stormed north for an hour or more. Then things got more challenging.

The passage between the most northerly of the islands and the coast narrows and is set about each side by underwater reefs. Piloting safely through the gap depends on accurately identifying islands and rocks from the pilot book descriptions. But as I peered through the spray, I struggled to distinguish one low island from the next. For a few moments, with Coral still forging ahead, I had an anxious time. Was that Inishgloria ahead, or had we already past it? Were we clear of the hidden reef jutting out from the mainland? Dave helmed while I checked and rechecked the pilot book. Then suddenly we were safely through the gap, passing through a patch of water where foam streaked across the passage, just as the pilot book told us to expect in heavy weather.

There was no time to relax. After the relative shelter of the inner passage we were suddenly exposed to the full force of the Atlantic. But it was not the regular swell we had encountered earlier in the day: the waves were sharp and chaotic, bunched up in peaks and troughs, their tops blown off in spindrift. We hauled in the sails to bring Coral close-hauled to weather Annagh Head, but rough seas knocked the wind out of the closely-reefed sail, so she didn't have the power to muscle through the waves. Coral faltered and dropped to leeward. I watched the rocks and surf off the headland draw close, closer than was comfortable: rocks that looked alarmingly jagged, covered in surf that looked particularly fierce and bright.

"Time for a judicious use of the engine," I said. Was I trying to sound calmer than I really was? We were all three holding on tight to stop us being thrown around the cockpit, so even getting to the engine controls was a challenge. Coral lurched as I reached for the throttle, throwing me across the cockpit. Susi grabbed at me by the tail of my waterproof, crying in some alarm, "Oh my god, I thought you were going over the side!" although I was only a bit bruised from my tumble. Once started, the engine did its business, powering us through the water so we cleared the head and then the enormous mass of Eagle Rock a mile or so along the coast.

Coral crashed into the waves, nothing elegant about her progress. The engine roared under our feet, with an unfamiliar whine from the propeller as it thrashed through solid water one moment, spun in foam the next. Sharp-peaked waves towered around us, lurching Coral viciously this way then that, each sidedeck under water in turn. Between the peaks deep troughs opened, holes in the sea we could peer down into, eerily dark and calm at the bottom. One wave picked the whole boat high in the air then dropped her directly into a trough, where she landed with a crash, the rigging shuddering, the hull throwing sheets of water high on both sides. There was a clattering from the cabin as crockery was thrown around in its racks; Susi looked anxiously down the companionway, but nothing seemed to be broken, just a tin of drinking chocolate flying out of the locker. Even in these severe conditions, never once did I feel Coral was at serious risk, never once ploughing into a wave or allowing one to actually break over the deck, but rather lifting bow or stern buoyantly to each challenge as it came. Was it scary? Well, scary enough for Susi to turn pale and reach for her lifejacket; scary enough for me to look up at the mast and pray there was no weakness in the rigging that would bring it down; although Dave seemed happy enough to watch the waves and exclaim at their size. I was just relieved that the steps we took to keep moving safely were sufficient. "Thank goodness for an engine that starts!" we agreed.

Once we were clear of Eagle Rock we turned north and east past Erris Head itself. The seas quietened somewhat, and with the wind on the quarter we turned off the engine and ran for the shelter of Broad Haven Bay, Coral rolling horribly in the following seas. There was shelter but not much comfort in Broad Haven, just an open anchorage in the Belmullet Channel. "Where have you come from?" asked a fisherman on the quayside where we landed in our dinghy. I said something about the rough water. "Ah," he said in masterly understatement. "It can be a bit nasty around Eagle Rock in a northwesterly."

The wind got up again that night. Sitting in the shelter in Belmullet Channel with Coral riding at her anchor and the wind roaring around her, I wondered about the day. Had I been foolish to set off in such fresh winds? Should I have anticipated the rough seas around Eagle Head? And I wondered, how much more violent can the sea get? We recorded 27 knots on our wind indicator, less than a full gale. What would the sea be like in storm force winds twice that speed, given that the force of the wind increases at least geometrically with velocity?

Despite the steep sharp waves, the water flying everywhere, the crash of the hull and the shuddering of the rigging I knew, alarming though it all was, that everything was going to be OK. But more than OK: as I reflected then, and since, on this experience I asked, "Was this, too, a moment of grace?" It was in marked contrast to my almost transcendental sense of merging with the night sky. But nevertheless it was a moment when I was totally open to everything around me. It was a time of intimate interdependency, of fierce beauty and determined action; a time of utter attention and presence.

We were stuck for two days and two nights behind the spit of land that shelters Belmullet Channel from Broad Haven Bay while strong winds from the northwest blew bands of heavy rain across us. The Belmullet Peninsula is flat and low-lying, stretching featureless around the anchorage; and we were miles away from the town itself. So we sat around in Coral's cabin getting rather bored and fed up. Dave and Susi played what seemed like endless games of cards while I tried to read, watching the weather forecasts for the opportunity to continue our journey. Sometimes these periods of enforced idleness bring with them a sense of developing camaraderie with lively conversation; but they can also, as on this occasion, result in 'cabin fever', claustrophobia, deepening irritation and lethargy. Our conversations became awkward and I felt an emotional distance developing between my two younger crew members and myself.

Eventually the weather improved, Met Éireann forecast fresh but not strong winds and a moderate sea. The next leg was to be a long one: I wanted to sail straight across the entrance to Donegal Bay to the island Aranmore—over seventy miles, at least twelve hours' sailing—rather than take the long diversion into the bay and then out again. This would be the longest sail that Dave and Susi had done so far, and while we talked it through together, I sensed they remained a little anxious. Maybe I was too concerned to keep them happy, which is why I let them stay in their bunks, leaving at seven, rather than leave at first light, as I would have preferred.

We left the shelter of the bay and headed north and west away from the low coast of County Mayo toward the cliffs of County Donegal. The wild weather of the past days had left an uneasy swell. The wind had dropped considerably and backed south of west, so our course took us more or less downwind. With the genoa goosewinged and a preventer line from boom end to the bows to stop the mainsail banging around, we took turns at the helm. All through the morning and into the afternoon Coral ambled along, her stern quarter lifting to the swell then dropping back as the wave passed underneath: pitch and roll, pitch and roll. It was an awkward and tedious motion. There was sufficient wind to keep us moving, but not enough to bring much pleasure or excitement, or to make good time. Keeping her on course required constant concentration from the person at the helm. It became clear that this was going to be a very long day's sail.

Once we had passed close to the Stags of Broadhaven, four

rocky islets emerging sharply from the sea, the weak early sun catching the thatch of grass on their eastern sides, our course took us well offshore. The coast of County Mayo, then of County Sligo, dropped back into a distant haze. For about half an hour we were right out of sight of land, and then the high ground of Slieve League and Malin Beg came into view on the far side of the bay. By teatime we were sailing along the Donegal coast. We might have enjoyed the scenery, the rugged cliffs rising out of the dark, edgy sea into the pale afternoon sky. But whilst we were making progress, it was slow progress; we were tired and still a long way from shelter.

Aranmore lies off the coast midway between Rathlin O'Birne Island on the northern corner of Donegal Bay, and Bloody Foreland, where the coast takes a decisive turn to the east. There are two approaches to the anchorage in the sound between island and mainland. The all-weather entrance is from the north, and to reach that we would have to sail to the west of the island and round Torneady Point at its northern extreme. There is an alternative approach through shoals, rocks and islands to the south, but this is only practicable in calm conditions, good visibility and with sufficient rise of tide. For a while I ignored the scenery, leaving Dave and Susi on watch in the cockpit, and sat at the chart table, going over the directions in the pilot book, scribbling tidal calculations in the logbook and estimating our time of arrival. For a while I thought we could just about make it through the southern approach, which would save us at least two hours' sailing. Then I realized it was stupid to even think about approaching tricky, unfamiliar channels on a lee shore with a dropping tide and fading light. I climbed up the companionway.

"I think it's unwise to take the southern approach with the tide dropping. We will have to take the long way round," I told them.

"How long will that take?" asked Susi.

"At least a couple of hours' extra." And as I told them I felt a glum silence descend.

Off the west coast of Aranmore the sea became more disturbed. Coral slopped about uncomfortably. I became increasingly worried about my crew, who sat in silence, tired and cold. I took the tiller and did my best to keep Coral sailing as fast as possible in the conditions, but the western side of the island stretched on interminably. Eventually we reached the point where we could gybe the main and make a safe course past the lighthouse and into the sheltered waters beyond. We had a few moments' delight as the sun dropped behind us, bathing us in yellow, lighting up the sails and drawing a deep orange brown from the coastline ahead. Very soon it touched the horizon in a final dazzle and then quickly set. As we rounded the northern tip of the island, darkness was approaching fast.

Once we had turned into the approaches to Aran Sound, the island rose up to starboard as a dark mass, silhouetted against the remaining brightness in the western sky. Soon we were faced with the challenge of finding our way in complete darkness. We could pick out one or two house lights and then, almost directly ahead of us, a light flashing.

"Flashing white every two and a half seconds." I counted out loud and checked the chart. "That's the beacon on Ballagh Rocks at the entrance to the Sound," I said. No longer worried about how long the journey was taking, I was again completely absorbed, piloting Coral into an unfamiliar anchorage, checking the sailing directions against what I could see. "Dave, will you steer directly for it while Susi and I look out for the lights on the leading line."

With Dave at the tiller and Susi and I looking out for the lights that would guide us into the sound, we approached closer and closer to the beacon on Ballagh Rocks. What had been a spot of light flashing in the distant darkness became bigger and clearer, until we could make out the shape of the lantern, the height of the beacon, and the luminous surf breaking against the rocks below. Dave, understandably anxious about steering directly for the breakers, allowed Coral's course to head off the direct line.

"Keep heading directly for the light," I told him, maybe rather abruptly, wary of hidden dangers to each side.

"We seem terribly close to the rocks," he replied. And I could see how it would feel like that.

"We are fine, a long way off yet," I tried to reassure him, "keep on the course."

It was not until we seemed very close that Susi pointed to the two occulting leading lights emerging from behind the island to starboard. They gradually came into line so we could, with some relief, turn away from the rocks and follow them along the transit into the anchorage, knowing that, even though we could not see them, Calf Island and Blind Rocks were safely to starboard, Dirty Rock and the mainland shore to port.

But Dave was still unhappy about being on the helm. "Which way do I turn to keep the lights in line?" he kept asking, not having the experience to keep Coral on the leading line in the dark.

I should have paid more attention to the anxiety in his voice, but I wanted him to stay on the tiller so I could pilot Coral to a safe spot to anchor. Once we were past Calf Island a new challenge emerged. 'Do not turn to starboard,' the sailing directions emphasize, 'until the peak of Moylecorragh comes in line with the Obelisk.' But in the pitch dark there was no sign of either peak or obelisk, just the lights on the leading line and a solitary flashing red in the distance on the starboard bow. I was taken aback: I had assumed that once we were in the Sound the way to the anchorage would be obvious. I slowed Coral right down and told myself that so long as we were on the leading line we were safe.

Susi had the pilot book in her hand. "That red light is on Black Rocks outside the harbour, right?" I said. Together we carefully identified what we little could see. We couldn't go into the harbour itself, which mainly served the ferry, but needed to find a spot to anchor in the bay between the Black Rocks and Calf Island. "I think anchorage must be in a bay to starboard over there," I said cautiously, pointing into the darkness.

I took over the helm from Dave—to his immense relief—and steered Coral off the leading line, edging carefully toward the shore. "Keep a good lookout each side and ahead," I told Susi and Dave. Dark shapes loomed up in front of us: a biggish vessel, which we realized was one of the ferries moored to a buoy overnight; the shore of Aranmore, dotted with orange streetlights; the vague shapes of moored yachts; and the outline of Calf Island. Although the Obelisk was still hidden in the dark, I gradually got my bearings and found a spot to anchor. It is amazing how much one can see on even the darkest night once one's eyes have developed their night vision.

It took a while to make sure the anchor was holding well, to stow the sails and tidy up the decks. We were all exhausted by the time we went below and made supper, although I was also elated at the successful piece of tricky pilotage. I should have noticed that Susi and Dave had been pretty alarmed: with no night sailing experience, they must have felt that we were blundering around in the dark with inadequate directions. Maybe if we had debriefed more before we went to bed I could have allayed some of their concerns, but I didn't. All I said before we turned in was, "We'll have a quiet day tomorrow exploring Aranmore."

But it wasn't to be. Yet again the wind got up overnight, blowing from the southeast directly down the Sound, so that Coral pitched around at an exposed anchorage. I was up from the small hours, keeping anchor watch. Dave seemed to sleep soundly, but I noticed Susi sit up and peer out of the cabin window several times. I guessed she was feeling uncomfortable and anxious. I too was on edge. While the anchor held we were safe, but when I looked aft I could see the waves breaking on the rocky lee shore. With the change in wind direction, I wanted us to move as soon as we could see what we were doing. At first light I checked the pilot book, and read the directions for Burtonport, a fishing harbour on the mainland side of Aran Sound, reached by the narrow but well-marked Rutland Channel between rocks and islands. We could get shelter there.

"This is neither comfortable nor very safe," I told them as I handed them mugs of tea at around six. "We need to move into Burtonport." Once we were dressed and in our waterproofs we gathered round the chart table and I went through the sailing directions.

"See the beacons on these rocks here and here," I pointed to the chart. "We have to pick them out and get on the transit between them to keep clear of Dirty Rock, which is here," I pointed again. "Once we are on that transit we should be able to pick out the channel markers, which are here and here."

Dave peered over my shoulder at the chart. "I don't really follow," he said. "I'd rather just leave it up to you." Quite unfairly, I felt a wave of irritation pass through me. I turned and looked him directly in the face.

"With this rain and all the spray that's around the beacons won't be easy to spot. They are just poles with triangular top marks. I need your eyes," I told him, and pointed out where the beacons were again.

Once underway and crossing the sound it wasn't too difficult to find the transit; Susi picked out the nearer beacon, then the more distant one. The leading line into the Rutland Channel passed rather close to where the water swirled about the rocky shore, but before I had time to worry about that we were in the deep and sheltered water. Even though the wind howled around us, and the stream swirled around in the channel, it was not difficult to follow the markers that led up to the harbour.

Burtonport is a tiny harbour at the end of a dredged channel. There is no space to anchor and no facilities for yachts, just one pier and a slip for the car ferry. Of course, it was full of boats sheltering from the windy weather. There was little room to manoeuvre as we looked around to find a place to moor. A local man, who had watched us come in all wet and bedraggled, called from the pier head, pointing out a space, and caught the lines we threw up to him. We had a few moments of frantic activity, getting lines ashore and secured, getting fenders out to keep Coral away from the metal piles.

Once Coral was safely tied up against the pier, with long lines set as springs so she would drop down safely with the tide, we climbed up the rusty metal ladder to the top. Dave and Susi decided to go off and find the shops. There was nothing around the harbour itself, but the pilot book suggested that there was a supermarket a mile or so down the road. It was with some relief, mutual, I am sure, that I watched them walk off together. I realized that they were both unhappy. If they had been frightened, that was my responsibility. But something else was going on: they seemed to be holding a bond between them that excluded me. But I soon forgot that as I turned to my own tasks, dragging the diesel containers from the depths of the cockpit lockers to top up the tank; filling water containers from the rather distant tap and struggling to carry them back along the pier and lowering them on a rope down into the cockpit. It was heavy work, and I could have done with some help. Once all this was done I made yet another cup of tea and settled down to wait for them. "We'll have to sort all this out when they get back," I told myself.

It seemed like I waited an age for their return. They said they had walked miles and still not found the supermarket. They had bought a few provisions at a local shop, and once we had stowed them I opened the conversation.

"Listen, we need to clear the air. We've had a difficult time, and I get the feeling neither of you are happy."

Susi immediately started to cry. "I just want to go home," she said. "I don't feel safe." I immediately felt for her: I remembered that feeling from when I first started sailing. "All last night I was looking out of the window worried that we were drifting on to those rocks," she continued.

"And I was up all night making sure we weren't," I pointed out, trying inadequately to reassure her. She poured out her worries about all the incidents of the past few days, which had started when she thought I was going to fall overboard in the rough water off Erris Head.

"I just want to go home," she repeated.

Dave took up the conversation, saying how he felt claustrophobic in Coral's little cabin and hated being dependent on me for everything. He too had felt unsafe. "It seemed sometimes that you were anxious about what was happening. That worried me. I'm used to being responsible for my own safety."

Something about that last phrase really irritated me and I nearly responded abruptly. I stopped myself just in time. "Listen! Just listen to how they feel," I told myself, as I realized just how far outside their comfort zones I had taken them. They seemed surprised when I told them how upset I felt that they had not felt safe. "It's been challenging, but I don't think it has been dangerous," I told them. "I'm really sorry you have been frightened. That is my fault."

We had a difficult conversation with a lot of heart-searching, including concerns on their part for leaving me on my own. In the end we agreed, I think mutually and amicably, that it would be best if they found a B&B and caught the morning bus from Burtonport back to the UK, while I continued on alone.

It didn't take long for them to find a B&B, pack their bags, and climb up the ladder. I watched them walk side by side along the pier, realizing I was feeling upset, relieved, and sympathetic all at the same time. I was happily on my own once more.

When people hear that I am sailing on the western coast of Ireland they often make comments admiring my courage, or ask about the dangers involved. To some extent these are sensible questions. This coast is exposed to the Atlantic with strong winds and enormous swell battering the shoreline at times. In several places submerged reefs run offshore for a mile or more. While in some areas there are many sheltered bays and harbours, there are also long stretches with little shelter and exposed headlands to negotiate. Help is always a long way off.

Is it dangerous? Probably less so than driving along a busy trunk road in heavy rain. It is, however, challenging: I have to be continually watching the weather, studying charts and sailing directions, making plans that I know will have to change; all this as well as sailing the boat and looking after myself. There is a boundary between acceptable challenge and foolhardiness, a boundary whose position is not always easy to determine: what appears to be a sensible plan in the morning can look foolhardy by mid-afternoon.

Hard physical conditions, challenges, even dangers, are necessary aspects of pilgrimage of all sorts. They are the experiences that help shake the pilgrim out of their everyday comforts and taken-for-granted assumptions. They are the challenges that we rise to, which draw forth our best and our worst selves, and so are necessary aspects of the learning.

Environmental activists Karsten and Allison Heuer once followed a herd of porcupine caribou in their yearly migration across northern Yukon and Alaska to the Arctic National Wildlife Refuge and calving grounds. Reflecting on their experiences, academic Shoshannah Ganz argues that this five-month journey can be seen as a pilgrimage not only for the humans but also for the caribou, engaged as they are in an ancient and instinctual movement that is under threat from oil drilling. For both humans and animals the journey is a hazardous affair, as Heuer points out, 'Four mountain ranges, hundreds of passes, dozens of rivers,

countless grizzly bears, wolves, mosquitoes, and Arctic storms—
those were the risks, that was the real story'.[1]

A major threat came from grizzly bears. Starving, having just
woken from their winter sleep, the bears follow the caribou in a
desperate hunt for food. Humans might be easier pickings. As
Allison protested, "Karst, this is crazy. We're following the
caribou to the calving grounds with a bunch of hungry grizzly
bears!"

What is the place of events like this on a pilgrimage? It is easy
to see them as the inevitable consequences of adventuring in
lonely places, or to dismiss them as foolish errors or sheer incom-
petence: the Heuers should have known about grizzlies, just as I
should have realized that the seas around Erris Head would be
rough. But in the context of pilgrimage they also carry some
teaching. They seem to be sent to test the pilgrim in some
manner, and the individual's worthiness is measured against
their ability to respond. But more than that, it often seems that
modern society does its best to remove risk and danger and
unpredictability from life. In doing so, it also removes us from
the natural world into the protected sphere that is 'civilization',
and in doing so takes away much that actually makes us human.
"Why do we go into the wilderness?" asked ecologist Anthony
Weston. After a thoughtful pause, his friend Tom Birch replied,
"Wilderness treats me like a human being."[2]

The first lesson is that the world, beyond and beneath human
constructions, is irrefutably real. Headlands are exposed, rocks
are hard, grizzly bears are fierce and hungry. The pilgrim may
start out with a whole range of hopes, fears and expectations, but
the encounter with the world will reveal its indisputable
presence. Whatever idealist, social constructionist or anthropocentric worldviews we hold are all challenged. Samuel
Johnson's friend Boswell thought Bishop Berkeley's arguments to
prove the nonexistence of matter irrefutable. Famously, Johnson
replied, 'striking his foot with mighty force against a large stone,

till he rebounded from it—"I refute it thus."'[3]

Headlands are exposed, grizzly bears are hungry and once we get past our flashy brains and technological wizardry we humans, just like the bears, are entirely dependent on the real existence of the thin layer of liveable space that surrounds Planet Earth.[4] We will crash into the factuality of climate change, the degradation of ecosystems, loss of other species, just as surely as night descended as we approached the Sound of Aran.

So the second lesson for the traveller as pilgrim is, are you alert for the signs—those that are obvious but more importantly those that are hidden—that warn of hazards? As wilderness guides and spiritual teachers continually ask, "Are you awake?" And the answer, for modern humans, must be, "No, we are sleep-walking into calamity."

The third lesson is, "Can you respond?" do you have the skill, resources and presence of mind to summon up appropriate action in response to the challenge? Can you respond without making the problem worse? In some ways pilgrimage seems to be about relearning life's fundamental lessons. I responded effec-tively enough in navigating Coral around the headland and finding the anchorage in the dark, but I do wonder what I would have done had Coral started sinking in the cold waters of the Atlantic.

Beyond immediate responsiveness lies a further challenge. My friend Malcolm Parlett writes that responding fully to situations is the 'heart of human living'. While we humans appear to be well designed for responding to the challenges of well defined emergency, he wonders how can we learn to respond to situa-tions of greater complexity, which have a longer timespan, where the evidence is less clear cut, and where there are extreme conse-quences if our choices are the wrong ones. A look at the long trajectory of human life on Earth suggests that ever since the agricultural revolution we have been obliged to develop solutions to problems thrown up by our previous inventiveness, at enormous cost to the less privileged humans, to other species, and to the Earth herself.[5]

Gary Snyder reminds us that 'The world is as sharp as the edge of a knife'; that the baby hare 'gets maybe one free chance to run across a meadow without looking up'. The wilderness pilgrimage not only takes us along that edge; it may also draw our attention to the precipice on which we all are teetering.[6]

I didn't want to spend a night alongside the pier. Now that the wind had dropped and veered westerly, it should be safe once again in the sound off Aranmore. With Susi and Dave away, I let go the mooring lines and motored back down the channel, which even at this second passing felt strangely familiar. As I started across the sound, the wind blew up yet again, still mainly southerly, bringing hard rain into my face. Was I mistaken in believing that the anchorage would be out of the wind? About halfway across, just as I was beginning to make out the landmarks on Aran, the rain suddenly hammered down, the wind increased and in a matter of minutes veered rapidly, almost flipped round, from southwest to nearly northwest. As I entered the anchorage the wind was offshore, the water quiet; it was wet and windy but nevertheless safe and snug. Even though it carried on raining hard, soon I was securely anchored.

Now I was on my own again, I wanted to make a fresh start. So after tidying the cabin and putting away the boots and lifejackets that Susi and Dave had used, I stripped off, washed, shaved, and put on clean clothes. I went through my charts and set waypoints for the next leg of the journey round Bloody Foreland. Elizabeth called, and we had a long conversation full of the intimate mutuality of 50 years of relationship. I cooked supper, creating a little ritual of making potato cakes, boiling up the potatoes with carrot and parsnip, mashing them with fried onion and a beaten egg, then crisping the cakes in the frying pan. Outside the rain stopped, the wind dropped back to nothing at all, although the heavy clouds remained.

I was just washing the dishes and stowing everything in its place, when I was startled by changes in the light outside. The sky over the hills of Aran suddenly—in a matter of seconds— filled with colour: a patch of yellow immediately above the hills, a halo of orange, and high above the heavy rain clouds deepened to purple. The rippling sea reflected the pattern of the sky. Between sea and sky lay the dark mass of the island, the line of its ridge sharply marked. The colours enveloped everything in a warm glow. I felt that the elements had given this difficult and complicated day their blessing.

Chapter Twelve

The Gestures of the Planet

*But more marvellous than anything else is the great fellowship that
exists between the ocean and the course of the Moon. For at [the
Moon's] every rising and setting, [the ocean] sends forth the
strength of his ardour, which the Greeks call "rheuma," to cover the
coasts far and wide; and when it retreats, it lays them bare. The
sweet streams of the rivers it abundantly mingles together and
covers over with salty waves. When the Moon passes on, [the ocean]
retreats and restores the rivers to their natural sweetness and level,
without delay. It is as if [the ocean] were dragged forwards against
its will by certain exhalations of the Moon, and when her power
ceases, it is poured back again into his proper measure.*

The Venerable Bede

The Reckoning of Time

I left the anchorage at Aranmore early the following morning,
taking advantage of now-moderate westerlies to carry me
northward. I rounded Bloody Foreland, although there is
nothing 'bloody' about it at all, just a long slope of grassland
down to the sea; the name is said to come from the rich red taken
on by the rocks in the evening sun. I had now left the western
coast of Ireland and was travelling eastward along the northern
coast. There were many places I would have liked to explore, in
particular Tory Island to the north of Bloody Foreland, but
autumn was approaching, nights were drawing in, and I still had
a long way to go. It was quite late that evening when I was
pleased to find a mooring buoy in Port Salon, a shallow bay just
inside Lough Swilly, sheltered from the fresh northwesterlies
that were forecast overnight and for the following day. I was
planning to slip out early in the morning and catch these winds

in the crossing to Scotland.

When I woke in the following morning I knew it was going to be a challenging day. The weather had been quiet when I turned in, but around midnight I was woken by the hollow sound of Coral's hull bouncing against the buoy and an uneasy motion in the water. The wind had picked up, veered northerly and was blowing directly down the lough against the ebbing tide. In the morning it was clear that the fresh winds had turned into a full gale and the mooring would become increasingly uncomfortable. In vain I searched the chart and the sailing directions to find a more sheltered spot: the only possibility was an anchorage across the lough, scarcely sheltered by the cliffs of Dunree Head.

I stayed there for two days and two nights. Tucked well in, Coral was at least out of the worst of the wind: in the exposed water out in the lough, frequent squalls scattered across the water blowing the tops off the waves and sending long streaks of white downwind. But she was not out of the flow of the tide, which ran hard round the shallow bay. She rode uncomfortably, suspended between the wind and the tidal stream, moving continually and restlessly in the water. For maybe half an hour between tides when the stream was slack she lay quietly head to wind, but the awkward motion would start again as soon as the new tide took hold of her keel. Each time she swung round I was concerned that she might pluck the anchor from the seabed; it was great relief that it held firmly; I imagined it burying itself deeper and deeper in thick sticky mud, as anchors are designed to do. There was nowhere else safer or more comfortable to go, so for the most part I shut myself in the cabin as Coral lurched around under my feet. Cold and continually alert, I kept peering through the wet cabin windows to make sure she was still in place. From time to time I would clamber into waterproofs and go on deck to check all was well. It is amazing how much discomfort one can put up with if necessary.

It was mid-September. With a new moon and thick cloud, the

nights were long and dark. Late afternoon of the second day the weather began to moderate: the low stratus that had covered the sky disintegrated and in its place chunks of heavy grey cumulus, torn into strange shapes by the last of the gale, raced across the sky. At sundown the cloud broke up enough to reveal blue sky and patches of pink cloud behind the grey; although the ensign was still blowing wildly the water surface was calmer. The Met Office forecast was much quieter weather the following day. I had a more restful night. At dawn, with a clear sky, the few clouds tinged with salmon pink from the rising sun, I set out to round Malin Head and sail on to Scotland.

Malin Head is the most northerly point of Ireland. It is also the point at which the flood tide that flows up the Irish Sea and through the North Channel between Ireland and Scotland meets its counterpart that has come directly up the west coast; and similarly, it is the place where the ebb tide divides. The tidal streams are complex and changeable, and in heavy weather they can kick up a dangerous sea.

I needed to leave early enough to pick up the first of the east-going tide round Malin, before it got too strong. It was scarcely daylight as I motored out of the lough, the shadowed cliffs on the eastern side standing over Coral, dark and gothic, mist pouring off the ridge and down the gullies. Once out at sea, as the sun began to bring a little warmth to the day, it was clear my timing was spot on: we soon left the head itself behind, the mainland coast dropped away, and I could feel the tide pick Coral up and carry her eastwards. As we passed Inishtrahull and its light-house, with the changing perspective the two halves of the island separated and then aligned again. I set the sails on a course for Islay, knowing that the tide would be more or less with us for the rest of the morning.

Those who stay on land, who maybe go to the seaside once or twice a year, know the tides from the way they cover and uncover beaches, fill and empty estuaries. Some may know of roads only passable at low tide; or read of swimmers carried away on a rip tide. Most people know vaguely that the tides are caused by the pull of the Moon; they may know that the greater range of spring tides takes place when the Sun and the Moon pull together. The full story of tides is far more complex and fascinating.[1]

Tides are indeed caused by the gravitational attraction of the Moon and the Sun. But this doesn't just pull the water upwards, it sets up a wave running across the oceans from east to west around the Earth. There are two tidal waves running round the planet: one directly caused by the pull of the Moon and Sun; the other, on the opposite side of the planet, caused by the centrifugal force of the Earth around the axis of the Earth-Moon system. To get the idea, imagine how the ponytails of two skaters holding hands and spinning together around a common axis are thrown outwards by the force of their circular motion. This means that in most places there are two tides each day.

Some tides are larger than others. Very simply, at new and full moons, when the Sun and Moon are aligned relative to Earth, their influence combines to create a greater tidal range ('spring' tides, a term possibly derived from the Anglo-Saxon word *springan* meaning to bulge); in between, at quarter moons, Sun and Moon pull against each other, so the range is smaller ('neap' tides, derived from the Old English *nep*, to become lower; or possibly 'without power'). As the Sun, Moon and Earth move around each other in their ever-changing elliptical orbits, the gravitational pull varies, so some spring tides are higher than others. Each month, each year and over longer cosmological cycles the character of the tides is in constant change.

In mid-ocean, the combined gravitational pull of the Moon and the Sun is only sufficient to raise the surface of the water some eighteen inches; so what is it that produces spring tides of nearly fifteen metres in places like the Bristol Channel and the

Bay of Fundy? Eighteen inches may seem slight, but this is sufficient to create a long-period wave, an enormous mass of water travelling around the globe at speeds of about 430 miles an hour, which is then shaped by the contours of Earth. As the wave encounters a continental shelf, its energy is compressed and it gains height, just as wind-driven ocean waves rear up as they cross into shallower waters. The tidal wave is further compressed in coastal waters and even more as it is forced up narrow channels and bays, all of which increase the tidal range significantly.

The tides are not just important for sailors: they have an important role in moving heat around the planet, lessening the extremes of climate oscillation. They also move nutrients around the globe, and the constantly changing conditions in intertidal zones bring about strong evolutionary pressures that contribute to the variety of life. It is quite possible that without a large moon and therefore significant tides, life would not have evolved on Earth.

It is often said that all living beings are influenced by the gravitational pull of the Moon. There is some evidence that the Moon has an immediate effect on living beings: just like the circadian clock which synchronizes to the cycle of day and night, there may exist a lunar rhythm that synchronizes with the phases of the Moon. But tides in the ocean are large-scale phenomena, and there appears to be little evidence to support claims that in humans it can change moods and influence women's menstrual cycle. For me, there is enough wonder at the evident way that tides influence life on earth: I think of them as among the 'great gestures' of the planet.

It was a new moon and spring tide on that September day as I crossed from Ireland to Scotland. The spring tidal range is always greater around the equinox, and in addition the Sun, Moon and Earth were at the point in an 18-year cycle when they were most closely aligned, causing a particularly large range and strong tidal flows.

After being cooped up and tossed around for the past two days, I was delighted to be on the move again. Coral bubbled across the sea at a comfortable pace: Ireland dropped away behind me; the Mull of Kintyre was just visible on the eastern horizon, and around midday the broken cliffs of the Oa, the peninsula at the southern end of Islay, came into view. I sat in Coral's cockpit, enjoying the sunshine, well out to sea and yet able to see from the land passing by that we were making good progress. Tired of snacking, I found a tin of mackerel in the locker and made myself a proper plate of fish, potatoes and green salad—the latter rather wilted but acceptable once doused in vinaigrette. All was very well in my world.

Travelling with the tides like this used to be a common experience. Coasting vessels would follow the stream, often anchoring to wait out the period of unfavourable tide. On traditional ocean voyages, ships would leave port on the ebb tide and follow routes that followed the currents and trade winds: the clippers sailed east about the globe, taking advantage of the strong westerly trade winds in the southern ocean; more notoriously, ships on the Atlantic triangle route crossed to the Caribbean on the southeast trade winds and returned on the southwesterlies with the North Atlantic Drift behind them.

I felt at this moment that I was not just having a pleasant sail: I was riding the waves of the planet. As I enjoyed the freedom of the open sea and appreciated the warmth of the sun and the good food, and as the water under her hull and the wind in her sails hastened Coral toward her destination, I experienced a profound sense of rightness and alignment that was beyond the simple pleasantness of the moment. Of course I was happy to be away from my unpleasant anchorage, but something more profound was also going on: I knew intuitively I was participating in this great gesture of the planet, linking myself and my ship through the water to the contours of the coast and the influence of the Moon and the Sun.

What is it about such moments when one experiences being part of a greater whole? The feeling is almost imperceptible, but I am sure it is there. One reaches for a leaf on a tree and suddenly knows that the carbon the tree draws from the atmosphere through photosynthesis is the stuff that forms one's body; one catches a blackbird in the eye and sees not just an ocular phenomenon but the presence of another living being; one learns of the tragic death of someone the other side of the planet and experiences for a moment a grief as if they were kin. Just as in my encounter with the night sky, I see all these as moments of grace when, to some extent, the boundaries of the separate self become permeable and one touches the whole.

But this was not to last. I was so pleased with myself, having got the tides right around Malin Head and across the open water, that I forgot to look ahead. I had intended to reach the Oa around slack water, but Coral made such good time that we were ahead of schedule. As I watched the cliffs ahead of me I slowly realized that we were no longer approaching them: Coral was actually going sideways, taken westward by the tide. I looked again at the sailing directions, and realized that I was sailing directly into the tidal race that runs around the Oa at the height of the stream. Annoyed with myself for not being properly prepared, I turned Coral into the tide, started the engine and set a course that I hoped would keep outside the race. It was a vain hope: the tide was too fierce. It drew Coral into the stream rushing past the Oa.

With the engine roaring at full power and, with the wind on the beam and a freshening breeze, the sails pulling strongly, Coral thrust her way through the water faster than I believed possible; yet we only inched forward, just creeping past the headland. One minute we were sailing across smooth, dark water, the surface covered with mysterious swirls; next, we were crashing over short sharp waves, the waters agitated as they flowed over an uneven bottom; then we would be surrounded by white, breaking water, picked up in the swirl of an eddy, breasting a line of breaking surf.

In the space of half an hour we had moved from riding with the forces of the planet to fighting against them. With the help of the diesel engine we were not defeated. But I felt no sense of triumph as Coral emerged from the race and I piloted her into Port Ellen: it wasn't dangerous, it was just silly, I thought at the time. On reflection, however, that is probably a narrow assessment. For the image of those strangely wild waters remains vivid in my mind, and the feeling of Coral fighting every inch to make progress is almost palpable in my body as I remember it. I hesitate to call this a moment of grace, but it was without doubt a marvellous meeting of the vast forces of the planet which have their own beauty, even as we have to work against them.

Spending months mainly alone in a small boat on the edge of the Atlantic Ocean I became more and more fascinated by this idea of participating in the great gestures of the planet. The influence of tides was immediately apparent, but I knew there were larger movements of water that influenced our life. Guidebooks often drew my attention to the influence of the Gulf Stream, suggesting that the temperate climate of the towns and bays along the western coast is brought about by the warm water it carries to our shores from tropical areas. There are particular places up and down the west coast where the Gulf Stream is said to bring particular warmth and where gardens have been established which support semi-tropical plants: at Tresco in the Scillies, Garinish Island near Sneem in the Kenmare River, at Oban in Argyle, even as far north as Inverewe in Wester Ross.

The ocean current that is popularly referred to as the Gulf Stream is part of a system of permanent currents—quite separate to those set up by the tides—that weave around the oceans. The

Gulf Stream proper flows from the Gulf of Mexico up the east coast of North America. It originates as a wind-driven current, but is accelerated by the spin of the earth as it travels north and becomes the western side of the great circular motion of the North Atlantic Gyre. In mid-ocean the stream divides, one branch heading eastward toward northern Europe which, when it reaches the western shores of the British Isles, is properly known as the North Atlantic Current. It is now part of the 'global thermohaline circulation', driven not by wind or the gravitational pull of the moon but by changes in the density of water caused by differences in temperature ('thermo') and differences in salinity ('haline').[2]

As the current travels northward, its density increases. At lower latitudes, this is brought about by wind-driven evaporation leaving behind denser, salty water. At high latitudes, surface water is chilled by arctic winds and its salinity increased further due to ice formation—when ice forms salt is excluded. Cold, salty water is dense and so plunges in two enormous surges or 'downwellings' to the ocean bottom, drawing warm surface water from the south to replace it. Hence the thermohaline circulation consists of warm currents at surface level and cold ones deep in the ocean. The cold dense water flows south to eventually upsurge into the Indian or Pacific Oceans maybe hundreds of years later. The system can be understood as an 'overturning' of the world ocean; the technical name is the Atlantic Meridional Overturning Circulation.

The generally accepted view is that the North Atlantic Current, by bringing warm water to northern European shores, helps create the temperate climate, in particular keeping winters relatively mild. Comparisons are often made with the east coast of North America at similar latitudes, for example Labrador, where average temperatures are lower and winters severe.

Global warming is increasing temperatures in the Arctic, bringing about an increased presence of fresh water from ice melt. This dilutes the salinity of sea water; it becomes less dense, and as a consequence, there is concern that the downwelling might decrease or even stop altogether, slowing or even halting the northwards flow of warm water. It is feared that such an event might plunge Britain into a significantly colder climate. The most recent research I can find suggests that the North Atlantic is indeed the only spot on the planet that is getting colder rather than warmer, an early warning sign that the thermohaline circulation in the North Atlantic is slowing down and may be less stable than previously thought.[3]

Over the past few years, some scientists have countered the orthodox argument, using climate models to show that the current actually does not carry sufficient warmth to make a significant difference to winters in northwest Europe. They argue that the northeastern Atlantic coast has a straightforward maritime climate maintained by the prevailing winds picking up the warmth retained by the mass of ocean water through winter. In this view, the anomaly is not the mild climate of northwest Europe but the cold one the other side of the Atlantic: after all, British Columbia, on the equivalent latitude on the Pacific coast, has a mild wet climate just like Britain. The cold of Labrador is explained by the influence of the Rocky Mountains, which diverts the jet stream south and allows arctic air to be drawn into northeast America.[4]

Whichever of the arguments is correct, and it is difficult for a lay person to make a judgement (although it seems that only a minority of scientists dispute the conventional view), the warming and moderating effect of the Atlantic Ocean on our climate is far more complex than the popular view suggests. It is simply trite to say, as so many tourist guides do, that an area is 'warmed by the waters of the Gulf Stream'. But my very brief and simplified summary of the ocean systems does show that our climate is intricately knitted into complex systems of the planet. Patterns elsewhere on Earth, whether they be the warming of the

Arctic or the influence of the Rockies on the jet stream, have significant impact on our climate.

We can experience and understand the influences on our weather, even if we cannot accurately forecast more than a few days ahead. When we stand on a high point in a fresh wind or bathe in sunshine we can feel the influence of weather systems on our bodies. If we are sailors or live near the sea, we can experience, understand and work with the flow of the tides; as we catch the tidal stream, we may intuit how we are riding the waves of the planet. But the larger, slower gestures of the planet, such as the thermohaline cycle and the long-term carbon cycle that moderates climate, while hugely important to our well-being, do not seem in any way experientially accessible to us. I find this immensely curious, a paradox my pilgrimage pointed to but has not resolved.

Chapter Thirteen

Meandering and Storytelling

me·an·der

(mē-ăn′dər)

intr.v. **me·an·dered, me·an·der·ing, me·an·ders**

1. *To follow a winding and turning course: Streams tend to meander through level land.*
2. *To move aimlessly and idly without fixed direction: vagabonds meandering through life. See Synonyms at* **wander.**
3. *To speak or write in sustained fashion on a number of loosely connected topics.*
4. *To be directed in various directions or at multiple objects: His gaze meandered over the church's façade.*

n.

1. *often* **meanders** *A bend, turn, or winding, as of a stream or path.*
2. *A portion, side trip, or episode in a longer journey.*
3. *A passage on a subtopic or digression in a longer piece of discourse.*
4. *An ornamental pattern of winding or intertwining lines, used in art and architecture.*

   thefreedictionary.com

At the end of my voyage around Ireland to Scotland, I left Coral to overwinter at Dunstaffnage Marina, north of Oban. At the end of May the following year, I prepared to leave home for a second summer of pilgrimage. My bags were packed. I had been up to the Polling Station and cast my vote in the General Election for the Green Party; put out the recycling; walked up for a final look at the garden and the orchard. I was taking the afternoon train to London and then on to Scotland. My plan was to spend until mid-August exploring the west coast and the islands, on what I was increasingly willing to call a sailing pilgrimage.

It was again a wrench to leave home, the place that has been the centre of my life for nearly 40 years and carries a deep sense of familiarity. It was particularly strange to leave in early summer, when all living beings were bursting into activity. As I walked up the footpath to the orchard I noticed that the May flower, which the previous week had been at a peak of glory — Elizabeth said it was covering the countryside in 'bling' — was beginning to fade. White petals fell around me as a light snowfall, dropping slowly through the air and littering the paths. In the orchard, the apple blossom was over; in its place fruit was forming on the trees, growing larger and taking on colour day by day. But maybe it was the wildflower meadow in the orchard I would miss most. Through the winter and early spring we had kept the grass cut to stop it overwhelming the flowers. While the grass was still short there had been a sprinkling of cowslips; now the yellow rattle was flowering and the black-eyed daisies were in bud. I imagined how through the summer different species would dominate in a glorious sequence, and that I would miss it.

I was also full of questions about the voyage itself. Would Coral be ready and all her gear working properly? How difficult would I find navigating on my own around the Scottish Islands? What would it be like to be away for three whole months, mainly on my own? How would I spend my time, and would I get bored, depressed and lonely as on previous voyages?

More important were the questions I asked myself about this voyage as pilgrimage, as holding the intention of exploring deeper connections with the more-than-human world. What would make it truly worthwhile rather than simply a personal indulgence? After two long voyages exploring the western edge of these islands, was there more to discover about deepening my conversation with the world? Of course, this was a silly question when I thought of the long periods reclusives spend in the wild: the Desert Fathers, the monks on Great Skellig, the yogins in

Himalayan caves. The question nevertheless haunted me, for the state of affairs on the planet seems so pressing that a contribution is demanded of me: would I be more useful working for Greenpeace, campaigning for the Green Party, or simply radically reducing my own ecological footprint?

But I kept coming back to my conviction that there is work to be done on the transformation of human consciousness if we humans are to create a civilization in balance with the ecology of the planet. How can we learn that we are part of the community of beings on Earth? Our present culture is so anthropocentric; we see the world from an exclusively human perspective and judge all things in terms of our own, usually short-term, interests. It is a huge leap to see human destiny as integral with the destiny of the Earth. And yet in these terrible times it is comforting to know that there is a great work to be done, changing the way we modern humans see ourselves.

In my more self-critical moments, all this sounds rather pretentious. But my voyaging was part of a quest for a different way of being a human. This was and is an enormous demand I place on myself: to make a contribution to what can only be seen as a millennia-long shift in the nature of consciousness. I was going sailing on my own on the west coast of Scotland because I was sure that immersion in the wild is an essential aspect of my quest. Since I believe that we humans need to rediscover that we are part of the ecological process, I must offer myself to the width of life, as expressed in the open seas. Only after that submission can I possibly hope to authentically influence anyone else.

My first week in Scotland was planned as a family holiday with my elder son Ben and his children Otto and Liberty. I had a day to fill while I waited for them to finish work and school and we could leave for the north. So, rather strangely, my pilgrimage began in the heart of London.

I took the tube from Highgate down to the Embankment and

walked along the Thames to Tate Modern. I wanted to see the Matisse exhibition, but when I got there found I needed to book in advance. I chose to go and sit with the Rothko murals instead. I stayed for an hour or more, sitting quietly in front of each canvas in turn, absorbed in the way the deep reds and purples seeped in and out of each other, in the throbbing sensation this created, while other visitors came and went. I found myself wondering what kind of human imagination can create such mysterious images. What might be the link between this extreme Abstract Expressionism, which I have always loved, and the qualities of ecological participation I am seeking to express? Seeing these paintings again reminded me of a visit to the Rothko Chapel in Houston, a place of vibrant quiet and sparse minimalism designed as a setting for Rothko's abstractions. The chapel creates an environment in which one is not so much looking at the paintings as participating with them.

I left Rothko behind and plunged back into the busyness of London, finding my way through the crowds in the Turbine Hall, across the Millennium Bridge and up to St Paul's. There I searched out another piece of modern art, Bill Viola's silent video installation *Martyrs*: four individuals, across four plasma screens, being martyred by earth, air, fire and water. The figures start in stillness. Then one of the four elements of nature begins to disturb them. Slowly at first, then with increasing violence, the water pours down, the flames envelop, the earth covers, the winds lash. Throughout, the figures remain still, their resolve, it seems, unchanged.

The video runs silently for seven minutes. I watched it through three times, utterly absorbed. It was both agonizing and strangely wonderful. Like Rothko's paintings, Viola's work seems not so much to be looked at as entered into. Then I turned away and climbed the stairs to the whispering gallery, where I had not been since I was a boy, and on up to the top of the dome.

From the Golden Gallery at the very top, more than 85 metres above street level, I looked over the roofs of London to the countryside beyond, although with no sense of any 'wilderness' in sight. It felt strangely appropriate that I should begin my pilgrimage here in the heart of London, at one of the great centres of both the Christian Church and Mammon.

All things evolved with the universe, including we humans, our culture and our technology. So too did all of this: this building, this city, all these people crowding into the gallery and all those I could scarcely see below me hurrying around, in their fancy clothes and make-up, with their smartphones and preoccupations. There is nothing else. All these sights of modern civilization are the universe experimenting with different ways of expressing itself. From this perspective all aspects of the human—the beautiful and the creative, the bizarre and the destructive—are aspects of a self-differentiating universe. We can see this as the outcome of random events if we wish; or we can see it as an expression of an intelligent creativity immanent in the whole. Sitting high up above the dome of St Paul's, it seemed to me that, since we are part of the expression of the universe, we are called to live our lives as creatively as we are able, as beautifully, as ethically and above all in intimacy with the Earth out of which we arise.

Strange to have these thoughts sitting up in St Paul's which is itself a monument to the human-centred Enlightenment consciousness that I am pushing against. But at that moment I also realized how false it is to distinguish the human from the more than human. Ecological wisdom will not come from separating the one from the other but from seeing how they belong together in intricate intimacy. We have to thoroughly understand the human project if we are to live as well as we might and allow the planet to live as well as it might.

As I made my way back down the stairs, through the streets and the underground back to north London, I tried to practise a discipline that may have Sufi origins, to recognize each person coming toward me, "This is my brother, this is my sister; this too is my brother and this too my sister." And so also are all the other beings on Earth.

What kind of travelling makes an ecological pilgrimage and what kind of story can we tell about it? My pilgrimage is certainly an adventure of sorts, and there are tales of derring-do to tell. But the pilgrimage is not intended as an opportunity to conquer the world, nor are pilgrimage stories accounts of heroic accomplishment.

I had originally intended in this second year to sail up through the Western Isles and the Hebrides, round the north of Scotland, through the Pentland Firth and back to the west coast through the Caledonian Canal. But I remembered how the challenging weather the previous September had made the last leg to Scotland such hard work; how I regretted rushing past places, particularly the coast of Donegal, where I would have liked to linger and appreciate. Most of all, I remembered how, by the time I reached Oban on the west coast of Scotland, I was so very tired.

This led me to rethink my second year's intention. As I studied the charts and thought about the long single-handed passages involved, I realized that my plans were overambitious and not really necessary. When I told people I was planning to sail around the west coast of Britain and over the top of Scotland they were impressed. It was a wonderful challenge, but too heroic by far. Not only would I overstretch myself, I would again rush past places where I might want to linger.

So I began to explore a different metaphor for the second year's journey; I decided that I would 'meander' round the Highland coast and the Hebridean islands. I reflected on how a meandering river winds through the countryside, its changing course guided by its own internal dynamics and in response to the land through which it flows. Meandering is a response to particular environmental conditions: a relatively wide valley, soft soil, a gentle incline. It is a self-reinforcing process: the curve of a river erodes the outside bank while depositing silt on the inside of the curve, resulting in even greater curvature. Maybe we all meander through life in similar fashion: small choices amplify themselves, and as Robert Frost tells us, 'way leads on to way' and every small choice 'makes all the difference'. The plans we set out with are little more than entertaining fictions.[1]

A river does, of course, flow with a sense of direction, meandering always down toward the sea; but its course may take it in great loops away from this destination. And a river does not meander all the time: where it flows over hard rocks, it may be forced into ravines, tumble through rapids or over falls. In similar fashion, the meandering pilgrim will at times hurry to reach a temporary destination, a safe anchorage in bad weather or a town where stores can be replenished.

The word meander is used metaphorically to suggest leisurely wandering over an irregular or winding course. 'Wandering' generally means to go without fixed purpose or goal, or to go by an indirect route. Henry Thoreau extolled the virtues of 'sauntering': 'We should go forth on the shortest walk, perchance, in the spirit of undying adventure, never to return'. He derives the word sauntering, maybe fancifully, 'from idle people who roved about the country... under pretence of going à la sainte terre — to the holy land.' A 'sainte-terrer' is a saunterer, a holy-lander. Or maybe, he says, saunter is derived from *sans terre*, meaning 'without land or a home', one who while having no particular home is nevertheless equally at home everywhere. And he too makes the link with meandering, saying that despite its wayward course the river is 'sedulously seeking the shortest course to the sea'.[2]

Thoreau is, of course, writing about walking, and much of the literature which appreciates the natural world begins in walking. Indeed, walking is sometimes taken as the paradigmatic means of meeting the world, not only for Thoreau but also for Wordsworth, Shepherd, Dillard, Macfarlane, and many others. Macfarlane notes at the beginning of *The Old Ways* that there is a link between 'paths, walking and the imagination'.[3]

When walking, we meet a full and complex world, a world of landscape, of hills and valleys, of trees and shrubs and mosses, of streams and lakes. Walking has a rhythm to it, as one step follows another. Robert Macfarlane writes of walking at its best as 'enabling sight and thought... paths as offering not only means of traversing space, but also ways of seeing, being and knowing'. His pace, he tells us, at 29.7 centimetres: 'it is a unit of progress and it is also a unit of thought', and quotes Kierkegaard among other walkers as writing 'I can only meditate when I am walking... when I stop I cease to think; my mind only works with my legs'.

Long distance sailing is different; it involves hour upon hour of doing very little, yet needing to be awake and attentive for those critical moments when intense activity is called for. We may watch the coast passing by, or look out for changing weather. We may attend to the waves, to the pattern of swell and ripple. On a long passage there may be little but slow movement of the sun across the sky. In some ways there is far less stimulus at sea, far less to look at, to be distracted by and to think about. And yet one learns to appreciate a different kind of detail. Long ago, when my sons were young, we used to while away the long hours in the cockpit by playing 'I-spy'. To make the game more interesting, we developed the rule that only items not part of or on the boat could be chosen to spy. Through this I came to realize the enormous variety of things to be seen. Just think how many off the boat words begin with 's': sea, sky, spray, stars, sun, spume, spindrift, seagulls are among the more obvious ones.

Crossing the English Channel one summer I spent the long hours in the cockpit reflecting on just how much I could observe and describe. As the French coast dropped behind us, we settled down on our course for Plymouth, moving fast in the moderate westerly on a starboard reach. The sun broke through high cirrus clouds dancing pinpricks of light, tiny sparkles over the surface of the water. As the sun climbed higher the sea took on a deeper, more uniform blue. Rain clouds gathered from the west, the breeze freshened, drops spattered on my face. Coral heeled over, carrying now just a fraction too much sail for comfort, charging through greeny-grey waves. There was blue sky ahead, no need to shorten sail; I chose to hold on until the squall passed.

From my perch on the windward side of the cockpit I looked down at the water below me. I could feel rather than see the long rhythm of the swell rolling up the channel and passing under the hull. Shorter, sharper waves gave a texture to the surface of the swell; streaks of white were blown from their crests. And at the next scale down, I watched how patterns of ripples fanned across the waves, decorating them in windblown wrinkles.

The movement was relentless: Coral rose with the swell, her bows pitched up; she rolled to leeward, then slid down the back of the swell, lifting her stern as she rolled back into the trough. Again and again the pattern repeated with each peak and trough, never exactly the same. Now and again a wave arrived out of sequence and hit Coral's amidships in mid-roll, arresting the regular movement and sending a shudder through the hull. The irregular movement knocked Aries, the windvane steering, off course; it swung around wildly before settling down again. The mainsail flapped as it lost wind, then filled again with a sharp crack; pots and pans crashed together in the galley; jars of jam and mustard rolled around in their locker. Then with a final flurry of wind and rain the squall passed and the blue sky was above once more.

In the Channel there was nothing in sight except sea and sky and the odd gannet. No ships, no land, no sign of other humans; even Ben and Otto were out of sight in their bunks. There was nothing here keeping me alive except human ingenuity and inventiveness: a seaworthy hull, sails to drive the boat forward, Aries to steer, GPS and charts to navigate. Yet here I was, entranced by the unfolding of the day, managing the boat, plotting our course, feeling alive. The wilderness of the sea was showing me again what it is to be a human being.

Toward evening the lowering sun threw dark shadows on the face of the approaching waves. Between the shadows the light caught the water, burnishing the surface with a metallic sheen. As the sun dipped below the western horizon, the full moon appeared in the southeast. The daylight faded, the colours drained away, the sea became heavily leaden, the sky a curtain of thin blue. Then at night the bright moon created a seascape full of new contrasts: lumpy dark sea separated from a profoundly blue sky by the sharp horizon, white horses and the ship's wake glowing in phosphorescence. The moon rose higher and threw a silver path across the sea that Coral followed as she sailed on northwards.

Later that night, after my watch below, I took over from Ben. "I thought I saw the loom of a light over there," he said, pointing northeast. "But surely it is too soon." He went below and I stared in the direction he indicated. Yes, there it was, just the hint of a light on the horizon. Then Coral lifted on a wave, I saw the pinpoint of a lighthouse, the loom of the light through the sky and a little later the regular three flashes that I knew to be Start Point. We were approaching home.

Sailing, I suspect, can bring a greater sense of emptiness than walking. Even more so at night, when the darkness envelops, and the cold draws you into yourself. I wonder, therefore, if the sailing experience is more naked, more like a retreat where one may spend hours just attending to breath, or attending to a landscape with an empty mind—as at the Buddhist retreat centre at Dzogchen Beara where the shrine room has a floor-to-ceiling window that looks out over nothing but sea. Emptiness indeed.

The idea of meandering and Thoreau's notion of sauntering can both be linked to that of 'holy uselessness'. If humans are to pay full attention to the world as it is we need to find ways to retreat from human plans and ambitions, which force an anthropocentric view and so reveal the world primarily as resources for human purposes. The Celtic monks took this to extremes in their *peregrinatio*, even casting themselves adrift at sea, happy to accept whatever the outcome might be.

But I am not a Celtic monk, I am not casting myself at the mercy of the divine, my 'holy uselessness' is not the whole of my life. I have purposes and commitments that I have chosen as worthwhile and authentic, of which this pilgrimage is only a part. My notion of meandering is not a purposeless wandering, for while not firmly goal-oriented it nevertheless implies an inclination. Just as a river follows a meandering course toward the sea, so a human may travel with some sense of a direction and purpose, while not allowing that to dominate their choices. Meandering suggests rather an emphasis on spontaneity and choice in the moment, influenced by circumstances and opportunities and by one's own inclinations. For me to wander at sea without paying attention to the wind and the tides, without choosing the appropriate time to round a headland or make a passage, would be foolish and irresponsible. The trick is to find the sweet point of wandering with intention.

As a river meanders it leaves behind it a record of its history: often an extensive fertile flood plain, layers of deposits, occasional oxbow lakes. A sailing yacht leaves a wake behind that very soon disappears into the ocean. As a pilgrim sailor I can leave another kind of record, in the stories I can tell, the meaning I can fathom from my journeying. But what kind of stories can be told?

Storyteller Geoff Mead, following the psychoanalyst A. B. Chinen, distinguishes between three kinds of stories: heroic stories, post-heroic stories, and elders' stories. It is a distinction that illuminates my understanding of pilgrimage.[4]

In hero's stories the protagonist, usually young and male, responding to a call to adventure, a quest to right wrongs, journeys out in pursuit of some more or less grand purpose and returns changed. The adventure involves trials and ordeals, meeting with helpers and mentors and substantial amounts of courage, magic and luck to overcome one obstacle after another. In the end, the hero marries his princess, becomes King and lives happily ever after. The story arc goes out and back. Clearly this fits in some ways with the pilgrimage journey that traditionally takes the pilgrim away from home, through adventures, trials and tribulations, to a sacred place and then home again. Jean and Wallace Clift, in their book *The Archetype of Pilgrimage*, call this the classic rite of passage: the separation and the sense of purpose; the liminal stage including release from social ties, the freedom, difficulties and dangers of the journey itself, the sojourn at the shrine and the encounter with the sacred; and then the return home, renewed and transformed. Joseph Campbell, in his book *The Hero with a Thousand Faces*, argues that all important myths share this underlying structure. The tales of Parsifal and the Holy Grail, of Jack and the Beanstalk, of Christ in the wilderness and the Buddha in his quest for enlightenment all show varieties of this pattern.[5]

Many women writers have criticized Campbell's emphasis on the heroic myth, saying it does not sufficiently account for the feminine experience. Sharon Blackie, for example, is unhappy with what she sees as the highly active, privileged 'swash-buckling, adventuring' hero. She thinks women need to make a different pilgrimage, and writes, 'A pilgrim isn't entirely sure whether she can save herself, let alone the world. She knows that something is lacking in her own life, that something is missing or broken... A pilgrimage asks that we give up everything so we might learn what is truly ours.' Chinen himself has attempted to

147

address this issue in his second book of women's stories. In her introduction, June Singer suggests the heroic woman's story is often one of plunging into the depths of the unconscious or underworld to break the conventions that bind women to their false selves: the stories of Inanna and Persephone's journey into the underworld are important examples. These are stories about the struggle of waking up and so are often subversive or dissident, telling tales of possibility beyond patriarchal assumptions.[6]

Mead tells us that the post-heroic story is different. Rather than going out and back, the post-heroic story goes *down* and back up, and in that way is similar to the women's stories. The post-heroic tale is not based on a call to adventure, but is a necessary response to something that has gone wrong, has been spoiled, has caused the protagonist to lose their way. It is what happens *after* the 'happily ever after' ending of the heroic story. The post-heroic story starts with downfall, often arising from the hubris that accompanies the heroic ego. The challenge of the post-heroic protagonist is not to slay metaphorical dragons and marry the princess, but to discover and stay faithful to that which he or she truly loves through long and difficult labours. There will be helpers and mentors along the way—the post-heroic protagonist has to learn to recognize them in order to gain their advice and support—but there are no magic interventions that solve problems with the wave of a wand. The post-heroic tale is about learning to be true to what really matters in life rather than obey the dictates of others or of our own egos; and it is about bringing back the true self to work in the world through mid-life and beyond.

This quality of story informs the idea of pilgrimage in a different way. A traditional religious pilgrim may well start from what has been spoiled: a sense of sin that needs forgiveness, maybe an act of gratitude for a prayer that has been heard. The challenges of the pilgrimage journey may well show the pilgrim what is most important to them. An ecological pilgrim may also start from the realization that the human race has spoiled and is spoiling the planet of which we are a part. There are no certain magical solutions that will encompass this challenge: new forms of economy and production, technological breakthroughs in low carbon energy, even geo-engineering, may make useful contributions. But they are not magic wands. We need rather to find ways to reconnect and be true to our wider ecological selves, the ways in which our identity is woven into the ecology of the planet. A 'spiritual' response is needed to support the pragmatic responses so that, in the words of religious scholar Douglas Christie, 'we do not continue to visit our most destructive impulses upon the natural world'. This, as I see it, is the task of the ecological pilgrim.[7]

It seems, then, that a post-heroic pilgrimage is less individualistic than the heroic pilgrimage. It may be less concerned about saving one's own soul or finding one's princess, and more concerned with contributing to a collective response. This has links with the Buddhist tradition of the bodhisattva path. Buddhist scholar David Loy tells us that the bodhisattva response to the suffering of the world is not personal salvation but a contribution to the collective. He writes, 'Instead of asking, "How can I get out of this situation?" the bodhisattva asks, "What can I contribute to make this situation better?"' In classical Buddhist terms, 'the bodhisattva takes a vow to help liberate all living beings'; an unachievable task but not a hopeless gesture. But, as Joanna Macy puts it, we can all be part of a Great Turning of our world, we can never know the outcome of our actions, never know what the collective response will be. Personal transformation and social transformation are two sides of the same coin.[8]

Geoff Mead tells us there is a third story arc, beyond the post-heroic, which he calls the 'elder tale'. In elder tales the protagonist drops personal ambition and withdraws from the demands of adult life; she or he stops caring what other people think and may break completely with social customs, and through this wonder, delight, spontaneity and magic return to life. A lovely example of this can be found in *The Snow Leopard*, Peter Matthiessen's account of accompanying the field biologist George Schaller on a Himalayan expedition. After a cold, dangerous and exhausting journey the travellers arrived at the Crystal Mountain monastery and eventually met the Lama, living as a recluse in a nearby cave. Crippled by arthritis, he moved only painfully with two crutches. His twisted legs meant he would never again leave the cave. Even so he was cheerful, open, natural and strong, smiling at the Crystal Mountain as he talked. Matthiessen ventured to ask him if he was happy: 'Of course I am happy here! It's wonderful! *Especially* when I have no choice!'[9]

The hero quest is a call to adventure and challenge to attain a goal; the post-heroic story tells of the work required to heal and mend that which has been spoiled; the elder tale is one of acceptance, of living with what comes. I can look at pilgrimage through any of these three lenses.

Chapter Fourteen

Silences

A man in Anatuvuk Pass, in response to a question about what he did when he visited a new place, said to me, "I listen." That's all. I listen, he meant, to what the land is saying. I walk around in it and strain my senses in appreciation of this before I, myself, ever speak a word. Entered in such a respectful manner, he believed, the land would open to him.
Barry Lopez
Arctic Dreams

To bend the ear to silence is to discover how seldom it is there. Always something moves... But now and then comes an hour when the silence is all but absolute, and listening to it one slips out of time. Such a silence is not a mere negation of sound. It is like a new element... The world is suspended there, and I in it.
Nan Shepherd
The Living Mountain

With Coral anchored in the sound between Mull and the smaller island Ulva, I took the dinghy ashore. The outboard had not been working properly since I left Oban, so it was a long row against the tide. "That looked tiring," commented a man drinking his coffee at the café at the top of the slipway; but actually it left me feeling well stretched and present in my body. I tugged off my seaboots, laced up walking boots, and, leaving my lifejacket in the bottom of the dinghy, headed inland. A map at the visitors' centre showed various trails across the island, and I chose the one that led along the southern coast toward Craigaig Bay, where I hoped to be able to see eagles. As I tramped under the trees I was distracted by glimpses of water to my right... surely it should be to the left... was I on the right track? I carried on, puzzled and preoccupied, until I was jerked into the present by the sight of an eagle soaring from behind the treetops and banking out over the loch. She flew low enough for me to see her primary feathers fingering out into the sky, subtly moving as she adjusted her flight. She circled twice and disappeared behind the trees again.

I stood still, open-mouthed and openhearted, waiting for her to return. Then a helicopter crashed overhead, followed by another, filling the air with a throbbing that shook my body and overwhelmed my hearing. They clattered off into the distance leaving me shocked and disoriented. Gradually the silence of the woodland and the eagle returned.

I continued along the path and turned a corner into a clearing. In front of me a five-barred metal gate between stone gateposts guarded the entrance to a church: a plain white building, quite recently painted, with bare stone quoins at the corners, and a small belfry at the end of a pitched slate roof. The gate creaked and wobbled precariously as I swung it open on rusty hinges.

The main church door opened into a dark vestibule with several doors to choose from. After some hesitation I found my way into what seemed to be a vestry, through a narrow passage behind a vast wooden pulpit, into the main meeting room. It was a square, open space, with a wooden floor and a high ceiling, flooded with sunlight from three large windows set with clear leaded panes on the eastern side. Cut flowers were arranged on the windowsills; I found it strange that while some were fresh, others were dried out and dusty. From the far end I looked back at the plain but enormous wooden pulpit, with steps leading to two levels and a canopy over the top that rose almost to the ceiling. I suspect the lower level was for reading from the Bible, with the upper reserved for the all-important sermon.

I discovered from a notice that this was a 'Parliamentary

church', one of five churches on Mull and Iona designed by the celebrated engineer Thomas Telford following an Act of Parliament which funded the building of churches in parishes without one. They all have a simple and inexpensive design, build on a T-shaped plan that allows a maximum number of parishioners to sit near the pulpit. The Ulva church was completed in 1828 when the island had a substantial population; the clearances that started shortly afterwards brutally removed two-thirds of the inhabitants.

I walked around quietly, feeling enveloped in a silence that noticed every move, echoing as my footsteps trod the floor. Even though the building is now used primarily as a community centre, it carried for me the feeling of a sanctuary. The silence held qualities different to those of the eagle, somehow drier, crisper, enclosed: a human silence rather than a natural one.

Out of the church and through the creaking gate I chose the pathway that led high over the centre of the island and, I hoped, toward my original destination. After climbing through muddy woodland to the open hilltops I looked down into Craigaig Bay, a small inlet protected by a scattering of grassy islets, and to islands beyond: Lunga and the Treshnish Islands, with Coll and Tiree in the further distance. The sea was calm; tiny squalls ruffled the surface into patches of ripples and a line of disturbance showed where the tide was racing round the headland. I watched another eagle, this one floating high above the cliffs. A hawk flashed past in the woodland below me, too fast to clearly identify but most likely a peregrine. Swallows perched on the fence posts and twittered at me, close enough for me to see clearly the orange patch under their beaks; as I approached, they fluttered along to the next post.

Farther down the hill, I passed through dense patches of foxgloves fading into a purple haze in the distance. Clusters of primrose, speedwell and low-lying honeysuckle grew in the shelter of lichen-covered outcrops. Now I became aware of a wider range of sounds: the twitter of smaller birds; a harsh cry of distress in the distance, suddenly cut off; then the single call of a cuckoo. All were contained within an underlying silence so profound that each sound seemed to hold a physical, three-dimensional presence.

Above Craigaig Bay I found a place to sit with my back resting against a rock. From here I looked down to where a passage between the rocks led to the sheltered beach. Up from the beach stood the stone walls that are all that remains of some cottages; and surrounding them the mounds and ridges that are all that is left of a field system, lazy beds and a water mill. For generations people here worked the land and fished the seas until they were burned out in the late nineteenth century. They seemed to have left a different kind of silence behind them.

'Silence' is a fascinating word. At a very simple level it can be taken to mean the absence of sound, or at least the absence of noise that is intrusive or irritating. But this is misleading. Silence is not an absence of sound but as Sara Maitland puts it in her *Book of Silence*, it is a 'positive presence... Perhaps it is a real, actual thing'. It is rather more difficult to say just what it is that is present.[1]

Certainly, as I sat on the grass above Craigaig Bay, I was reaching outward with my listening as if seeking to touch something elusive and fragile: the call of the birds, the whisper of the wind; maybe even the trace of the now-absent sounds of those people who once lived here. Maybe I was reaching into the gaps between the sounds, to hear that which was occluded. Sometimes I felt I was also trying to reach behind those present and past sounds to a sense of an underlying cosmic silence, maybe to what the ancient ones called the music of the spheres.

But the silence was also about me. It was about a certain quality of mind and attention. Sara Maitland describes 'an interior dimension to silence, a sort of stillness of heart and mind which is not a void but a rich space'. This 'rich space' certainly is one that is stilled, relatively emptied of internal chatter and self-absorption. But it is nevertheless awake, alert, full of imaginative response to my surroundings.

"Why do you go sailing on your own?" people often ask me. I usually reply that the presence of other humans seems to demand conversation, and however attractive that is, it fills the rich space of internal quiet and overwhelms the possibility of opening to the underlying silence of the world.

So while silence is a positive space, it is a space that opens only when 'I' am no longer filling it. By 'I', I mean in particular my self-importance and self-concern, my attachment to my own purposes, all of which create a deafening internal 'noise'. Silence, in the extended, positive sense of the word, seems to arise when external 'quiet'—the absence of intrusive noise—meets an internal quietude. This meeting is a delicate place: the external quiet may be unexpectedly disrupted, as my encounter with the helicopters suggests; my quietude is continually threatened by egoic concerns. This is the kind of silence prized, according to Barry Lopez, by the Tukano Indians of Brazil when they speak in praise of 'The Quiet': a 'realm of life that could not be sensed until one overcame the damage done to perception by long exposure to inescapable noise.[2]

Solitude helps open this inner quietude, especially when accompanied by an intentional practice such as meditation and prayer. In the company of others it helps to agree to avoid ordinary chatter. Sometimes, quietude arises through social conventions, such as the formal silences that mark moments of remembrance or mourning and the reverence that is customary in holy places. The physical rhythms of walking are often said to lead to an internal quiet. So too do the extended periods in long-distance sailing where there is nothing to be done but attend to the movement of the boat through the water. All these are brought together in the discipline of pilgrimage.

The qualities of quiet and quietude create space for calmness and joy. All sense of division fades away: no longer separate things, no split between inner and outer, no conventional judgements of good and bad. The mind becomes coherent and with it the world; everything is just as it is. And in this, human being and world meet each other. Peter Matthiessen's sense of the land at Crystal Monastery, high in the Himalayas, catches exactly this quality:

> There is so much that enchants me in this bare, silent place that I move softly so as not to break a spell. Because the taking of life is forbidden by the Lama of Shey, bharal and wolves alike draw near the monastery. On the hills and in the stone beds of the river are fossils from blue ancient days when all this soaring rock lay underneath the sea. And all about are prayer stones, prayer flags, prayer wheels, and prayer mills in the torrent, calling on all the elements in nature to join in the celebration of the One. What I hear from my tent is a delicate wind-bell and the river from the east, in this easterly wind that may bring some change in the weather. At daybreak, two great ravens come, their long toes scratching on the prayer walls.[3]

Toward the end of the afternoon I left the grassy slopes above Craigaig Bay to return to Coral. At first, the pathway carried me over soft turf, but it then gave way to a track laid with coarse stone chippings that continually shifted underfoot. Soon my mood sank. I was tired, footsore, trudging heavily, irritated with the distance and the rough path. It was as if, after a charmed day, my prima donna self felt the landscape owed it some ease: I wanted a quick return to the comforts of civilization, a cup of tea, a comfortable seat. I was alarmed at how quickly I become irritated, even angry at my surroundings, just because they didn't meet my expectations. The silent place where I met the world became overwhelmed with self-pity. Luckily, I caught myself at it and was able to laugh: what nonsense it was that my 'Holy Roman Ego' thought it has a privileged place in the scheme of things. So I interrupted my trudging, chose to walk upright, seeking a balanced Tai Chi gait and an open awareness. I imagined myself as walking *with* the landscape rather than against it, and immediately felt lightened and less tired. Once more the flowers were bright, birds were singing and gentle waves breaking on the foreshore. I was nevertheless very pleased to get back to the landing place and treat myself to a cup of tea with a cream scone before rowing back to Coral.

Chapter Fifteen

All This Will Pass

By evening I have sunk into a deep depression. I wandered around Tashkurgan in the gathering gloom thinking black thoughts. There are moments in all long journey when the whole business of travelling seems utterly stupid. One feels homesick, tired, and above all bored. Nothing pleases. Everything palls.
William Dalrymple
In Xanadu: A Quest

From Ulva I had sailed north past Ardnamurchan and spent nearly two weeks centred around the fishing port of Mallaig exploring the Small Isles, the lochs on the southern coast of Skye and Loch Nevis. Steve had driven north with his partner Melanie; he joined me for a few days while she stayed in a cottage in the upper reaches of Loch Nevis. These were two weeks full of the ups and downs of pilgrimage: moments of delight and insight followed quickly by depression and a sense of pointlessness.

I found the whole area is outstandingly beautiful; picturesque scenery in the best sense of that word. It has been the backdrop to conflicts, historical horrors and heroism; they have been written about, painted, photographed. This area seemed to me to be so familiar, so full of cultural referents, that it was difficult to take in afresh, for itself, so to speak. I felt that whatever I wrote would be clichéd. As I passed my 70th birthday the very idea of an ecological pilgrimage seemed simply ridiculous. Yet this was also a time when I settled more deeply into my journey and laid the ground for some of my deeper understandings of what I was seeking.

After passing Ardnamurchan I spent a night of torrential rain at

Arisaig. In the morning, I took Coral out through the intricate passage between rocks and shallows at the entrance to the anchorage. My attention was focussed on identifying the navigation marks—nothing more than thin 'perches' sticking up from the rocks—and keeping Coral in deep water. It was not until I was past the last of the marks and in the open sea that I raised my eyes to the horizon, where rested the long outline of Eigg. The rain had washed the atmosphere clear and the day promised to be bright. I made an instant decision: rather than sail directly up the coast to Mallaig, as I had planned, I would take a long detour around Eigg, one of the Small Isles to the south of Skye. Muck, the smallest of the group, lies to the south and west of Eigg; to the north and west is Rum, the largest and most mountainous; and beyond Rum is Canna with its close companion Sanday.

Leaving the mainland behind, Coral bubbled happily through deep blue water under clearing skies—the Sea of Hebrides at its most benign. At first, Eigg was no more than a long low ridge on the horizon; as I approached, the volcanic outcrops and precipitous cliffs at the northern end, the greener fields to the south, all became clearer. For a while, the cloud-covered mountains of Rum were visible through the saddle in the middle of the island, then hidden as I got closer. Low-lying Muck came into view to port and I steered Coral through the sound between Muck and Eigg, close under 'an Sgurr', the vertical chockstone block at the southwest end. Then, almost as in a film sequence, the mountains of Rum slipped into full view again as I rounded the southwest corner.

I turned northwards between Rum and Eigg. By this time, the sun was high in the sky, the sea had turned to a startling luminescent blue, the clouds had lifted completely and the peaks stood clear against a paler sky. While Muck is flat and low and Eigg appears as a long ridge, the mountains of Rum rise sharply from the sea to half a dozen separate summits, the remains of a huge ancient volcano.

I anchored for an hour or so in the Bay of Laig for lunch and a snooze. As I turned back toward Mallaig, lowering cloud blew in from the southwest, the peaks disappeared, and by the time I reached the mainland both islands were concealed in a wet greyness.

A few days later I set out from Mallaig late one morning, making for Canna, the most westerly of the Small Isles. It was again a lovely day, with sunny intervals. The sea was sea smooth and the wind just strong enough to push Coral along pleasantly. I could see right up Loch Nevis, overlapping mountain slopes reaching into the distance; across to the Sleat Peninsular and the craggy Cuillin peaking up behind, their heads in the clouds. But south and west, Rum was enveloped in cloud right down to sea level. "This isn't going to last," I told myself, "there is going to be rain soon." And then the wider thought popped into my mind, "All this must pass."

I had just finished reading Elizabeth Kolbert's book *The Sixth Extinction*. This is a first-rate journalist's account of the many ways in which the human impact on the planet is directly or indirectly bringing about the disappearance of other species and ecosystems. Frogs are disappearing because international travel is spreading a fungus around; coral reefs are threatened by ocean acidification and warming; many creatures are threatened by climate change; and more still by the destruction and fragmentation of habitats. Most megafauna, as well as our Neanderthal cousins, were wiped out shortly (in evolutionary terms) after human arrival in their territory. The book is engaging and deeply alarming.[1]

I had also been reading Charles Eisenstein's *The More Beautiful World Our Hearts Know is Possible*. He argues that we humans need to move away from a 'story of separation' in which we see ourselves as apart from the wider world, toward a story of 'inter-being'. In many ways his book overlaps with the perspective I take in this book. One of his most important points is that many of our actions to 'save the world' derive from the story of separation, and in that sense can be seen as contribution to the problem they attempt to address.[2]

But I found this a strangely irritating book, too full of sweeping statements and over-sure of itself. In particular, the proposition that a 'more beautiful world' is possible needs to be set against the reality of the present crisis, including the extinction spasm. As Kolbert clearly articulates at the end of her book, we humans are part of an extinction event that began early in human prehistory, is caused by human presence and is accelerated by modernity. The very things that make us human, our use of symbol and language, 'our restlessness, our creativity, our ability to cooperate to solve problems and complete complicated tasks', change the world. And they change the world in a way that pushes beyond the limits of the current ecological order, bringing about widespread extinctions just as surely as an asteroid did for the age of dinosaurs.

Somehow, the unsettled weather played a counterpoint to these thoughts in the back of my mind. I found myself wondering just what qualities of interbeing are possible on a catastrophically impoverished planet. In a moment of reflective melancholy, as the wind picked up and blew in a scattering of rain drops, I wrote these lines:

All this will pass:
This moment of insight
This calm sea and gentle winds
This sunshine and showers, these patterns of clouds
These homely houses with their gardens and fields
These towns, harbours, ships
These waters and all that live in them
And this human man.
Even the mountains come and go.

As I worked Coral past the Point of Sleat and round the west of Rum squally rain showers hit us from the west, blowing this way then that as the wind was deflected through the mountain passes and accelerated down to sea level. One moment Coral heeled over extravagantly, speeding through water flattened by the heavy rain. The next moment, the wind whipped round to head her: with no pressure on the sails she lurched upright, sails cracking. For half an hour or so my attention was taken with the demands of sailing. Then the squalls passed, the clouds lifted and Coral settled down again to a comfortable amble through the water. In the clear air that so often follows rain, the sea turned leaden, the sky a washed-out blue, separated by the sharp razor slash of the horizon. In the middle distance, the brilliant white of a gannet soared past the dark mass of the Cuillin, the dramatic mountain range at the southern end of Skye.

Science teaches that our world is in constant evolutionary change. History shows that cultures rise and fall. The Buddha taught that all things are empty and impermanent. The Taoists hold that the 'ten thousand things' arise from and fall back into the 'pregnant emptiness at the heart of things'; the Christian tradition reminds us that 'all flesh is as grass, and all the glory of man as the flower of grass', that 'the grass withereth' and fades away. It is easy to know this to be true intellectually while everyday life continues its habitual path and we are fooled by the myth of permanence.[3]

But in those few moments, just before the squalls hit, I knew the truth of impermanence in a different way — directly, incontrovertibly, at the heart of my own impermanent being. All this must pass, this moment and these mountains. And yet there remains this instant of awareness and beauty.

Canna is the most westerly of the Small Isles, hidden from the east behind Rum. The peak of Compass Hill — so called because it is full of iron and causes a magnetic anomaly — makes a good visual landmark, emerging as one clears the northernmost point of Rum. The well-sheltered natural harbour, the only one in the Small Isles, is tucked in the southwest corner between the island and Sanday.

The land immediately around the harbour is lush meadowland, rising gently to the base of the volcanic outcrop that soars high to the north and east. In contrast, Sanday is low-lying and rather featureless, apart from the elaborate St Edward's Church, now deconsecrated and used as an arts centre.

Steve and I walked through a wet meadow full of buttercups and clover, the yellow wild iris sharp against the dour grey of the basalt cliffs. Swallows flew overhead and chirped at us from on the wire fences. We sat in the sunshine munching apples, looking at the dark clouds hanging over Rum; Canna, being relatively low and to the west of Rum, has less rainfall. As on Ulva, I felt enveloped by a silence that had depth and spaciousness through which the cry of a lamb, the call of an oystercatcher, the twittering of woodland birds, even the sense of my own heartbeat, were all thrillingly clear. Then a lone cow standing in the corner of a field started to bellow, filling the air with a deep trumpeting that bounced repetitively between the basalt cliffs above the meadow. And yet behind the sound I was still conscious of the underlying silence that contains it all.

Steve's call for my attention, "Peter!", was almost shocking as it cut through both the silence and my reverie. I turned to see him gesticulating toward the high crags. Following his pointing arm, I saw what was exciting him: an eagle, beating its wings hard to gain height and avoid the mobbing crows, soared across toward Compass Hill. It circled for a while, a dot against the sky, then swooped down so we lost sight of it against the hillside.

Later, we walked across the machair on Sanday amongst a profusion of wildflowers—it was almost impossible not to tread on the spotted orchids, there were so many of them. The rain had blown through and the air was again sparklingly clear. We sat at the top of the low cliffs looking east across the Sound of Canna to the steep west side of Rum; west, back to the basalt terraces of Canna; and north to the Cuillin and beyond along the west coast of Skye.

I woke early. All was quiet. I lay in my bunk half asleep for a while, wondering where I was. Then I remembered: I was afloat in Coral on still water in the middle of a ring of mountains at the southern end of Skye. Today was my 70th birthday and I was anchored in Loch Scavaig.

After a few moments, I swung out of my bunk and went on deck to look around. First I checked that Coral hadn't moved overnight. The anchorage at Loch Scavaig is a tight pool surrounded by mountains that rise steeply from the water's edge. I had to crane my neck to see their tops. The anchor is set in soft mud, so the holding is poor and the sailing directions warn of fierce squalls dropping down the gullies even in calm weather. But all was well: the tide was high, the pool full to the brim; still water mirrored the rock faces; Coral and the other yachts lay quietly, anchor chains hanging vertically into undisturbed water, their flags flopping listlessly.

I stood in the cockpit, almost, but not quite, part of the stillness that infused everything around me. It was a stillness filled with the soft sound of tumbling water—more than a trickle, less than a downpour—from the waterfall that drops hundreds of feet down a crack in the cliff. Absorbed in the sight and the sound, I noticed how in some places the water poured over the boulders, in others buried itself behind fallen debris. It seemed there was something infinitely precious about the way the unceasing sound merged with the stillness.

Beyond the waterfall a line of jagged peaks caught the morning sun, while the anchorage itself was still shaded by a lumpy rock face on the eastern side, curiously patterned with fissures and gullies. It was a wonderful place to wake, especially on my birthday; and also a strange place, a place of forbidding rock faces, squally winds, seals, seabirds, ravens and eagles.

Clouds drifted almost imperceptibly across the sky. The occasional call of an oystercatcher broke through the underlying murmur of the waterfall: I love the way those birds seem determined that you know of their presence. The only movement I was aware of was an Arctic tern. She flew over the water on her delicate wings, hunting, dipping just below the surface in pursuit of fish. Was she the same tern that Steve and I had watched fishing late into the previous evening? If so, she was a very busy bird! Then another sound, somewhere between a cough and a sneeze, alerted me, and I scanned the surface: there was nothing to be seen, until I noticed a pattern of concentric ripples. Through my binoculars I saw the smooth head, black eyes, and whiskers of a seal, looking at me looking at her.

But for all the charms of this place my mind was haunted with questions. What had taken me away from the intimacy and familiarity of people and things I love on this day of all days? What was I seeking and what was I meeting? This place was startlingly beautiful, remote yet hugely popular and much visited. All around were the signs of human colonization: there were half a dozen yachts, a bothy for climbers, and I knew that quite soon the first of the tourist launches would arrive pouring visitors in their brightly coloured outdoor clothes over the landscape. From where I stood I could see chunks of plastic along the shoreline, greasy patches from oil spills. I was moved by the beauty and by the underlying pain, the mess that is left after we humans have colonized a place.

I asked myself again, what was I looking for on this long slow journey? I found I had no answer. I looked back over my seventy years of questions and struggles and ambitions: I had explored many questions and accomplished much of what I set out to do. Maybe there was nothing now to find. Maybe what I was looking for was always right in front of me. Maybe I just could not see what it was.

I scribbled my strange, lonely thoughts in my little leather notebook, but then cast it aside. I am a writer, I told myself, but what am I a writer of? I judged my words harshly, as inadequate and as intellectualized cliché. "What is it that you are still looking for, you strange old man?" Then an answer came: I was looking for some healing of the human heart and some means of healing the destruction we have brought about by intent, by mistake, and simply through our existence. Maybe the Earth can take only so much of this curious, restless animal. Maybe there is no healing. Just grief.

Feeling rather sombre but less depressed after my musings, as I stood in the cockpit the world gradually woke up. Cloud gathered over the mountain ridge and a glimmer of sun broke through over the mountains in the east. The bright green grass and the white bothy reflected more vividly on the surface of the loch. A breath of wind dropped down from the mountains and Coral swung around her anchor chain. Steve stirred in his bunk and called up to me, "Happy Birthday!" I knew he had smuggled presents and a cake on board, and that I must shrug off my gloomy thoughts, pretend to be surprised and behave like a birthday boy. I clambered down the companionway and put on the kettle for tea.

Later, we took the dinghy ashore, tying her up awkwardly behind the launch that had just landed a group of tourists. "Lovely place!" we greeted the boatman who was sitting waiting for his passengers to return. "Aye! And to think I have to spend an hour and a half just sitting here every day," he replied with a laugh, gesturing at the scenery.

We climbed the metal steps on to the shore. "Cross the stepping stones for the best view of the loch," the boatman advised us. We followed the path past the rapids where the fresh-water Loch Coruisk drains over polished rocks into the sea, and clambered unsteadily over the "stepping stones"—actually a pile of unstable round boulders through which the water runs. We soon came to a small shingle beach at the bottom of the loch from where we could see over the water toward the jagged mountains at the far end. The loch and corrie were scooped out of the basalt and gabbro by glaciation some 10,000 years ago; its name means 'Cauldron of the waters'. Today, the cloud hung low all around and the water looked deep and mysterious. It 'broods an atavistic nervousness', as geologist Richard Fortey puts it. Steve and I sat separate for a while in the deep silence, watching the clouds gather and clear over the jagged peaks. Eventually the midges drove us to move. I walked over to where he was sitting; he looked up and simply said, "This is it, isn't it?" In a way, he answered all the tortured questions that had plagued me that morning.[4]

While Steve was sailing with me, Melanie was in her cottage at the top of Loch Nevis on an estate owned by the musical producer Cameron Mackintosh. We had dropped her off at Mallaig with Merlin the dog to catch the local ferry to Inverie on the Knoydart peninsula, from where she was picked up in a workboat by Norman, one of the men working for the estate, and taken up the loch to the little bay at Tarbert. We met after our excursion around the Small Isles at the pub at Inverie, and after a huge supper of fish and chips, Melanie went back to Tarbert on the workboat, while Steve and I stayed on Coral overnight and followed her in the morning.

I had been nervous about going up the loch to Tarbert because, according to the sailing directions, anchorage was unsafe in the bay: there is poor holding as the bottom is soft mud over hard rock; and as with all the sea lochs it is liable to sudden squalls blowing down the hillsides. But while we were away, Melanie had arranged for us to moor overnight on one of the estate buoys.

The bay at Tarbert is narrow with high bluffs on each side and a narrow shingle beach at the head, from which a track leads across a small grassy field and disappears inland. A small stone jetty protects a landing place where several boats are lying ashore, alongside piles of seagoing equipment—old buoys, piles of plastic fishing crates, nets and coils of rope. Toward the centre of the beach, rusty rails run down into the water from a winch above the high water line, installed long ago to haul out the herring boats that landed their catch here. Before the harbour at Mallaig was built in the nineteenth century, Tarbert was a seasonal centre for the herring industry: the fish landed here were taken overland to Loch Morar and on to more distant markets.

Today, Tarbert is quiet but not deserted. A small community of estate workers are rebuilding and restoring the cottages on the estate as holiday lets, one of which Melanie had taken for the week. As soon as we had picked up the buoy, an open workboat came buzzing around the headland, Norman at the helm with Melanie and Merlin on board.

We spent that day at Melanie's cottage, and in the evening walked back along the path high above the loch. On the beach outside one of the cottages the estate employees were partying, saying farewell to a young Englishman who was returning home after an internship. Whisky was flowing freely. It would have been uncivil not to accept the invitation for a dram, and then another. We were shown around the cottage our hosts had restored, invited to admire the workmanship in the stonemasonry and carpentry. Eventually I was able to break away and motor out to Coral in the dinghy.

For a while I sat in the cockpit listening to the continuing party noises from the shore and looking westward down the loch to where the sun was dropping behind the mountains on Skye. It rested, a spot of brilliance poised between two peaks, then sank from view, leaving the sky a glow of orange, deepening into crimson. The remains of the day's fair weather clouds, high above

the peaks, darkened as the sun lit them from behind, their under-
sides turning purple as the light finally faded.

"What is it about sunsets?" I asked myself through a haze of
good malt whisky. I can get quite cynical when I see people
snapping away with their cameras at a dramatic evening sky. Yet
here I was doing it myself. This sunset was an ordinary, yet quite
extraordinary, sight: the planet at its dramatic best. Maybe, I
thought as the darkness gathered, sunsets engage us strongly
because they offer us a moment when our minds are stilled yet
our hearts are caught up in a transition far greater than
ourselves. A gap opens in our everyday reality—what I have
already called a moment of grace. We can almost feel the Earth
turning under us, even that the whole solar system is moving
around us. Our attention is drawn beyond our little selves to a
wider sense of being that is even beyond the Earth. Maybe at
such moments we are aware that the world about us is beyond
human control and we are part of a mystery far greater than
ourselves.

Coral was safe on the estate's mooring buoy, so I slept soundly,
although with too much alcohol inside me to have a really restful
night. In the morning, the wind was from the north, cold but
light. The sky was clear, and I could tell that when the sun rose
it would be a fine day; although never as warm at sea as on land.
It was a lovely day for sailing and after the interlude with Steve
I was on my own again. I dropped the line from the mooring and,
once away from the narrow head of the loch, sailed down toward
the Sound of Sleat. I was on my way north again, and, once in the
Sound, I set Coral close-hauled, tacking back and forth against
the wind. The starboard tack took me over to the lush green of
the Sleat peninsula on Skye with its scattering of settlements
dotted along the coast. The port tack took me back toward the
mainland, where the rough hills of Knoydart rise above the
rocky shoreline. On the Skye shore, the anchorage behind the Isle

of Ornsay looked attractive, but was open to the northerly wind. I turned Coral and headed back across the Sound toward the entrance to Loch Hourn. The pilot book listed several anchorages there, but clouds were gathering on the mountaintops and the loch looked dark and forbidding. I remembered the squalls that blow without warning down the mountainsides. I would explore Loch Hourn another day.

I tacked Coral out into the Sound again and headed a few miles further north to Sandaig Bay, a sandy inlet protected from the north wind by the low Eilean Mor and Fraoch Eilean, where I would be quiet for the night. From the anchorage I could see right down the smooth waters of the Sound of Sleat, past distant Eigg with its sloping skyline and the sharp drop of the dramatic pitch-stone ridge, and out into the Sea of Hebrides. Nothing was stirring, which felt odd after the busyness of Mallaig, with its ferries, fishing boats and marina, and my social time at Tarbert.

In *Ring of Bright Water*, Gavin Maxwell's account of living with otters, Sandaig Bay, where he had his cottage, is disguised as Camusfeàrna. For Maxwell it was a secret place. He describes scrambling down the steep path alongside the burn, 'so steep that neither the house nor its islands and lighthouse are visible from the road above, and that paradise within a paradise remains, to the casual road-user, unguessed'. I was looking at the same scene Maxwell describes, but from the other direction: the 'wide shingly outflow of the burn'; the chain of islands, 'rough and rocky with here and there a few stunted rowan trees and the sun red of patches of dead bracken' with the lighthouse at the end and the 'small beaches of sand so white as to dazzle the eye'.[5]

Despite being in such a lovely and in a way significant spot, I sank into despond. I experienced a nagging sense of meaninglessness: it was such a struggle to keep going, and my so-called pilgrimage seemed pointless. Was there anything new to say? And would anything I wrote make any difference? I outraged myself by writing in my notebook, 'It's just one damn loch, one damn mountain after another'. Maybe I was feeling lonely having left Steve and Melanie at Mallaig. Maybe I was just tired and cold after a long day tacking against the wind. Maybe these emotional ups and downs are inevitable aspects of pilgrimage; one can't stay in an exalted state all the time. But when such feelings arise, as they do quite regularly, the insights that 'all this must pass' and the gorgeous, transformative experience of the sunset simply disappear.

Chapter Sixteen

Wind and Weather

The general synopsis: High 100 miles west of Rockall, 1030. Low Fisher 1012 slow-moving with little change.
Hebrides
Wind: North or northwest 4 or 5.
Sea state: Moderate.
Weather: Fair.
Visibility: Good.

Nights alone on Coral are rarely unbroken. Often the wind shifts and changes its tone in the rigging; sometimes I have go on deck in my pyjamas and tie back the halliards to stop them rattling on the mast. When the tide turns Coral may swing around, the anchor chain clanking in the stemhead or growling as it scrapes along the seabed. Or the changing tide may bring a swell into the anchorage so she pitches and rolls in the water. Often I dream of wild winds and vast waves far out to sea. On waking, before anything else, I listen to the wind and crane my neck to look at the sky through the hatch; as soon as I get out of my bunk I go on deck to see what the weather is doing. With my first cup of tea I check the tide tables: even though I usually have them written down for a week ahead, I want the times of high and low water firmly in my head, and to be sure to know when tidal streams we may encounter that day start and stop. Every day and in every way the weather matters and the state of the tide matters. I will be warm or cold, wet or dry, safe or precarious; I will make a fast passage or find myself battling against the elements. There can never be a retreat to *terra firma*, into a house or car. I must sail Coral in relation to the wind and sea, know each moment where I might seek shelter.

I woke after a peaceful night at anchor in Sandaig Bay to blue sky and gentle northerly winds. It was a promising start to the day. Since I had to wait for the tide to turn before I could pass through the narrow Kyle Rhea between Skye and the mainland, where the stream runs at up to 8 knots, I spent the morning on domestic chores. I stripped off and washed from head to foot, including all the intimate places that need special attention—I am always proud that I can do a full body wash in two inches of water in a small bowl. Then I shaved my month-old beard—it was quite respectable, but very grey, and made me look like my father in a way I found disturbing. I washed some socks and pinned them to the guardrail to dry, and generally tidied the cabin. There was still plenty of time before the tide turned, so I just sat in the cockpit enjoying the peacefulness. The sun came out for a while, then the clouds covered it again; the white sand glowed in the bright light; a big workboat passed slowly down the Sound, pushing an enormous bow wave in front of it.

After lunch I hauled up the anchor and continued north. I was pleased to find I had got my calculations right so I entered Kyle Rhea just as the tide was turning, so Coral was whisked through the narrows and carried on the tide through the Kyle of Lochalsh and under the Skye Bridge. Out in the wider waters of the Inner Sound the north wind was sharper and colder, and now was blowing against the tide I had used so favourably. It was dead on the nose for the course I had planned round the north of Longay and Scalpay to an anchorage in the south of the Sound of Raasay. Biggish waves were rolling toward Coral, and I realized how lucky I had been with the quiet waters of the trip so far.

I could have turned back, but of course I didn't. As Coral pitched in the rough waters, I had to scramble to keep my balance as I set her as close to the wind as she would go. Once settled to her course, with Aries looking after the steering, she charged into the waves while I hunkered down under the sprayhood. A quick tack north took us clear of Longay, but was I clear of the reefs beyond? I hesitated: should I pass between the reefs and Longay through the passage marked by a green buoy; or put in another tack and take the longer route to windward of the reefs? I decided to take the shorter route, past the green buoy.

I had avoided reefing while close-hauled to keep as much power through the waves as possible. As soon as I turned her off the wind, Coral was overpowered and hurtled toward the buoy. I realized I would soon be manoeuvring close to a lee shore with too much sail up. Wrong decision, maybe, but too late now. Aries couldn't cope with the excess wing in the mainsail, so I took over and steered as cleanly as I could toward the buoy. We cleared it successfully, and I immediately had to scramble, with the shore rather close, to get Coral back on the wind and sailing more stably. My heart was in my mouth for a second or two when she surged toward the rocks rather than clawing away from them, but soon she was safely on the new course. Am I frightened at such moments? At the moment of action I am too busy. It is later, in the middle of the night, that the "what ifs?" really arise!

But the day was by no means over. I reached the shelter of the southern end of the Sound of Raasay and tried a couple of places to anchor, both of which were unsatisfactory, still too exposed and uncomfortable, so I had the anchor up and down twice. The two lochs nearby on Skye didn't seem very good alternatives so I decided to press on north the extra three miles to the shelter of Portree.

Winds arise due to differential pressures between masses of warm and cold air. There is a general pattern to circulation of the atmosphere: the sun warms the air over the equator, the air rises, developing an area of low pressure over the equator. The rising air meets the stratosphere and is turned toward the poles, cools and drops, causing high pressure in mid latitudes. This flow of air is diverted by the rotation of the Earth and develops into the regular patterns of wind around the planet that are known as the 'trade winds' because for centuries they provided the most convenient routes for long distance sailing.

More locally in the North Atlantic, warm tropical air meets cold polar air along an unstable boundary. As pockets of warm air intrude into the cold, they rise, drawing in more air and creating winds. The rotation of the Earth causes this emerging weather system to spin anticlockwise and travel eastward, intensifying as it goes. As the moist tropical air rises, it condenses as clouds and eventually precipitates, usually when it meets high ground on land.

The sequence of low pressure areas, and their associated warm fronts bringing rain followed by cold fronts bringing bright skies, are the origin of the wet and changeable weather we experience in the British Isles. Conversely, high pressure areas develop where cold air falls and moves outward, creating an area of clear skies and light winds.

I am continually making sense of the weather patterns while at sea, listening to the forecast from the Met Office, checking online sites, downloading pressure charts as I try to estimate conditions through each day, maybe the next, even (more speculatively) several days ahead. What I am looking out for is the pattern in the weather. Maybe there is a series of depressions, each bringing that characteristic pattern of changing wind direction: becoming more southerly (backing) to start with; then, with gathering clouds and the threat of rain, moving to the southwest or west (veering) and gathering in strength. After the warm front that carries the rain passes, the wind typically veers again, often quite sharply, to the northwest, the skies clear bringing clear and brisk weather.

I am also looking out for high pressure areas, which may be an extension of the permanent high pressure over the Arctic, or of the Azores high in the subtropical North Atlantic. The polar high often brings clear weather and a cold wind; while the Azores high brings warmth, moisture, and misty conditions.

When high pressure is centred over the country, fine weather with lighter and more variable winds predominate.

Finally, I am thinking of the way the shape of the land will influence the wind: how it may be gusty around headlands or blanketed by high ground; how the rapid warming of the land through a summer day will cause local low pressure so that sea breezes develop; how wind flowing against the tidal stream may cause rough water and overfalls.

What I am looking out for is an indication of wind strength: most summer depressions pass to the north of the British Isles and bring with them good sailing winds; but a deep depression will bring winds of gale force or more. High pressure zones may bring fine weather, but often with very little wind. Where high and low pressure meets there is often a steep pressure gradient between them and strong or gale force winds.

Sailing toward Portree, a fresh north wind was blowing down the east side of a polar high centred over the North Atlantic. Earlier in the day the wind had been light and I was in the sheltered lee of Skye. In the afternoon it gathered force, funnelled down the Inner Sound, possibly amplified by an afternoon sea breeze as the land warmed up. I was maybe a little careless in thinking this through at the time, maybe too ambitious to press on, leaving me exposed by late afternoon.

Three miles on to Portree didn't seem very much, really, even into the wind. But the Sound is completely open to the north, and not only had the wind increased but it was funnelling rollers down the sound, some of which were breaking. With the engine at full revs we moved forward well enough, but pitched quite spectacularly. Many of the waves Coral was able to shoulder aside with just a bit of spray. But the bigger ones seemed to come in pairs: the first would lift her bows high in the air, so she came crashing down into the next one. Sometimes she hit the second wave foursquare, sending huge sheets of water to each side; other times she seemed to plough into it, so that a mass of solid water poured over the deck. The cockpit sole was awash with water, the sprayhood leaking, the crockery crashing around in its racks below so I was sure that everything would be smashed. All this time I stood precariously balanced in the cockpit, looking over the sprayhood, watching each wave and Coral's response. My face was covered in salt, my glasses thick with spray, but I didn't feel it right to crouch in the cockpit while she was doing all this hard work. It was then I noticed how cold my face was without a beard!

On and on we went, wave after unrelenting wave. The sun sank behind the high cliffs and in the shadow the evening turned cold. The contrast between the still bright sky and the darkness at the bottom of the cliff made it difficult to judge my distance away from the rocks along the shoreline. Would I reach Portree before it was completely dark? Eventually I was able to turn into the wide entrance of the inlet which leads to the harbour; although this meant turning across the waves, setting Coral rolling as well as pitching. Soon we were in the shelter of the inlet and the bliss of calm water. The visitors' moorings under the wooded promontory on the north side of the harbour were well out of the wind, with a long pick-up line that was easy to catch with the boathook, and a substantial mooring line with a large eye I could just drop over the cleat.

And then it all seemed worth it: the world had offered a series of challenges and Coral and I had risen to them. My arms ached, my shoulders were stiff, my neck seemed to have a crick in it; and I was so very tired. And while I had made mistakes along the way, and while others might have made different choices, I was pleased to be in a truly sheltered place for the night.

After resting a couple of days in Portree and filling up with food and water, I sailed on north and anchored for a couple of days at the top of Loch Sheildaig, an extension of Loch Torridon on the eastern side of the Inner Sound, reaching deep into the mainland. The sky was deep blue all day and for the first time that summer I was hot! Huge rounded hills, great masses of rock, rise abruptly from a small strip of land by the water's edge. At Sheildaig village a row of homely white houses are strung along the shore, utterly dwarfed by the hillside that rises behind them. In every direction, foreground hills overlap those behind which again overlap those in the far distance. I felt the landscape round the loch had a magical quality to it; it brought to my mind the 'misty mountains' of Tolkien's fantasy world. As I sailed around the loch, especially when passing the low finger of rock that separates Loch Shieldaig from Upper Loch Torridon, the low foreground moved relative to the higher background, revealing new perspectives moment by moment.

This place is the origin of the term 'Torridonian sandstone', which is used a lot in my guidebooks. The hills, as I learned from my geology book *The Hidden Landscape*, are composed of ancient sandstone overlaying the even more ancient Lewisian gneiss: 'the Torridonian sediments covered a Precambrian landscape floored by the Lewisian that was already ancient and eroded'. I was ever so slowly getting the hang of geological terms, wondering yet again why I did not learn any of this at school.[1]

While I was exploring the Loch, the Met Office issued a gale warning. Although the whole country was sweltering in sunshine, a deep area of low pressure out in the North Atlantic was headed toward northern Scotland. Strong winds (gusting to Force 9, severe gale) were forecast to sweep across the northwest that night and through the following day. I needed to be in a secure anchorage overnight to sit out the bad weather.

I moved Coral to a bay in the corner of the loch that, so the sailing directions told, offered shelter and good holding for the anchor. And I waited. Every hour I checked on my phone for updates to the forecast from the Met Office. The warnings continued, but strangely enough, even in the late afternoon there was little sign of a change of weather. The sky remained blue from horizon to horizon, apart from the usual clustering of fair weather cumulus around the tops of the hills. At the very end of the afternoon I noticed the high stratus clouds that were the early signs of a warm front approaching, heralding the depression. Ominously, the barometer remained high, even rising slightly through the day. When the gale arrived, pressure would drop dramatically: very high winds were on their way.

I had done everything I could to prepare: the anchor was well dug in, with plenty of chain paid out; there was nothing loose on the deck; everything in the cabin was safely stowed away. But the sun carried on shining strongly as it sank toward the horizon, the wind remained light, and so the waiting was a little surreal. Doubtless I would not think so in the middle of the night. I went to bed with a sense of foreboding. I wanted to be awake when the gale struck, but I needed to be rested.

It wasn't until about four in the morning that the winds came suddenly on us, gusting fiercely between the hills, throwing Coral one way then the other. I managed to keep dozing for a while, peeking out of the cabin window every now and then to check the transit marks I had noted: a telephone pole aligned with the corner of the white house. Each time I looked, they remained in line, so I was reassured that the anchor was holding... until around 5.30 I realized it wasn't. The marks moved steadily apart and other features on the shoreline began to move past each other. I could stay in my bunk no longer.

After dragging warm clothes and waterproofs over pyjamas, I hurried on deck to sort things out. Coral was heeled over, drifting sideways toward the middle of the loch, but in no immediate danger. I worked away at the windlass to raise the anchor, and once I had it clear of the water I saw it had picked up an enormous bundle of weed, so heavy I could hardly lift it, even with the windlass. Nothing for it but to lie on my belly on the wet deck, reach under the pulpit with my arms over the bows, pull away the stalks of slimy seaweed, dropping them back into the water, until I had it clear. In the cockpit once more, I motored back into the bay. Re-anchoring single-handed was a struggle: I had to motor just beyond my chosen spot, cut the engine and clamber up to the bows to drop the anchor before the gusts blew the bows sideways downwind. Each time I missed the moment I had to take Coral through the whole manoeuvre again.

I lost count, but I think it was four times during that gale that the anchor dragged and needed to be hauled up, cleaned off and reset. After the second occasion, I dragged out the backup anchor, a huge 60lb CQR, from the bottom of the cockpit locker and tried with that. I had never needed to use it in twenty years of sailing Coral. I set and reset the anchor, sometimes with one, sometimes two. Nothing seemed to work; indeed, the big anchor seemed more of a nuisance than a help.[2]

Each time I hauled up the anchor—careful to wear rigger gloves and to pull with my legs rather than my back—I felt myself at the utter limit of my physical capabilities. Soaked through with rain, spray and sweat, my arms ached, my back was sore, and I was simply exhausted. Each time I struggled with the anchor, there was little voice of alarm in the back of my head saying, "You can't do this on your own." And each time I found that, once I started, my head was clear, my body ready, and I did what was needed. The challenge was both alarming and satisfying, but I am not sure how many more times I could have done it. Eventually I must have hit lucky and found a place on the bottom where there was no weed and some stiff mud. I added extra scope by shackling a heavy rope line to the end of 30 metres of chain. At last, Coral stopped moving.

Once finally settled, I sat in the cockpit and stared at my new transit, now aligning the telephone pole with the second window on the house. In the lulls between gusts, Coral lay still and the loch seemed quiet. There was a moment of tranquillity in our little bay, just the moan of the wind tormenting the trees on the hillsides and the tumbling waves further out in the loch. Then, as if the wind was preparing itself, a howl sounded from afar, louder and higher pitched as it came our way. It hit Coral with a wild shriek, shaking the rigging, blowing the bows round and heeling her over. Lying at an angle, the wind caught her broadside; she was thrust downwind of the transit. I held on tight, anxious the anchor was dragging again, expecting that any moment it would pull out, or the warp would break. But each time everything held and when the next lull came she swung round and moved sedately back into position.

At times I found myself talking to the wind, saying, "That's enough, please stop now." I realized that I was tensing my body with each gust, using up energy I might need for real work, so I tried to find a way to enjoy the wind, to be in tune with it, rather than fight it. Of course the wind was just doing what it does, howling through the pressure difference between low pressure to the north and high to the south.

Early afternoon the rain came: sheets of wetness blowing down the loch, soaking everything, reducing the visibility to a few hundred yards and forcing me into the cabin. But the rain was also a sign that the worst was over. Gradually the wind eased, the gusts faded away—not without a last few shrieks, but shorter, less intense. I found I had dozed off for a bit, and then, quite suddenly, it was calm, with even a few patches of blue sky. By evening the sea that had been a turmoil of white water was tranquil, stretching through the loch northwest out to sea. The hills reappeared from behind the low cloud, once again giving the place the appearance of an illustration from a fantasy book. But there was no fantasy about my aching limbs and back: I was very tired and went to bed early.

Chapter Seventeen

Earth Time, Eternal Now, Deep Time

Four billion years… What can we make of such a span? During that time the surface of the Earth has been shaped, reshaped, and reshaped again, and that new shape once more redesigned. Life has appeared, diversified, suffered crises, moved from sea to land to air, developed the consciousness to learn about its own past. Over the area now occupied by our small island the sea has advanced and retreated many times… Risen from dust, we could yet return to it.
Richard Fortey
The Hidden Landscape

When I am sailing, I often pick up pebbles from the seashore. Usually, they seem interesting at the time, but soon lose the significance of the moment of collection, clutter up the cabin and are eventually discarded. As I travelled north up the Highlands coast, I collected three contrasting pieces of rock that developed a particular significance. The first was a pebble of pink granite I collected on the beach on the southwest corner of Mull. I had anchored Coral in the tight little bay at Rubh' Ardalanish and gone ashore to explore, picking out this rock as I returned. It was startlingly pink when I lifted it out of the cold water; when dry it was more subdued but still remained strongly coloured, its coarse crystalline structure evident to the naked eye. Granite is an igneous rock, its crystals formed in intense heat and pressure under the Earth's surface, cooling as it bubbles through in dome-shaped formations. My piece of granite erupted some 50 million years ago as part of the major Earth movements that formed the Highlands. In geological terms it is contemporaneous with the columnar volcanic basalt, most celebrated on the small island of Staffa, but generally common across this area.

I found my second piece of rock among the massive rounded hills of Loch Torridon: a pebble from the foreshore, deep browny-red, composed of fine, even particles with no crystalline structure apparent. This is Torridonian Sandstone, a sedimentary rock more ancient by far than the igneous rocks of Mull and Skye. Composed of the eroded fragments of earlier formations and deposited about a billion years ago as a low relief plain, it has weathered through eons of time into the rounded mountains that characterize this landscape.

My third piece of rock came from yet further north. It is rough and craggy, with a crystalline structure more coarse even than the granite. On one side, bands of dark and light crystals are scattered with gleaming dots of fools' gold; the other side is pinky-red embedded with bits of mica. This is Lewisian gneiss, collected from the far northwest. This rock originates in the Precambrian era, up to three billion years ago, a metamorphic formation forged by the transformation of even older rock by enormous heat and pressure as the crust of the primal Earth solidified. These rocks were already ancient and eroded when the sandstone was laid down, and are among the oldest on the planet.

I collected these rocks as I travelled through and dwelt within these geological landscapes, contemplating the ancient rocks, picking over them on the foreshore, reading about them in the geology books in my ship's library. And through this dwelling and contemplation I entered into experiences of time quite different from the clock time of my everyday life.[1]

The first intimations of the disruption of my sense of time came early in my Scottish voyage when Coral was at anchor between the low, grassy island Inch Kenneth and the huge basalt cliffs at the entrance to Loch na Keal on the west coast of Mull. I approached the sheltered anchorage cautiously: it is guarded by underwater reefs with no clear indications of the passage between them. Once safely in and settled, I looked around me. Coral was anchored between the hard and the friable. Inch Kenneth is formed of sedimentary rock where ancient conglomerates and limestone outcrops have broken down to give good grassland. The cliffs, in contrast, are volcanic in origin: sequential eruptions laid down layers of Triassic basalt; over time these eroded into terraces that step down the hillside before dropping hundreds of feet to the sea. At the base of the cliffs, by the road along the shore, stand three tiny white cottages. In many ways they are quite insignificant, but also a testament to human ability to create living space in the most unlikely places.

I decided to stay put for a day. It was early in this second year of my pilgrimage, I needed to settle in, take things gently. The following day was raining and windy, and I saw no point in getting wet and uncomfortable and so stayed another night. I devoted periods to formal meditation, quietening my mind then opening to the land around me. With the rain spitting and fresher winds rocking the boat, as well as my restless mind, concentration was difficult. In time, however, I was able to really attend to these cliffs. I watched them through the day as the sun moved across the sky, casting shadow in the morning and lighting their peaks with orange in the evening. I noticed the details of the streams tumbling down, glimmering where the light caught the falling water. I absorbed the contrast between the cottages at the foot of the cliffs and the enormity of the 200–300 metre drop. All this attention provided me with a tiny sense of intimacy, of being in place rather than watching scenery. And I was struck by the contrast between my human impatience, my restlessness to get on, and the simple presence of these cliffs.

I was glimpsing time at the limits of human imagination. While the basalt rocks are geologically quite young, they were formed long before the ancestors of the *homo* species emerged. And yet those little cottages appear so permanent, so part of the scene. There was a lesson about the nature of time here, but at this early stage of my pilgrimage I was not yet ready for it. I needed to get further into the experience and allow it to disrupt my everyday sense of time more thoroughly.

Late one midsummer evening some weeks after my stay at Inch Kenneth, I put aside my book and climbed the companionway to the cockpit. Coral was anchored in the pool off Tanera Beg in the Summer Isles, a few miles north of Ullapool. The sun was just touching the peak of the Eilean Fada Mór to the northwest, throwing a rich golden light on to the sandstone rocks that circle the anchorage. A heron stood in the deep shadow along the shoreline, motionless, poised to strike. A few gulls cried harshly; there was a twittering of land birds from the shore. The flag halliard rattled lightly against the backstay. Otherwise silence.

Opposite the sinking sun, the three-quarter moon was rising into a just-blue sky over the line of mountains on the distant mainland. The low sunlight lit up the ridges and cast the valleys into shadow, giving the mountains a dimensionality and body even though they were in the far distance.

The sky was clear apart from a few wisps of dark cloud over the peaks: a slack weather system with patchy cloud and light, variable winds had persisted for the best part of a week. The sea reached calm all the way to the mainland shore, tiny ripples moving dark shadows hypnotically across the surface. The tide was falling, revealing the reefs at the entrance to this pool and uncovering the coral beach, ghostly pale in the failing light, where an oystercatcher was busily hunting along the water's edge.

Night was coming, and yet at this time of year and at this latitude it would be scarcely dark, especially with the near-full moon high in the sky. In the time it took to scribble a few words in my notebook, the sun had disappeared, the distant mountains seemed to be in a greater light, the moon had risen higher and was more clearly defined in a darkening sky.

My everyday life is dominated by clock time: I wake and retire, have my meals, arrange to meet people, pretty much by the clock. This remained true at the start of my voyage, as I religiously consulted the almanac for the times of high and low water for the week ahead and noted them down in my tidal atlas. But as the pilgrimage unfolded, while there remained a sense of time passing, this was increasingly marked, not by the digital regularity of clocks, but by the natural rhythms of the planet that I shall call 'Earth time'.

Two months into my ecological pilgrimage, anchored in the Summer Isles, I was saturated in Earth time. I experienced time passing not by one digital metric but by a series of overlapping rhythms: the sun rises and sets; the moon waxes and wanes; high tide moves forward about 50 minutes each day; I get hungry and I eat, tired and I rest. The passing of weather systems brought a longer beat to the rhythm. When slow moving or slack weather systems predominated—as in the 'long hot days of summer'—little changed to mark the passing of time. But when depressions move in quickly from the Atlantic, bringing fresh, changeable winds, they stir up a sense of change and even urgency. Clock time never disappeared completely, of course; it simply became another strand in the weave, only salient when, for example, I needed to know the start of the favourable stream through a narrow passage.

As clock time fades in significance and a more direct encounter with the wild world distracts attention from everyday preoccupations, social constructions of reality fade away. This allows for a second experience of time that I call the 'eternal present': those moments when differences between self and other, inner and outer, are transcended and time appears to stand still. At such, often tiny, moments it was as if there was a crack in the cosmic egg through which a different world opened that was nevertheless the same world.

Later in my pilgrimage, leaving Scalpay in the Outer Hebrides, it was more of a performance than usual to get out of the harbour and on my way.[2] It took a while to get the dinghy on board and properly stowed. The anchor chain came up black and sticky, spreading mud all over the foredeck, taking several buckets of sea water and a lot of scrubbing to clean up. As I motored out of the harbour there were unfamiliar rocks and reefs to negotiate. And once the mainsail was hoisted and set, it was clear that there was very little wind, and to make any progress at all I needed to rig the inner forestay and hoist the big No.1 genoa, a big sail that sweeps the deck and reaches nearly as far aft as the cockpit, rather than just unfurl the working foresail. For nearly an hour I seemed to be constantly on the go from cockpit to foredeck and back again.

Once settled, with all sail set, Coral sailed elegantly toward Skye, rippling the unusually smooth waters of the Little Minch, making just over three knots. But soon the wind faded. Coral's speed dropped below three knots, then two, and after creeping along for half an hour or so, to nothing at all. "Let it be," I told myself. "There is plenty of daylight, we are not unsafe or uncomfortable." I allowed Coral to drift about in the middle of the sea.

The day was pleasantly warm. Loose cloud covered the sky, the sun shining fitfully through the gaps. The wind was even more fitful, ruffling the water, promising some action, but fading into nothing very much. Ahead lay Skye, a dark silhouette; astern, bright sunshine picked out the outcrops of gneiss on Harris, and fair weather cumulus marked the whole line of the Outer Hebrides from Barra to Stornoway. The quiet sea, undulating like a dimpled mirror, threw shallow reflections this way and that. Sea and sky took on the same luminous silvery grey, meeting in the far distance north and south at a horizon that was diffuse and uncertain.

Now I had stopped fiddling around trying to get Coral to sail, I was open to the wonder of the moment. Held in a space between two lands, and with the sea merging into the sky, the sky into the sea, I lost myself into this wider, silvery world. My sense of self became as diffuse and uncertain as the horizon. I was still present, but with no sharp distinction between in here and out there; I became part of the quiet presence of the world.

As Gary Snyder puts it so nicely, such 'sacred' moments take one away from one's little self into the wider whole. If I have learned anything in three long seasons of sailing on the western edge, of pilgrimage in search of a different kind of relation to the Earth on which we live, it is that these sacred moments arise quite spontaneously and unexpectedly. They certainly cannot be forced, although I notice they often come when I step back from preoccupation with the demands of sailing and pilotage. But on occasion, they arise in the midst of such preoccupations.[3]

Sailing north, making for Ullapool, in strong and gusting winds, I secured the double-reefed mainsail with a preventer and poled out the genoa with the spinnaker boom. Through the morning Coral blew fast but not uncomfortably up the coast toward the headland Rubha Reidh, safely keeping well offshore. I made myself coffee, then soup and a chunk of bread for lunch, after which Coral had passed the headland and it was time to gybe round on to a reach into outer Loch Broom. (Sailors will know that gybing involves bringing the mainsail across from one side of the boat to the other. Done properly, it was a safe manoeuvre; uncontrolled, it can be dangerous.) I started the routine of getting Coral ready for the turn: I rolled in the genoa; then, secure with lifejacket and harness, I clambered cautiously forward to the exposed foredeck to lower and stow the spinnaker boom.

It was only when back in the cockpit that I looked astern at the following sea. The waves seemed bigger than I had expected, the troughs between them deeper. For a moment I hesitated. Could I really do this safely on my own? The grey-green surface of the approaching wave looked cold, relentless and implacable: a small hillside of water, then another, then another. I watched the waves for a few short seconds and my fear dropped away. Now, in recollection, I would describe this as a moment of direct meeting, when I was simply present in this wild sea with no thoughts and no self-concern. By watching the waves roll toward Coral's stern, I tuned myself to their rhythm: without conscious decision the moment of action arrived. I hauled in the mainsail hand over hand and jammed it firm in the cleat; then leaned against the tiller with my thigh and held it there. Coral's stern came round through the waves and the mainsail, constrained by the tight sheet, flipped safely through its short arc with a sharp crack. I slowly paid out the sheet so Coral settled on to the opposite tack, driving eastward into the loch. With the mainsail safely gybed, I rolled out the genoa again and, after peering through the spray into the distance and comparing what I could see with what was shown on the chart, set a course to pass to the south of Priest Island.

In many ways there was nothing special about this. I was on my own in rough and windy weather, but a gybe is just a gybe, one of many on a three-month voyage. But in the weeks that passed, the image of those implacable waves rolling up behind Coral's stern kept returning, until I found some illumination in David Hinton's book *Hunger Mountain*, in which he explores the wisdom of the ancient Chinese poets and sages. In contrast to the everyday Western experience of the self as separate from the world and acting intentionally as a 'transcendent spirit centre', Hinton considers the terms *wu-wei* and *tzu-jan*. *Wu-wei* means 'not acting', in the sense of 'acting without the metaphysics of self'. By being absent or self-less while acting, Hinton suggests that, 'Whatever I do, I act from that source and with the rhythm of the Cosmos' (the 'I' in the sentence must be read ironically, in the sense of 'this particular being'!). *Tzu-jan* is usually translated as 'suchness', and points to the spontaneous unfolding through which the world burgeons into presence. And while I don't want to get into absurd and unsustainable claims of selflessness, it does seem to me that at the moment of the gybe I was so sufficiently tuned to the boat and the wind and the sea that the action was accomplished with an elegance that was not just of my own making.[4]

These tiny moments when time stands still, or maybe more accurately becomes irrelevant, are easy to overlook or to see as insignificant. They are not in themselves overwhelming transformations of consciousness, but nevertheless are profoundly important in calling forth a different relationship with the world: no longer out there as landscape, but recognized as a subjective presence of which we are part. The challenge, the creative opportunity, is quite simply to be open to these moments when they arise.

Further north again, the sea around Coral turned a bright turquoise blue as I sailed past Rubha Coigeach into Enard Bay. The low shore ahead, gnarled and lumpy gneiss, was pierced with many small inlets and scattered with small islands. From out at sea I could see the succession of sandstone mountains, Stac Pollaidh, Suilven and Quinag, rising as a line of sculptured forms above the gneiss platform.

I found an anchorage that night in the small but sheltered Loch Roe. The sailing directions refer to a high bluff that distinguishes the entrance; but there seemed to be high bluffs all along the coast, and I found it difficult to discern the way into the small loch against the background of gnarled crystalline rocks merging into each other. On first approach, I sailed past the entrance before I realized my mistake. With the sails down I motored back, close along the shoreline. "Ah! that must be the bluff of rock, there are the offshore rocks marked on the chart." I steered closer into what looked like a narrow entrance, ready to retreat at a moment's notice. The little bay ahead ended in a beach strewn with seaweed and plastic litter, but a passage to starboard opened between a tidal island and a patch of floating bladder wrack that indicated an underwater reef. Beyond was a tiny pool, deep, with just room to swing an anchor. A sheer cliff of crystalline gneiss stood high above the cockpit to one side, a line of rocks and tidal islets provided shelter on the other. And in the distance, the ridge of Quinag rose above the flattened landscape, clearly visible across the top of the loch.

The tide rose until the pool was full to the brim. The swell from the sea found its way between the islets, moving Coral gently around. Enchanted, I sat in the cockpit till late, watching the light play on the rocks and mountains as the sun went down, absorbing an unfathomable sense of geological time. This was the place I had been looking for, a place that offered a glimpse of a world both eternal and made anew in every moment.

Just what is it about these different rocks and mountains that I found so satisfying to see, to be in the presence of? Apart, that is, from the fascination of their different origins; apart from their beauty and grandeur, the way they shapeshift with the changing light; and apart from the contrasting landscapes they give rise to?

It seems to me that there is something simply inconceivable to the human mind about their age, their origins, their history; and that this is an opening of a third dimension I call 'deep time'. Confrontation with the age of the Earth, and beyond that the Cosmos, allows a glimpse of time as the container of all possibilities. Dwelling with these mountains—by which I mean spending time with them, meditating on them, studying their origins—gave me some sense of deep time quite different from what I have called Earth time and the eternal present. We can measure their age, but the age we derive is really beyond our grasp: truly, whose mind can encompass three billion years? We might also consider that, in terms of time passing, the Sun and Earth and solar system are more or less halfway through their lifespan. If we struggle to consider three billion years of rock formation, or four and a half billion years of the Earth's existence so far, how inconceivable is it to think of the evolutionary possibilities that are latent in another four and a half billion years before the whole is swallowed in the red giant that the Sun will eventually become?

Contemplating these issues, I have come to think of deep time as close to the Taoist notion of Absence, the pregnant emptiness from which all things appear and to which they return in a process of perpetual transformation. We cannot know this absence directly, but we may get a suggestion of it through the ancient presence of these rock formations and mountains. They seem to point beyond time in any human sense to a timelessness at the heart of existence.

Chapter Eighteen

Fragility

For the last twenty years I have owned some islands. They are called the Shiants: one definite, softened syllable, 'the Shant Isles', like a sea shanty but with the 'y' trimmed away. The rest of the world thinks there is nothing much to them. Even on a map of the Hebrides the tip of your little finger would blot them out, and if their five hundred and fifty acres of grass and rock were buried deep in the mainland of Scotland as some unconsidered slice of moor on which a few sheep grazed, no one would ever have noticed them. But the Shiants are not like that. They are not modest. They stand out high and undoubtable, four miles or so off the coast of Lewis, surrounded by tide-rips in the Minch, with black cliffs five hundred feet tall dropping into a cold, dark, peppermint sea, with seals lounging at their feet, the lobsters picking their way between the boulders and the kelp and thousands upon thousands of sea birds wheeling above the rocks.

Adam Nicolson
Sea Room: An Island Life

From Loch Awe I sailed across to Stornoway in the Outer Hebrides, and after a few days exploring Lewis set off down the coast in long tacks against a southerly wind toward the Shiant Islands. I passed weathered cliffs of ancient gneiss, low and rough, with sparse vegetation, the occasional opening to a loch. As there are practically no landmarks and very few signs of human settlement, I found it difficult to get a clear sense of forward progress: it was as if I was just tacking out toward the middle of the Minch and turning back toward the land. Then I spotted the lighthouse at Gob na Miolaid nestled into the cliff face, and beyond it the islands appeared over the horizon. But I stopped overnight in Loch Shell and set out again in the morning so as to approach the islands early in the day.

The Shiant Islands are an isolated group, separated from Lewis by the Sound of Shiant, notorious for its strong tides, overfalls and underwater hazards. A line of islets and rocks stretches a mile west from the islands toward the mainland, the last of which, known as Damhag, lurks underwater, although often marked by breaking waves as well as the green passage buoy. When I first read about these islands and studied the sailing directions, I doubted whether I would be able to visit: they are very exposed and offer little shelter. But it seemed I was lucky: the weather was quiet, with a smooth sea and enough wind to sail. I was thrilled that I would be able to reach them but also cautious, carefully noting landmarks and consulting the GPS to confirm my position.

The little archipelago is made up of three main islands, two of which are joined by a natural boulder isthmus. Together they form an open pool to which I was heading. The Shiants are columnar basalt, the most northern of the volcanic chain that stretches south, through southern Skye, the Small Isles, Staffa and Mull to the Giant's Causeway off northeast Ireland. These rocks, full of cracks and fissures, look as if quite recently thrust out of the Earth, contrasting strongly with rugged gneiss of the Outer Hebrides and the smooth Torridonian sandstone of the northwest mainland.

As Coral sailed closer, I could make out more detail. To starboard the line of rocks stretched out toward the mainland like a row of worn-down dragon's teeth. I was well clear of any danger there. Ahead were the spectacular northern cliffs of Garbh Eilean, octagonal columns of basalt rising high above the tumbled debris of scree that sloped steeply to the water's edge. The low sun picked out the high points of the columns and cast deep shadows into the fissures between them. On the more gentle and sheltered slopes, I could see sheep grazing on bright green patches of grass dotted with rocky outcrops.

I steered Coral through the confused water of the tidal stream that poured out between the two northern islands Garbh Eilean and Eilean Mhuire. The calm pool opened in front of me, littered with specks of white as if some giant had cast handfuls of torn-up paper across the surface. Soon Coral was surrounded by puffins, with the distinctive markings around their eyes and their wonderful coloured beaks. The air was full of puffins too, so full it reminded me more of a cloud of mosquitoes than a flock of birds. Those afloat seemed to be juveniles, pufflets (puffins live up to forty years but do not mate for the first five years), while those airborne were clearly adults, tirelessly flying out to the fishing grounds and returning with sand eels hanging from their beaks to feed their chicks. These adults were so intent on their business that they often seemed not to see Coral, passing within feet of the mast and only diverting at the last moment.

It is very difficult not to anthropomorphize puffins. They do remind one of neatly turned out, rather insecure, self-important people. As I took Coral slowly across the pool toward the anchorage, steering through the floating flocks, the pufflets swam energetically ahead, looking anxiously from side to side as if to say, "I am not really bothered by this great white creature." But when Coral drew too close for comfort, their heads bobbed this way then that even more urgently while they made up their minds whether to dive or take off. Diving is the more elegant choice: a neat flip takes them beneath the surface, leaving concentric rings of ripples. In contrast, taking off is usually a bit of a mess: their wings don't seem to give much initial lift, so they splash frantically along the surface, wings and feet flapping away, often to crash inelegantly back into the water.

It took me a while to get Coral settled. The usual anchorage is by the isthmus that connects the two most westerly islands, Garbh Eilean and Eilean an Tighe. This is protected from the prevailing westerly winds, but open to today's light easterlies. These volcanic islands rise abruptly from the seabed, the bottom shoals steeply and consists of boulders, so there is no sand or sediment of mud into which the anchor can sink and get a good grip. It took a little while before I was happy that the anchor was holding, with Coral tucked into the corner between the isthmus and the precipitous cliffs of Eilean an Tighe. As soon as I had a moment to look about, two young men carrying backpacks and wearing serious outdoor clothing crossed the isthmus, their figures moving across the boulder film-like against the still lines of the seascape. They disappeared up the cliff of Garbh Eilean and I saw no more of them during my stay. But I was not entirely alone.

Once I had Coral safely anchored, I soon realized that there were nearly as many razorbills as puffins in the pool. They are also auks, but rather bigger, distinguished by a black beak with a white line across it, joining a similar line across the face to the eye. The razorbills seem on the whole less nervous than the puffins: I saw one swimming quite happily within a couple of yards of Coral; it seemed quite unfazed as I moved about the deck. When it decided to dive I was able to watch it turn tail up and, once underwater, open its wings to fly down beneath Coral's keel, the bubbles of air around its feathers gleaming as they caught the light.

Looking up again across the pool, I realized that there were tens of thousands of puffins and razorbills. There were, of course, other birds: shags, black-backed gulls, kittiwakes, fulmars, guillemots, the odd gannet and, for me the most impressive, the skuas, big, heavily-built seabirds, brown, with two white stripes on their wings. I remembered how, off the coast of Ireland, I had watched one attack a gull and make it regurgitate its meal. Skuas are known as 'kleptoparasites' because of their habit of stealing food this way. But I am sure that given half a chance they would snatch a puffin chick, as would the big gulls. I imagined the links in the local food chain: marine plankton feeding sand eels, sand eels feeding baby birds and baby birds feeding skuas and gulls.

I took the dinghy ashore to land with some difficulty on the big round boulders of the isthmus. From there I scrambled up the rocks to find a path that led across the relatively flat area on the west side of Eilean an Tighe toward the cottage, owned, as are all the islands, by the Nicolson family. Just past the cottage a spring was covered with a protective sheet of wood and a saucepan lay nearby: this was the source of clean fresh water for the cottage. I scrambled up toward the heights of the island. It became rough underfoot. I kept looking for a clear path, but only found sheep tracks that promised to lead me up but soon petered out. Eventually a haiku formed itself in my mind:

Is this a path
Or just where the grass seems flattened?
And does it matter?

I expected that once I reached the top I would be able to look down on Coral floating safely in the pool far below me and take a photograph of her anchored in this remote place. From the high point I could see across the pool, but no sign of Coral. Of course, I told myself, she is hidden under the cliff. But, slightly panicked nevertheless, I hurried north along the ridge, walking at first, then scrambling down into wet gullies and up on to solid outcrops, worried that I might twist an ankle, telling myself that she was secure and would not have blown ashore, while at the same time imagining disaster. It seemed to take an age to get to the top of the cliff... and there she was: I could look almost straight down at her. Of course she was safe, but I had got myself hot and bothered.

Happy to be back on board, I spent the afternoon watching the birds and enjoying the changing light. A few yachts visited, but none stayed for long. A couple of fishing boats chugged through the pool. As the long northern evening drew in I began preparations for the night. The weather was calm enough for it to be safe to stay overnight at the islands, but I wanted to move to a more secure anchorage. The dark cliffs and the stony isthmus looked too close, and if the anchor were to drag Coral would soon be ashore. Even if the light winds persisted through the night, it felt wrong to sleep while she was anchored off a lee shore where there was poor holding.

So I hauled up the anchor and motored round the end of Eilean an Tighe to the western side of the isthmus. This anchorage is open to the swell of the Little Minch and the water disturbed by the tidal movement through the Sound of Shiant. Despite this, with the light wind blowing Coral away from the islands, she felt safer. Two Danish yachts had already taken the best positions but I was able to find a spot where the anchor held closer inshore.

In the early evening the crews of the Danish yachts returned from their expeditions ashore, and soon there was a whiff of diesel and rattle of anchor chains as they left the anchorage and disappeared north round the end of Garbh Eilean. Where would they spend the night, I wondered. With their departure I felt suddenly alone and vulnerable. I got out my iPhone and checked the forecast yet again, even though that meant waiting impatiently for the weak signal to load the page. I looked again at the anchor chain: it was hanging almost vertical with plenty of scope out. I worked out how I would leave the anchorage in the dark if I needed to; there was plenty of sea room to the southwest. There was no rational reason why I should not stay safely overnight, so I took myself in hand, sat down quietly, made myself breathe properly and look out at the world around me rather than inwards to my anxieties. I might feel exposed, just a speck in a vast sky and expanse of sea, but I could relax and appreciate it.

The evening wore on, the light faded and I became enveloped in the quiet mystery of twilight. Coral pitched gently on the light swell. Little waves rolled continuously up to the stony shore and broke with a hollow crash on the boulders. Looking up at the mound of Garbh Eilean, I could no longer make out the details of the basalt columns; it loomed dark against the evening sky. On Eilean an Tighe the little cottage stood out ghostly white, then, as the light faded away, merged with the hillside behind. Looking over Coral's stern, past the line of rocks and islets that stretches toward the mainland, I searched the surface of the Sound for a glimpse of the flashing green light on the buoy that marks Damhag. All I could see was the grey sea and the distant hazy line of Lewis.

The word that keeps coming to my mind to describe this evening is 'fragile'. It is as if the word itself wants to be used, and it captures both the strength and the vulnerability of my situation, and of all humans, for at root, despite the veneer of civilization, we are all unprotected in a wild world and the wild universe.

Something that is fragile is stable; it holds its form firmly, yet a small perturbation can easily destroy it. A fine wine glass that gives delight for years may shatter into fragments with a careless knock. When the edge of my favourite chisel is honed until it is only a few molecules thick, it makes a clean cut in the wood, but can be easily damaged by an unexpected nail. A fragile object often brings together both beauty and functionality.

Fragility itself may also afford a certain strength. The snowdrops that emerge early through the frost shake on their thin stems, beautiful to our human eyes, broken by a clumsy footstep. Yet in their fragility is their ability to sway rather than break in the rough winter winds. As in the practice of Tai Chi, there is an essential strength in yielding.

It is easy to see the fragility in individual things. Yet it is often the ecosystems of which individual things are a part that are truly fragile. The spring blossom on apple trees can so easily be blown about by unseasonable winds or frozen by a late frost. That blossom depends on bees and other insects for pollination.

If the spring is warm and the insects emerge before the blossom, the cycle of pollination is disrupted. The puffins I have been watching all day depend on the sand eels that proliferate in the seas nearby: the warming of the sea and the impact of fish farms and overfishing may threaten this relationship.

Complexity theorists have taught us to see living systems as resilient and able to return to equilibrium following disturbance. A wide range of influences may cause populations of puffins and sand eels to fluctuate from year to year, but the relationship remains stable. If new factors cause change outside the normal variation—if warmer seas bring about a marked shift northwards of warm-water plankton so the marine food chain is disrupted and there are fewer sand eels near the puffins' traditional nesting sites—the system as a whole becomes less stable, with greater variation and bigger fluctuations. If these changes persist, then the system may reach what is known as a 'tipping point', at which the stability of the relationship fails and catastrophic change occurs. While the puffin population on the Shiants is holding up, the thousands that until recently nested on the southern cliffs of Iceland have all but disappeared; it is thought that warmer waters have encouraged mackerel to migrate into the area and devour the small fish the puffins depend on. Such catastrophic changes may lead to the emergence of new order: the puffins have disappeared, but the gannets, which feed on the mackerel, are prospering. In the greater scheme of things, such a catastrophic change can be understood as creating an evolutionary opportunity, a place in which maybe a new order of puffins may emerge.[1]

The fragility of ecosystems can also be hidden. The basalt columns that form the Shiant Islands appear strong and stable, but are weakly jointed; over time, wind and waves penetrate the joints, allowing large chunks to break away. This undermines the stability of the cliff face so that a whole section may tumble into the sea.

A robust system is one that when perturbed will fluctuate wildly but in time return to stability within the original order. A fragile system is one in which the zone between stability and the tipping point is relatively narrow and the feedback loops that maintain stability are relatively weak: a small perturbation can tip it into catastrophic change with no means of recovery. Sailing these sparse seas I do my best to arrange things so that the little ecosystem focussed around Coral is well within the zone of stability: I try to leave a good margin of error around rocks and shoals, reef the sails early in strong winds, use plenty of scope when anchoring. I don't want a catastrophic failure in the integrity that keeps my vessel afloat. But the essence of voyaging as adventure and as pilgrimage is to tease around this zone. Fragile situations are often where novelty and beauty and discovery lie.

Our attention has been drawn to the fragility of Planet Earth by the space programme. Ever since the early Apollo missions, pictures of planet Earth from space have been widely available, starting with the famous 'Earth Rising', taken as Apollo 8 emerged from behind the moon. This has been called 'the most influential environmental photograph ever taken'. For, it is argued, now that humanity can see the Earth alone within the vast reaches of space, we will realize her beauty, fragility and significance and band together to protect and preserve her as our home.[2]

Astronauts report that they spend much of their spare time on missions simply 'Earthgazing'. In the video *Overview*, NASA engineer Nicole Stott tells us, "I think you start out with this idea of what it's going to be like, and then when you do finally look at the Earth for the first time you're overwhelmed by how much more beautiful it really is..." Shuttle astronaut Jeff Hoffman goes further: Earth "... looks like a living, breathing organism, but it also at the same time looks extremely fragile." From Earth, he says, "on a clear day you can see the big blue sky that seems to go on for ever. How can we put enough stuff in it to fill it up with things that really change it? And yet, when you see it from space then it's this thin line that is just barely hugging the surface of the planet." And Ron Garon, who served on the International Space Station, remembers, "When we look down on the Earth from space we see this amazing, indescribably beautiful planet... It's really striking and it's sobering to see this paper thin layer and to realize that that little paper thin layer is all that protects every living thing on Earth from death."[3]

Edgar Mitchell, who was the Lunar Module pilot on Apollo 14 and the sixth person to walk on the moon, was one of many astronauts to reflect deeply on their experience. His view was that it is not just that you get to see the beauty and fragility from space, but there is also a shift in consciousness which he described as close to the ancient Yoga Sutras of *savikalpa samādhi*. There is as a direct experience of interconnection: "You see things as you see them with your eyes but you experience them emotionally and viscerally as ecstasy and a sense of total unity and oneness... It's rather clear to me as I studied this that is was not anything new, but was something that was very important to the way we humans were put together."

Just as Mitchell, when he read the ancient accounts of *savikalpa samādhi*, found they reflected his own experience, as I watch the video and listen to the astronauts speaking I feel their experience is not so very far from mine as I sat in the twilight off the Shiant Islands.

Of course, I am not among those who first saw Earth rising from behind the moon; I have not watched the shadow of night move across the face of the Earth; nor I have experienced the thin blue line of the biosphere clinging to the curve of the planet. And yet, as Mitchell pointed out, the astronauts' experience of oneness is nothing new. I think we may idealize their experience and in doing so see the capability of experiencing oneness as something special, something extraordinary, something for which we have to go outside the planet. Maybe it is better to see it as a dimension of human consciousness that we modern humans have neglected and marginalized, rather than something only available from outer space. Maybe a better way to celebrate the astronauts' experience, the way that 'Earth Rising' might change human consciousnesses, the way it might kick-start a true environmental movement, is to realize our own capacity for such experiences. These are capabilities that we must bring back to ourselves, and not just to our pilgrimages into the wild, but into our homes, our gardens, our cities, the everyday world around us and our relationships with other humans.

Zen masters teach us not to seek the extraordinary, not to look for special or 'sacred' places. To seek that which is special stops us from seeing what is before our eyes: the specialness of the everyday, how everything rolls together in being and nonbeing, how we are every moment part of a living planet. We may need a space mission, a sailing pilgrimage or some kind of retreat to divert us from the habits of mind through which we see a world of separation. Yet the experience of interbeing, the direct experience of interconnection, is the experience of seeing the world as it is, in its essential nature.

I sat out late, enchanted by my surroundings while still feeling strangely vulnerable, reluctant to go to bed. Through the evening the inexhaustible stream of puffins flew overhead; the skuas and black-backed gulls continued their patrols around the cliff tops. If I peered out to sea I could just make out the white flash of gannets on a late search for fish. As the darkness finally gathered, my long watch was rewarded by the waxing crescent moon rising, a deep red, between the two dark humps of the islands. The overhead stream of puffins ceased, and I too was at last content to climb down the companionway and sleep.

Chapter Nineteen

Pilgrimage at Home

Every creature on earth returns to home.
Clarissa Pinkola Estés
Women Who Run With the Wolves

Nature is not a place to visit, it is home.
Gary Snyder
The Practice of the Wild

My few days at the Shiant Islands effectively marked the endpoint of my pilgrimage. I returned to northern Skye, where I picked up a call from Elizabeth telling me her mother had fallen. At first it seemed she had only cut herself slightly, but the wound became infected, her elbow turned out to be broken and she was admitted to hospital. Elizabeth didn't want me to return home immediately—I had arranged to sail back to Oban with a friend in a week's time and didn't want to let her down—but asked me to stay within mobile phone range, which effectively ruled out exploration of the southern islands of the Outer Hebrides. So while I enjoyed the final ten days it took to sail back to Oban, my mind was now of getting Coral settled back in Dunstaffnage Marina and returning home.

Once home, I was immediately absorbed in domesticity and family affairs. Elizabeth's mother took a turn for the worse, Elizabeth herself became unwell with the stress, and my first priority was to support her as she attended to her own health while helping her mother convalesce and return home. I put the challenges of pilgrimage to the back of my mind, although I never forgot them completely. In time I was able to return to sort through my notes, photographs and videos, rekindle my memories and write the story of my pilgrimage.

In the months following my return home, even when distracted by family worries, I found myself reliving experiences from my pilgrimage, at times quite vividly. Through the winter, on those clear nights when a few stars managed to shine through the city light pollution, I felt a yearning for the gorgeous arc of the universe that I had witnessed on night passages. When I sat in our orchard, shielded from the hum of traffic by the high stone walls, I relived the silences I had entered into on Ulva. As spring arrived the palpable absence of the cuckoo's call—I have not heard one in Bath for many years—took me back to their almost constant calling on the west coast of Mull. As the long evenings of summer drew out I was taken back to even longer evenings in the northern isles, recalling watching the light change with the gradual lowering of the sun and the arrival of the full moon.

These experiences returned to me in full sensuous detail. It is as if certain moments had left their mark on me as a layer of carnal impressions imprinted on my body. Once these moments come into my mind I can move around within them, noticing again the precise way that oystercatchers hurried along the line where tiny waves were breaking on the coral sand beach.

Of course, not all of these recalls were pleasant. I could also re-experience the gale while anchored in Loch Torridon, feel myself lying on my belly, rain and sea spray rattling on my full waterproofs, as I reach over the stem to clear hunks of seaweed that had caught in a ball around the anchor. I can feel the mooring cleats sticking into my ribs, the rain dribbling down from my hair, the slimy wetness of the seaweed, the deck rolling beneath me as Coral blew out of the shelter of the anchorage into the full gale raging in the open waters of the loch. But whatever the quality of the experience, as these moments of recall passed, I was left with feelings of gratitude and quiet bliss, realizing how significant my pilgrimages have been for how I experience my relation to the world in which I live.

In contrast, I realized how easy it is in everyday life to be distracted by the seductions and entertainments of city life that continually separate the human from the more-than-human: living in a comfortable house, walking on overcrowded pavements dodging my fellow humans, travelling by car or train, enclosed and distanced from the world rushing past the window. As I wrote my story, drawing out the most significant themes from my pilgrimage, I realized that I needed now to bring my experiences back home and incorporate them into my everyday life. I remembered Satish Kumar's view that pilgrimage was not a matter of how far you travelled, but whether you could keep mind and heart open for whatever is emerging. While every person probably needs to have a particular place they call home where they live in their most intimate human relationships, an ecological pilgrimage invites us to realize that we are indigenous Earthlings, and that Earth herself is home.

The three pieces of rock I brought home with me served as an important reminder. Soon after arriving home, I told the story of my descent through layers of time to Elizabeth. As I did so, I passed each piece of rock to her in turn, explaining where I collected them and their geological origins. She listened intently and responded with delight, telling me that holding the stones helped her connect with my story and my pilgrimage.

I was often invited to talk about ecological pilgrimage and to read from my earlier book *Spindrift* at literary and ecological events. I took my rocks with me and passed them around as I told my story. People seemed to immerse themselves in my story as they held the rocks: the obloid pink granite pebble sits smooth and heavy in the palm of the hand; the smaller piece of sandstone invites one to rub it with the thumb while holding in the fingers; the jagged gneiss demands you turn it over to examine its different facets and run a finger along its sharp edges. The physical presence of the rocks appeared to give the listeners a deepening sense of engagement.

I placed the rocks in the middle of our dining room table, where they stayed through the winter, a reminder and stimulus for occasional conversation. As the New Year awakened they were put away and replaced by vases of spring flowers. As I finish this writing a year and more on, I hunted them out and put them on my desk again: they hold my memories, and are a way of bringing my pilgrimage home.

A pilgrimage is not over simply because the travelling is completed; the return home is integral. Many writers have referred to three stages of pilgrimage or ritual: separation—the breaking of the bonds with home and habits; transition—the inner and outer journey with its experiences that may change the pilgrim; and incorporation—after the intense learning of the transition phase, having shed our old skin we absorb the changes into a new sense of ourselves. This latter is not something that happens either quickly or immediately, but requires an extended process of reflection and digestion. Once family affairs were more settled, it was time to think in terms of bringing my pilgrimage back home, incorporating it into my everyday life.[1]

The first theme from my pilgrimage is the challenge of separation. Each time I left to go on pilgrimage I struggled with the challenges of separating myself from home. I do experience a yearning to be away, but the habits and relationships of the everyday exert a strong pull, so that I feel total sympathy with Bilbo Baggins as he resists the call of adventure. One can always find some reason not to leave: the moment is not propitious; there is an important task that needs to be attended to. And once one has left home, there is the pain of separation. On pilgrimage, after the excitement of setting off, there came a point when my whole being was screaming out to return home. The most extreme example was in the Scillies, when the feelings of homelessness and the enormity of the challenge ahead threatened to overwhelm me.[2]

As part my practice of bringing pilgrimage home I undertook some short excursions I called 'pilgrimages from home'. I found these everyday pilgrimages mirrored the challenges of leaving on a longer pilgrimage voyage: again and again I wanted to break away but avoided the moment of separation.

The second major theme of ecological pilgrimage was the experience of moments of grace: that capacity that integrates the diverse parts of the experience: the physical with the mental, the conscious mind with the unconscious, and the human with the more-than-human. At these times there is a loosening of the boundary between self from the wider whole in an experience of intense presence. Drawn up into the infinity of the starry sky, watching the Skellig Rocks emerge from the fog, even fighting the tidal race off Islay, I found myself present not so much *in* the world about me, but rather present *with* the world, with its sights and sounds and smells running *through* me. As the Trappist mystic Thomas Merton put it, 'The deepest level of communication is not communication, but communion. It is wordless. It is beyond words, and it is beyond speech, and it is beyond concept.' Maybe my clearest memory of this presence with the world was when anchored off the Shiant Islands: the fragility of my own position merged not just with the fragility of the islands but with the biosphere as a whole.[3]

Back at home, I find moments of grace are not necessarily such big affairs. Looking up from my computer, I glance out of my study window. It is early in the morning, and the low autumn sun lights the trees on the hillside below me. The leaves on the chestnut tree are fringed with brown; a maple glows yellow, while the ash trees are only just on the turn; I can just make out the profusion of red berries on the hawthorn trees; and in the valley below the city gardens are studded with the deep red of copper beech. For a few moments the whole landscape glows;

then it fades as a cloud covers the sun. This is no more and no less than a lovely autumn day in the West Country, but my glance turns into a gaze such that for a while I am *in* the autumn colours, just as these colours run through me. My deeper understanding of grace alerts me to the simple value of such moments.

Another theme from sailing pilgrimages was the experience of deep silence. I first attended to this while walking on Ulva, as clattering helicopters invaded ears that had become accustomed to the quiet. This led me to notice the different qualities of sound and silence in the church, the wooded areas, the coast; and attend to how sounds emerged from and fell back into the underlying silence.

In his BBC *Reith Lectures* exploring music and silence, the pianist and conductor Daniel Barenboim opened by telling his audience that 'although sound is a very physical phenomenon, it has some inexplicable metaphysical hidden power'. He pointed out that sound 'does not exist by itself, but has a permanent, constant and unavoidable relation with silence': the first note of a piece of music, the first sound 'comes out of the silence that precedes it'. If we don't keep putting energy into making that sound, it dies away. So music 'becomes rather than is there—it's not about being, but about becoming'. Traditional Chinese music similarly includes 'non-sound' elements—silences, interruptions and rests—so that 'Listening was not primarily about the ear: it required a freeing of the mind so that other non-sensory stimuli could be perceived'. Not just music, but all the sounds of the world arise out of a profound underlying silence; and when the energy that brings them into being is spent, they fall back into it.[4]

This experience of underlying silence is available whenever we are open to it, when we are not absorbed in with internal or external chatter: on entering woodland on a still day; at the moment that car alarm finally stops; in those seconds when the conductor, hands held high, holds open the emptiness at the close of music, resisting the onset of applause that will fill it. The folk myth tells us that when a sudden silence falls in a conversation, an angel is passing through.

As I have attended to my experience of silence and reflected on Barenboim's lecture, I have realized profound silence is present at all times. I have an exercise to explore this. First, I listen to the obvious sounds around: at my desk I hear the tap of the keyboard, the faint hum of the computer, the protestations of my cat demanding I open the door so she can sit on my lap. Next, I listen to the more distant sounds: there is the rumble of a bus on the road outside, the patter of rain on the conservatory roof. Then I listen for the sounds that are present but I cannot hear: the regular throb of heartbeat, the whine of my nervous system, the cries of children playing on the far side of town. Finally, behind even that I reach toward the underlying silence from which, as Barenboim points out, all sound arises and into which it falls. At those times when I manage all four stages of the exercise without my mind running off on a tangent, I find myself part of a profound stillness that underpins the noisy busyness of the world.

There are many ways I notice this. As one form of 'pilgrimage at home', my friend David and I go walking together. We take our notebooks, and when something engages our attention we see if we can write haiku in response, always giving ourselves permission to write 'bad' haiku. We call these walks 'hunting for haiku', partly in order not to take ourselves too seriously; but also because we like the idea that haiku are there to be discovered in 'haiku moments' rather than laboriously composed. Walking amongst the grazing sheep on the water meadows at Tewkesbury, where noisy crows perched on fence posts and foraged on the ground, and the distant Abbey loomed over the town, the underlying silence opened between the immediate sounds and I wrote this haiku:

Abbey bell rings sweet quarters
A crow's four harsh caws
The silence between

On another intentional pilgrimage I visited Bath Abbey. I found a seat about halfway down the nave and was immediately drawn into a depth of an ancient silence. There were the foreground noises: the low voices of visitors, the crackle of brown paper as a lady attendant unwrapped fresh flowers to arrange at the pillar near my pew, the busy preparations for the celebration of Holy Communion. There were the background noises: the buzz of traffic, the high notes from a busker in the Abbey Yard singing an incongruous love song. Dropping behind these I was enveloped in a deep and penetrating silence that reached back, at least in my imagination, to become one with the silences I had entered into on Ulva and Shiant. Through that silence came an impulse to say the Lord's Prayer, followed immediately by the even more ancient Om Mani Padme Hum. I said both; they seemed equally appropriate.

In his *Reith Lectures*, Daniel Barenboim tells us that when a musician plays, they give and take away energy from sounds. When energy is withdrawn from a note it dies away with what he describes as a 'feeling of death'. I suspect this speaks somewhat to my experience of attending to the way sounds arise out of and fall back into the underlying silence. Death is also that which is unborn: in attending to silence I am open to the whole of creation, as the 'ten thousand things' of Taoist philosophy take form and let go, appearing and disappearing in constant transformation.

Our everyday life imposes itself on the wider world. I am writing these sentences in the week preceding the ancient festival of Samhain, All Saints in the Christian calendar, Halloween in popular culture. About halfway between the autumn equinox and the midwinter solstice, Samhain marks the beginning of winter, the dark half of the year. The clocks have just been put back, and the media are full of complaints about the inconveniences caused by the time change. This 'daylight saving' can be seen as one of the most gross attempts of civilized society to impose its mechanical time on to the rhythms of the natural world.

A second imposition is light pollution. From my home in Bath, if I am lucky, on a dark night I can see just a handful of stars. The planets stand out more, and I was thrilled last year when Jupiter, Venus and Mars were visible, hanging together brightly over the roofs of our row of Georgian townhouses. But that is unusual: my vision is severely impoverished by the light pollution of the city. This means that the kind of encounter with the night sky that I experienced during long night passages is not available to me.

On pilgrimage I found myself much more directly in contact with what I called the 'grand gestures' of the planet—dawn and dusk, the night sky, the tides, the weather. I also found myself moving away from clock time into the natural rhythms of earth time, touching on occasion the eternal present and deep geological time. These themes from pilgrimage are much more difficult to bring home to an urban setting: clock and calendar time impose a regularity on my life; I am increasingly out of touch with the weather; have less need to attend to the phases of the moon; and the archaic geological structure of the world is concealed from me under a skin of concrete and asphalt.

To counter this disassociation and keep myself in touch with these grand gestures, I have attempted to build into my life simple ritual practices that draw my attention back to the world. The most successful are very simple: most nights, before I retire, I open the back door and look out into the night. I note the domestic lights in my neighbours' houses, take in the pattern of streetlights across the valley, look up into the night sky and to the distant horizon in the west. I sniff the air, picking up the damp of rain or the scent of flowers, listen for the call of owls and the grunt of urban badgers; then I lock the door and go to bed. In another little ritual, on the short walk across the courtyard I look up and consciously take in the night sky. This week I was drawn to a full moon lighting the south-facing side of the crescent houses: it shone through the glare of the streetlights, casting my shadow on the ground; but as I passed, my neighbours' security lights flicked on, their blaring light impertinent and disrespectful. The moon is magnificent even through these obstacles, but its fullness has none of the consequences it has at sea—for the light it provides for passage making and for its effect on the tides. After my long pilgrimages these simple acts of noticing feel important.

Some of the ways I attempt to bring pilgrimage home require larger commitments on my part. Toward the end of summer, I set out on a day-long intentional pilgrimage, walking across the valley from my home on the southern hills to Lansdown on the northern side, following the first section of the Cotswold Way. The official path took me from the city centre through Victoria Park, across the city golf course, up into the affluent suburbs on the northern slopes before plunging down into Weston village. After tramping along urban streets I was relieved when the path finally left the city on the lower slopes of Penn Hill. I stopped and ate my picnic lunch; and then continued through the farming countryside to the north and west of Bath. At last I could see the foot-worn line of a proper path stretching along the side of a valley, even though hemmed in between two barbed wire fences. I continued on, up Kelston Round Hill, through Shiner's Wood and steeply up again to the Cotswold plateau, where the Way followed a zigzag maze, wiggling between the Lansdown racecourse and golf course, before finally reaching the main road and stopping at the site of the Civil War Battle of Lansdown Hill.

As I walked, I experienced how the valley is almost

completely taken over by human activities. The city is a major tourist and shopping destination; the suburbs are marked by the elegant houses and fancy cars of the affluent middle classes. The farmland is so closely managed that little survives that is not 'productive' in human terms. Most of the fields showed the uniform green of fertilized ryegrass, dotted about with the telltale black plastic bales of industrial farming. I did pass one extensive area of meadowland that is allowed to grow without use of chemicals, although it seemed ironic that a notice was required to inform passers-by of this. The hay meadows of past years have disappeared and along with them much of the insect and bird life; and even the woodlands I passed through were actively managed.

There is some beauty in this human domination: as I crossed the valley my perspective on the Georgian architecture of Bath continually changed; in particular the long crescents changed shape from different viewpoints. Accustomed to the particular view from the north side, I enjoyed seeing how the older parts of the city nestled into the heart of the valley; the suburbs reach up the lower slopes of the surrounding hills, but the city is nevertheless surrounded by green space.

Despite this human domination, my walk allowed me to get a new measure of the valley. I walked down one side, across the level ground and up the other side, placing one foot in front of the other again and again, getting tired and footsore. All this gave me a physical sense of place, a sense that I had missed over nearly forty years of looking across or driving through. I was reminded of Thoreau's emphasis on sauntering; of Gary Snyder's assertion that we learn a place on foot, that place and scale need to be measured against our bodies and their capabilities; of Macfarlane's account of walking the 'old ways' and the tracks we human animals leave as we walk. In this walking to some small extent I connected myself physically to the limestone geology with the River Avon looping through its heart. When, rather out of breath, I reached the top of Kelston Round Hill, I was blown about by the brisk west wind and confronted with the almost 360° panorama that takes in parts of Wiltshire, Somerset, Gloucestershire, the Severn Valley, and beyond, the mountains of Wales. I felt this placed my home within the context of its bioregion. In walking across the valley, I reconnected with the physical imperative of pilgrimage: one doesn't get a full sense of the world we are part of by sitting still, or from the windows of a motor car.[5]

For another pilgrimage at home I decided to sleep one midsummer night under the open sky in the orchard. I was immediately confronted with the challenge of separation. Midsummer night I was too weary after a week of climbing up and down scaffolding to repair and repaint our conservatory; the following night, a family crisis kept me at home; the third night I thought it unwise to sleep outside immediately after an osteopathy treatment. The fourth night, I made it. I carted an old sleeping bag, a warm blanket, a mattress and a bivvy bag up the lane and found a flat place to make my bed. It is important to take care of 70-year-old bones. Then there was the strange process of saying goodnight to Elizabeth, leaving her to sleep on her own; locking the front door behind me and walking in my night clothes through the twilight; unlocking the orchard door and settling down in the corner under two apple trees and an oak tree.

Once I was snuggled into my sleeping bag, I felt the contrast with nights on Coral: the earth underneath me was surprisingly solid: there was none of the pitching and rolling I experience when sleeping on water. And this solidity brought with it a different sense of silence: there were no ship's noises and just a little background hum from traffic, which soon died away. The trees made a faint breezy noise as the branches moved slightly. It was a still silence, a silence of absence. I lay there for a while musing: what was I up to? Should I go to sleep or stay awake and watch? Was I completely mad? Would it get really dark or remain a midsummer twilight? And with those wonderings I fell asleep.

I woke in the middle of the night. The sky was much darker. The low moon was shining through a gap in the clouds, giving them shape and texture. It shone under the branches of the apple tree, through the tangled network of meadow grasses and on to my face. In contrast, the sky directly above me, framed by the black silhouette of the branches—the smooth curves of apple leaves, the jagged edges of oak—was more uniformly dark, almost featureless. Yet as I gazed into it, strange, darker patches floated past, maybe black, maybe deeper blue. I told myself these were patches where the cloud had thinned allowing a glimpse of the sky beyond. Yet as I looked into them, they appeared as cracks or crevasses in the substance of things: I might think I was looking up at the sky, but with a tiny shift in perspective I was looking down into great depths. Of course, as I was held on the earth by gravity, I was hanging off the Earth as much as resting on her. My feeling that there was neither up nor down reflected a wider reality.

A tiny breeze blew through and brought me back to an ordinary reality. I felt the air soft on my face, present and palpable, as if a viscous liquid had wrapped itself around me. I drew in the complex smell of the meadow: the scent of flowers, the tickle of pollen, the sweet rotting of humus. But now I was awake I had to get up to pee, struggling out of my sleeping bag, rocky on my feet for a moment. Once upright, the light from a bedroom in a nearby house, until then concealed behind the orchard's high wall, assaulted my eyes. It was almost painful. I hate it when my night vision is spoiled by bright lights: once my eyes are accustomed to darkness I want to hold it around me like a cloak; it always feels strange to me that people habitually strip the night bare with bright lights.

Back in my sleeping bag I was soon asleep again and

dreaming, just like on any other night in any other place. I woke briefly as dawn slowly crept in. All was very still, very quiet, except for the distant noise from airplanes. Then a solitary blackbird started its flowing song; I listened intently for a while, and then dropped back into sleep. A little before 6.00, I finally woke. Above me five parallel contrails had been drawn across the sky, disintegrating quickly into mare's tails. The stone walls were glowing in the golden light of the morning sun. The air was now full of birdsong: the jackdaws at their conversational best, pigeons engaged in never-ending grumbling, blue tits and wrens cheeping and chirping in the background.

I was slightly cold and a bit stiff, but lay still for a while thinking about the night. There was surprisingly little to say about it all. I felt deeply content. But I needed to stretch and I needed to pee. My night was over. I had touched something special, and there was no need of more words to describe it.

Another theme from my pilgrimage was the occasional brush with danger: rounding Erris Head in seriously rough seas; days and nights at anchor in gale conditions; hitting the keel on a rock. Back at home, danger is hidden: although we worry about road accidents, serious illnesses and terrorism, everyday life for most Europeans in the twenty-first century is extraordinarily safe. Modern society channels its energies into a life that is free of challenge and of nature and of risk. We have insulated ourselves from the natural world, so that danger, unpredictability and risk all disappear. There are of course the terrible dangers associated with the vast changes to Earth brought about by human action: climate change, ecological disruption, the increased potential for epidemics, the movement of vast numbers of people fleeing violence or poverty. But for many these dangers are concealed, only to burst forth on our television screens at dramatic moments.

The experiences I have described as states of grace, as

presence with the world, have to be won. Freya Mathews, in describing her panpsychic philosophy, tells us 'to win through to the inner presence of the world, we need to venture into the world itself. We have to face enigmas, difficulties, mortal perils. We have to risk ourselves. It is only by walking out into the world alone, facing the elements in all their ferocity, the wild animals, the stalkings and hauntings that attend our solitude, that we can turn to the world and truly ask, "Who are you?"'[6]

I ask myself, especially when I am feeling rather old and glum, where is that man who found the way through the rocks in the dark at Arranmore, who anchored and re-anchored Coral in the gale in Loch Torridon; who, in wild weather in the approaches to Ullapool, climbed to the mast and single-handed put a third reef in the mainsail? The pilgrimage and its risks are important because they are a corrective to modernity's driving preoccupation with ease and security. They cannot easily be replaced in an everyday urban life.

The most regular and significant of pilgrimages at home are my everyday visits to our orchard. These are visits that have no purpose—not to tend to trees, cut the meadow, repair stone walls—other than to draw myself back into a deeper sense of presence with the world. They manifest all the themes of pilgrimage I have explored so far.

To make the most of these brief visits I am learning to cultivate a practice of separation in which every detail echoes a major pilgrimage: leaving the everyday, getting ready, setting off. On a gusty day in late summer, after a morning work at the computer, writing, preparing my teaching or just keeping up with correspondence, I put my computer to sleep and tear myself away from the screen. I choose coat and shoes appropriate for the weather and put them on attentively. I close the front door behind me and walk across the courtyard and up the path, not hurrying, attending to the swing of my legs, the changes underfoot as I move from asphalt to the trodden earth path. As I walk, I glance at the views over Bath, listen to the city sounds rising up the hillside, take in the trees along the way. I notice how the haws are already beginning to colour up and the squirrels are attacking the yet-to-ripen hazelnuts.

It takes five minutes, maximum, from house to orchard, a symbolic leave-taking of the everyday. I have walked this path so many times in the past forty years. The challenge, on this so-familiar path, is not to rush, but to walk quietly with good attention for my surroundings, and so to turn what is a regular habit into a daily pilgrimage.

I reach the door to the orchard, set into an arched opening in the high stone wall. I made it myself, when we first bought the orchard, with a robust ash framework clad with tongue and groove pine boards; I set it so it fits precisely into the opening, curved at the top to match the arch of the stone, keeping the orchard itself completely private. I reach for the key hidden in a crack in the wall, turn it in the lock, click the latch.

As the door swings open and I step inside I feel immediately released. There is always a wonderful sense of calm inside, of stillness, even though everything is blowing around in the gusting wind. I breathe a little deeper, settle into myself, take the red chair into the hazy sunshine, look around and listen. What is it that is so peaceful about this place? Certainly, it is in part the quality of quiet, how the external sounds are dampened and made less intrusive by the high stone walls. But it is not just the absence of sound that makes for peace: there is a rhythm here, a pleasing sense of enclosed space, in the young trees reaching out of the soil into the air around them, in the movement of branches, the paths cut through the meadow grass.

Of course: it is also a place to worry! Have the raspberries got a virus? Have I pruned the apple trees right? Why does this blackberry not thrive? Should I thin out the close cropping apples? Then there is the bigger question of when I will need to get my scythe out to cut the meadow grass—not until the flowers have set their seeds, but before the grass is wet and flattened. These are all really pleasurable worries: it is hard work sometimes, but the questions are good ones.

But I am not worrying now, I am sitting still. If I listen carefully, I can hear the faint drone of traffic climbing Rush Hill, a background thrum of tyres carried on the fresh west wind. But I prefer not to attend to that, rather to listen to the wind clattering through the ash trees just over the wall. The sound rises and falls as gusts blow through under bands of clouds, which also sprinkle raindrops on my notebook. The wind bounces off the walls, spinning eddies around on the meadow grass, making the same spiral patterns as squalls blowing across the surface of the sea.

The intense yellow rattle and the glorious white and yellow of the daisies have now passed, and meadow grass is turning shades of brown, seed heads ripening alongside later-flowering blue vetch and purple knapweed. The apple trees are hanging low with the burden of fruit, which is just beginning to colour up pink. A gust draws me to look up: a magpie is flying hard into the wind, its long tail streaming behind. Jackdaws sit, as if on sentry duty, on the chimney pots I can just see over the top of the wall. There is quite a flock of them since the youngsters fledged: just now they are idly calling to each other in sporadic conversation; toward evening they will rise up together for their evening flocking, flying over the rooftops and out over the valley before going to roost in the tall trees the other side of the main road.

After sitting around I get up and walk around to inspect the trees: three old Bramley's Seedlings and the dozen younger apples, pears and plums we have planted. While I enjoy the mellowing colours on this quiet day—the ripening apples, subtly bright against the damp stonework of the walls and the dull bronze of the turning grass—I also feel a little melancholy as high summer is passed and the first of August, the festival of Lughnasadh, approaches. This is traditionally the beginning of harvest time, the season of mists and mellow fruitfulness. As I notice the waning of the year, I notice the waning of my own life as I move out of active life. I was a professor, I ran all sorts of projects, people would come to me for advice and want to work with me. In my early retirement I sailed off on three ambitious voyages, mainly single-handed. Now Coral is sold, and I am moving maybe into another phase of life. Is that OK? I think so.

I stand there, watching the sunshine light up the meadow flowers, fading, but still smothered in insects: a white-tailed bumblebee explores the hollyhock flowers; a smaller bee climbs over the vetch; a trio of small white butterflies flutter together; there are many more whose names I have not learned. It occurs to me that this is something Elizabeth and I are doing for the world: we are allowing space for this mass of pollen and making a place for insects. Is that enough to be doing in a world in ecological crisis? Is that the right thing, the sufficient thing, to simply care for and love the world in its beauty? Of course it is not enough, and yet it is utterly important. I remember the poets: Rainer Maria Rilke, who tells us, 'The more looked-at world wants to be nourished with love'; and Mary Oliver, whose 'Instructions for living a life' tell us to 'Pay attention. | Be astonished. | Tell about it'. That seems to be what I am trying to do.

It is such a sweet sorrow, to watch at the turning of the year and the turning of one's life, all against the background of ecological devastation. And then my attention turns again: I come out of my musings to look up at the big apple tree. I notice how this summer's growth has sprouted beyond the fruiting, how the new branches are criss-crossing each other; how the tree is overcrowded in places. I start thinking forward to the winter's pruning, how I will cut back here, thin here and encourage growth there. And as I stand there puzzling, I find I have entered into the presence of the tree: I am back with its hybridness, into its me-and-you-ness.

Clouds thicken, a gust of wind blows through, shaking the

branches and spattering heavy drops of rain. I hurry back to the house.

Thank You

I offer my thanks to the many people who helped make these voyages possible. The Rustler Association lent me a big pile of charts of the west coast of Ireland; Graham Rabbits was particularly generous in lending me his personal copies of guides and sailing books. My old friend Ian Galloway let me use his charts of the west coast of Scotland and the Hebrides. Simon Nelson kept an eye on Coral while she was moored at Schull. Damian Ward and his colleagues at Clifden Bay Boat Club offered hospitality, kindness and practical help at a critical stage of the Irish voyage. Mairin Glenn discovered via Twitter that we were close to her home in Belmullet and welcomed us with showers and supper. Many others—those who helped me at anchorages and marinas, who serviced Coral's equipment, who provided advice and guidance along the way—must unfortunately remain anonymous.

Thanks then due to those who came with me. Steve Reneaux was a stalwart companion for the passage out and the following year in Scotland. He was endlessly cheerful in the face of my sometimes grumpiness, and deeply appreciative of the whole experience. Suzanne Paulus and Pimaree Ginggeo were fortunate to have calm seas for our exploration of the Skellig Rocks and Blasket Islands; thanks in particular for many stimulating conversations. David Clarke and Suzanne Kuhn were not so lucky on the passage round the northeast of Ireland: you had a tough time in some heavy weather; thank you for hanging in and contributing for as long as you did. David, thanks too for the GoPro footage that I used in the YouTube videos.[1] Phoebe Swan joined me for the last leg back from Mallaig to Oban, painting the sea from the coachroof as we sailed past Ardnamurchan. Sorry this bit of the journey didn't make it into the book.

Some people journeyed with me in spirit. It was a strange

comfort that while I was sailing round the Hebrides, Elsa Hammond was on her own adventure rowing single-handed across the Pacific. David Manzi-Fé continued to exchange haiku with me even while recovering from major surgery. At one point he messaged me:

One old man on the sea
Another old man on a sea of morphine.

Thanks next to those who supported me during the writing of this book. My writing group—Emma Geen, Jane Shemilt, Mimi Thebo, Sophie McGovern, Susan Jordan, Tanya Atapattu, Victoria Finlay—were a constant source of support and constructive criticism. Rob Porteous, Elsa Hammond, Helen Sieroda and Julia Guest commented helpfully on several chapters; and Julia also generously filmed and edited the YouTube video.

Mark Cocker kindly read an early version of the manuscript and offered support and rigorous critique. Too much about the weather, he complained. There is still a lot of weather in the book, Mark! Katrina Porteous helped me develop insights into silence. Thanks to Martin Palmer for several conversations about pilgrimage; to Sarah Bird for reading the final draft and providing much constructive editorial advice; to Sue Gent for drawing the elegant and accurate the charts in the front papers.

A version of Chapter 14 was published as Reason, Peter. "Time and Ecological Pilgrimage." In *Participatory Research in More-than-Human Worlds* edited by Michelle Bastian, Owain Jones, Emma Roe, and Michael Buser. London: Routledge, 2016.

A version of Chapter 5 was published as Reason, Peter. "Moments of Grace". *EarthLines* 9 (2015): 13–18.

Thanks to Stamati Crook for permission to use part of one of the late Chan Master John Crook's poems from *The Koans of Layman John*, 2009, p. 20.

Notes and References

Chapter One

Epigraph: Berry, Thomas. *The Dream of the Earth*. San Francisco: Sierra Club, 1988, pp.123–124.

1. Earth in Pictures: https://www.theguardian.com/science/gallery/2012/dec/06/black-marble-images-Earth-in-pictures

2. The term 'more-than-human world' was first coined by David Abram. Wikipedia provides a useful definition: '... the broad commonwealth of earthly life, a realm that manifestly *includes* humankind and its culture, but which necessarily *exceeds* human culture'. Abram, David. *The Spell of the Sensuous: Perception and Language in a More-Than-Human World*. New York: Pantheon, 1996.

3. For origins of apple trees: Deakin, Roger. *Wildwood: A Journey Through Trees*. London: Hamish Hamilton, 2007; Pollan, Michael. *The Botany of Desire: A Plants-Eye View of the World*. New York: Random House, 2002.

4. For hybrids see Latour, Bruno. *We Have Never Been Modern*. Translated by Catherine Porter. Hemel Hempstead: Harvester Wheatsheaf, 1993.

5. For symbiotic evolution: Margulis, Lynn. *The Symbiotic Planet: A New Look at Evolution*. London: Weidenfeld & Nicolson, 1998, pp. 5–7.

6. Modern humans: I use the term 'modern' humans to refer to those of us deeply entrenched in the Western worldview that has its origins in the Enlightenment thinking of the eighteenth century. See for example Toulmin, Stephen. *Cosmopolis: The Hidden Agenda of Modernity*. New York: Free Press, 1990.

7. Carson, Rachel. *Silent Spring*. Boston: Houghton Mifflin Company, 1962. Originally published as 1962; Buckminster Fuller's *Operating Manual for Spaceship Earth* was first

published in 1968; Meadows, Donella H., Dennis L. Meadows, Jørgen Randers, and William W. Behrens. *The Limits to Growth*. New York: Universe Books, 1972. Revised editions were published in 1992 and 2004; Gore, Al. *An Inconvenient Truth: The Planetary Emergency of Global Warming and What We Can Do About It*. Emmaus, PA: Rodale Press, 2006; Intergovernmental Panel on Climate Change http://www.ipcc.ch/

8. Berry, Thomas. *The Dream of the Earth*. San Francisco: Sierra Club, 1988.

9. Universe Story: Swimme, B. & Tucker, ME. *Journey of the Universe*. New Haven: Yale University Press, 2011; Swimme, BT & Tucker, ME (Writers). *Journey of the Universe: An Epic Story of Cosmic, Earth, and Human Transformation*. USA: Yale University, 2011; Swimme, BT & Berry, T. *The Universe Story: From the Primordial Flaring Forth to the Ecozoic Era—A Celebration of the Unfolding of the Cosmos*. New York: HarperCollins, 1992. An account of human displacement from the centre of things can be found in Tarnas, Richard. *Cosmos and Psyche: Intimations of a New World View*. New York: Plume; and at https://youtu.be/h4Ji907EXvc

10. Cooper, David E. *Convergence with Nature: A Daoist Perspective*. Totnes: Green Books, 2012, p. 39.

11. Secular Society: Taylor, Charles. *A Secular Age*. Cambridge, MA: The Belknap Press of Harvard University Press, 2007.

12. Seed, John, Joanna Rogers Macy, Pat Fleming and Arne Naess. *Thinking Like a Mountain*. London: Heretic Books, 1988.

Chapter Two

Epigraph: Kumar, Satish. *Earth Pilgrim: Conversations with Satish Kumar*. Dartington: Green Books, 2009, pp. 21–22.

1. We are only talking to ourselves: '... if we do not hear the voices of the trees, the birds, the animals, the fish, the

mountains and the rivers, then we are in trouble... That, I think, is what has happened to the human community in our times. We are talking to ourselves. We are not talking to the river, we are not listening to the river. We have broken the great conversation. By breaking the conversation we have shattered the universe. All these things that are happening now are consequences of this "autism".' Berry, Thomas and Thomas Clarke. *Befriending the Earth: A Theology of Reconciliation Between Humans and the Earth.* Mystic, Connecticut: Twenty-Third Publications, 1991.

2. Reason, Peter. *Spindrift: A Wilderness Pilgrimage at Sea.* Bristol: Jessica Kingsley Publishers (originally published by Vala Publishing Co-operative), 2014.

3. Helpful references on pilgrimage have included Clift, Jean D. and Wallace B. Clift. *The Archetype of Pilgrimage: Outer Action with Inner Meaning.* Mahwah, NJ: Paulist Press International, 1996; Coleman, Simon and John Elsner. *Pilgrimage, Past and Present: Sacred Travel and Sacred Space in the World Religions.* London: British Museum Press, 1995; Westwood, Jennifer. *Sacred Journeys: Paths for the New Pilgrim.* London: Gaia Books, 1997; and the University of York Pilgrims and Pilgrimage website at http://www.york.ac.uk/projects/pilgrimage/ See also the editorial of Orion Magazine Sept/Oct 2014.

4. Peregrinatio: Hebrews 11:13–16. See Introduction, Bunyan, J. (1678). *The Pilgrim's Progress* (NH Keeble Ed., Oxford World Classics ed.). St Augustine, *The City of God.* Trans. Gerald G. Walsh. New York: Image, 1958. Leopold, Aldo. *A Sand County Almanac*: Oxford University Press, 1949.

5. Liminal space: Christie, DE. *The Blue Sapphire of the Mind: Notes for a Contemplative Ecology.* New York: Oxford University Press, 2013, p. 233.

6. Goodwin, Brian C. *How the Leopard Changed Its Spots: The Evolution of Complexity.* London: Weidenfeld and Nicolson,

1994.

7. Kumar, Satish. Interview in *The Spark* by Fiona McClymont. Bristol, February 2014.

8. Snyder, Gary. *The Practice of the Wild*. New York: North Point Press, 1990, p. 94.

9. Paul Theroux, remark on BBC *Saturday Live*, 9 June 2013. On early extinctions: Kolbert, Elizabeth. *The Sixth Extinction: An Unnatural History*. London: Bloomsbury, 2014.

10. Palmer, Martin. *Sacred Land*. London: Piatkus, 2012.

Chapter Three

Epigraph: Opening lines from Matsuo Basho's classic work of haibun *The Narrow Road to the Deep North*.

Chapter Four

Epigraph: Tesson, Sylvain. *Consolations of the Forest*. Translated by Linda Coverdale. London: Penguin Books, 2013, p. 4.

1. Matthiessen, Peter. *The Snow Leopard*. London: Picador, 1980, p. 15.

2. Paul Theroux, remark on *Saturday Live*, BBC Radio 4, 9 June 2013.

Chapter Five

Epigraph: Le Guin, Ursula. *A Wizard of Earthsea*. London: Puffin Books, 1971, p. 47.

1. Niebuhr, Richard Reinhold. "Pilgrims and Pioneers". *Parabola* 9, no. 3, 1984: 6–13, p. 12.

2. William Blake, *Vala or The Four Zoas*.

3. Bateson, Gregory. *Steps to an Ecology of Mind*. San Francisco: Chandler, 1972, in particular "Style, Grace, and Information in Primitive Art" and "Conscious Purpose versus Nature".

4. Bateson, Gregory. "Consciousness Versus Nature". *Peace News* 1622 (July 28), (1967): 10.

5. On *Gracias*: Julia Alvarez. "The Practice of Gracias". *Orion*,

34 (5), pp. 7–8. October 2015.

6. Berry, Thomas. *The Great Work: Our Way into the Future*. New York: Bell Tower, 1999. Carol Ann Duffy, "Moments of Grace".

7. Storm, Hyemeyohsts. *Seven Arrows*. New York: Harper & Row, 1972, p. 5. Storm is a controversial figure for many reasons, and many dispute the authenticity of his teachings. However, his books nevertheless contain much wisdom.

8. As told by the late Chan Master John Crook on a Western Chan Fellowship retreat. A slightly different version of this story can be found in Daido Loori, John. *Teachings of the Insentient*. Mt. Tremper, NY: Dharma Communications Press, 1999.

Chapter Six

Epigraph: Snyder, Gary. *The Practice of the Wild*. New York: North Point Press, 1990, p. 93.

1. Ende, Michael. *The Neverending Story*. London: Puffin, 2004. First published in German in 1979.

2. This is the story as told by Geoffrey Moorhouse in *Sun Dancing*. London: Phoenix, 1997.

3. Christie, Douglas E. *The Blue Sapphire of the Mind: Notes for a Contemplative Ecology*. New York: Oxford University Press, 2013. See also Reason, Peter. "Review, *The Blue Sapphire of the Mind: Notes for a Contemplative Ecology* by Douglas E. Christie." *Resurgence & Ecologist* No. 281, (2013): 60–61; and at https://peterreason.net/2013/04/26/the-blue-sapphire-of-the-mind/

4. Otto, Rudolf. *The Idea of the Holy*. Translated by JW Harvey. New York: Oxford University Press, 1923; Eliade, Mircea. *The Sacred and the Profane: The Nature of Religion*. Translated by Willard R. Trask. New York: Harper Torchbooks, 1961.

5. "How to Be A Poet". In Berry, Wendell. *Given: Poems*. Emeryville, CA: Shoemaker & Hoard, 2005.

6. Panspsychic or panexperiential philosophies have been articulated by a range of authors including Alfred North Whitehead, Freya Mathews and Thomas Berry. Whitehead, Alfred North. *Process and Reality: An Essay in Cosmology*. New York: Macmillan, 1929. Mathews, Freya. *Reinhabiting Reality: Towards a Recovery of Culture*. Albany: SUNY Press, 2005. Berry, Thomas. *The Sacred Universe: Earth, Spirituality, and Religion in the Twenty-First Century*. Edited by Mary Evelyn Tucker. New York: Columbia University Press, 2009.

7. For a contemporary Buddhist view of the world see for example Crook, John H., *World Crisis and Buddhist Humanism. End Games: Collapse or Renewal of Civilisation*. New Delhi: New Age Books, 2009. For a Taoist view see in particular Hinton, David. *Hunger Mountain: A Field Guide to Mind and Landscape*. Boston & London: Shambhala, 2012, p. 17.

8. Lopez, Barry. *Arctic Dreams: Imagination and Desire in a Northern Landscape*. New York: Charles Scribner's Sons, 1986. Also, *Of Wolves and Men*. London: John Dent and Sons, 1978. New York: Charles Scribner's Sons, 1978. For discussion of collapse of mundane and sacred see Tydeman, William E. *Conversations with Barry Lopez: Walking the Path of Imagination*. Norman, OK: University of Oklahoma Press, 2013, pp. 55–56. I have borrowed the term 'moral gaze' from Robert Macfarlane. *Landmarks*. London: Hamish Hamilton, 2015, p. 211.

9. Snyder, Gary. *The Practice of the Wild*, pp. 94–96.

10. Marsden, Philip. *Rising Ground: A Search for the Spirit of Place*. London: Granta, 2015.

11. On the aura of sacred places: Palmer, Martin. *Sacred Land*. London: Piatkus, 2012, pp. 3–5.

12. On sacred dream: Berry, Thomas. *The Dream of the Earth*. San Francisco: Sierra Club, 1988, p. 197.

Chapter Seven

Epigraph: Pullman, Philip. *The Subtle Knife*. London: Scholastic, 1997, p. 288.

1. Kaepernick's protest echoes that of African-American athletes Tommie Smith and John Carlos, who raised their fists in a Black Power salute during their medal ceremony at the 1968 Summer Olympics.

2. Hinton, David. *Hunger Mountain: A Field Guide to Mind and Landscape*. Boston & London: Shambhala, 2012. Quotations taken from pp. 3–4, 18–19, 32.

3. Deakin, Roger. *Wildwood: A Journey Through Trees*. London: Hamish Hamilton, 2007, p. ix. The full quote from Keats is taken from Andrew Motion, *Keats*. London: Faber and Faber, 1997, pp. 210–227.

4. Bate, Jonathan. *The Song of the Earth*. London: Picador, 2000, pp. 103–110.

5. Robinson, Tim. *Connemara: A Little Gaelic Kingdom*. London: Penguin Books, 2011.

Chapter Eight

Epigraph: Bauman, Zygmunt. "From Pilgrim to Tourist—or a Short History of Identity." In *Questions of Cultural Identity*, edited by Stuart Hall and Paul du Gay. London: Sage Publications, 2011, p. 29.

1. Robinson, Tim. *Stones of Aran: Pilgrimage*. London: Penguin, 1989; *Stones of Aran: Labyrinth*. London: Penguin, 1997. Following quotes all from *Stones of Aran*.

2. Evans, Paul. *Field Notes From The Edge: Journeys Through Britain's Secret Wilderness*. London: Rider, 2015, p. xi.

3. Cocker, Mark. *Crow Country*. London: Vintage, 2008, p. 105.

Chapter Nine

Epigraph: Crook, John Hurrell, *The Koans of Layman John*, Lula, 2009.

1. On Connemara granite: Robinson, Tim. *Connemara: A Little Gaelic Kingdom*. London: Penguin Books, 2011, pp. 257–9; later on names p. 168.

2. Sailing directions: I was using the eighth edition of *Sailing Directions for the South and West Coasts of Ireland*, compiled over the years by members of the Irish Cruising Club (the first edition is dated 1930; a ninth edition has since been published).

3. I am grateful to Martin Palmer for a conversation confirming my hunch about the location of Christian buildings.

4. Cunliffe, Barry. *Facing the Ocean: The Atlantic and Its Peoples 8000 BC–AD 1500*. Oxford: Oxford University Press, 2001. Macfarlane, Robert. *The Old Ways: A Journey on Foot*. London: Hamish Hamilton, 2012.

5. On pilgrimage: Coleman, Simon and John Elsner. *Pilgrimage, Past and Present: Sacred Travel and Sacred Space in the World Religions*. London: British Museum Press, 1995, p. 66. Various translations and renderings of the Tao Te Ching are available, including those by Gia-Fu Feng and Jane English; David Hinton; Ursula Le Guin; Thomas Cleary; and Robert Ames and David Hall. For a powerful account of the disorientation that may occur in pilgrimage, see Jay Griffiths' account of her experiences on the Camino de Santiago. Griffiths, Jay. *Tristimania: A Diary of Manic Depression*. London: Hamish Hamilton, 2016.

6. By inquiry I don't just mean academic research, but the kind of life and community inquiry articulated in the many forms of participative action research. See for example the three editions of the *Handbook of Action Research*, the first two of which I co-edited with Hilary Bradbury. Also Marshall, Judi, Gill Coleman, and Peter Reason. *Leadership for Sustainability: An Action Research Approach*. Sheffield: Greenleaf, 2011.

Chapter Ten

Epigraph: Robinson, Tim. *Connemara: A Little Gaelic Kingdom*. London: Penguin Books, 2011, p. 142.

1. Robinson's account of the chapel can be found in *Connemara: A Little Gaelic Kingdom* on p. 145.

2. On Macdara and stormy weather: Roderick O'Flaherty, quoted in Robinson, Tim. *Connemara: A Little Gaelic Kingdom*. London: Penguin Books, 2011, p. 140.

3. Who was Macdara? Robinson, Tim. *Connemara: A Little Gaelic Kingdom*, p. 141.

4. "Saint Mac Dara's Island. A report written by R.A.S. Macalister in 1895 for the Royal Society of Antiquaries of Ireland." http://www.aislingmagazine.com/aislingmaga zine/articles/TAM25/SaintMacDara%27s.html

Chapter Eleven

Epigraph: Snyder, Gary. *The Practice of the Wild*. New York: North Point Press, 1990, p. 23.

1. On Caribou pilgrimage: Ganz, Shoshannah. "'A Living, Breathing, Pulsing Web': Being Caribou as Canadian Ecological Pilgrimage." *Synaesthesia* 1, no. 2 (2009): 51–59. Heuer, K. *Being Caribou: Five Months on Foot with an Arctic Herd*. Toronto: McClelland and Stewart, 2006, pp. 10 & 93.

2. The story of 'why do we go into the wilderness' is told by Jim Cheney in "Truth, Knowledge and the Wild World". *Ethics and the Environment* 10, no. 2 (2005): 101–135.

3. Boswell, James. *The Life of Samuel Johnson* (1791). Quotation retrieved from http://www.samueljohnson.com/refutati .html

4. I have borrowed the term 'flashy brains' from Gary Snyder's essay "The Etiquette of Freedom".

5. Parlett, Malcolm. *Future Sense: Five Explorations of Whole Intelligence for a World That's Waking Up*. Matador Books, 2015. This phrase was in a draft but omitted from the final

version, but it seems so apt that I nevertheless include it here! The long trajectory of human life on Earth: Harari, Yuval Noah. *Sapiens: A Brief History of Humankind*. London: Vintage Books, 2011.

6. The world is as sharp as a knife: Snyder, Gary. "The Etiquette of Freedom". In *The Practice of the Wild*. New York: North Point Press, 1990, p. 18 & p. 4.

Chapter Twelve

Epigraph: The Venerable Bede, *The Reckoning of Time* (De temporum ratione) https://www.scribd.com/doc/245646239 /Bede-Bede-the-Reckoning-of-Time-Liverpool-University-Press-Translated-Texts-for-Historians-Liverpool-University-Press-1999. Bede's discoveries were recently discussed in a blog by Jon Garvey at http://potiphar.jongarvey.co. uk/2014/06/23/how-the-venerable-bede-got-us-to-the-moon/ and mentioned by broadcaster Melvin Bragg in *The Matter of the North* http://www.bbc.co.uk/programmes/b07q76b9

1. On tides: McCully, James Greig. *Beyond the Moon: A Conversational, Common Sense Guide to Understanding the Tides*. New Jersey: World Scientific, 2006.

2. Atlantic Meridional Overturning Circulation: Kump, Lee R., James F. Kasting and Robert G. Crane. *The Earth System*. 2nd ed. Upper Saddle River, NJ: Prentice-Hall, 2004; Harding, Stephan P. *Animate Earth*. Foxhole, Dartington: Green Books, 2009.

3. Cold spot in Atlantic: http://www.realclimate.org/index. php/archives/2015/03/whats-going-on-in-the-north-atlantic/#more-18156; Is the Gulf Stream slowing? https:// www.youtube.com/watch?v=EmiVhT5cHpw

4. Gulf Stream: Seager, Richard, "Climate mythology: The Gulf Stream, European climate and Abrupt Change". http://www.ldeo.columbia.edu/res/div/ocp/gs/ (accessed 8 April 2014); Seager, Richard. "The Source of Europe's Mild

Climate." *American Scientist* 94, no. 4 (2006): 334; Seager, Richard, DS Battisti, J. Yin, N. Gordon, NH Naik, AC Clement and MA Cane. 2002. "Is the Gulf Stream responsible for Europe's Mild Winters?" *Quarterly Journal of the Royal Meteorological Society* 128, (2002): 2563–2586.

Chapter Thirteen

Epigraph: The Free Dictionary

1. Robert Frost, *The Road Not Taken*
2. Thoreau, Henry David. "Walking". *Atlantic Monthly* (1862).
3. Macfarlane, Robert. *The Old Ways: A Journey on Foot.* London: Hamish Hamilton, 2012, pp. xi & 24–27.
4. Mead, G. *Coming Home to Story: Storytelling Beyond Happily Ever After.* Bristol: Vala Publications, 2011, p. 119. Chinen, AB. *Beyond the Hero: Classic Stories of Men in Search of Soul.* New York: Tarcher/Putnam, 1993.
5. Clift, JD & Clift, WB. *The Archetype of Pilgrimage: Outer Action with Inner Meaning.* Mahwah, NJ: Paulist Press International, 1996. Campbell, J. *The Hero with a Thousand Faces.* First published by Bollingen Foundation, 1949.
6. Sharon Blackie, http://singingoverthebones.org/2016/01/24/the-heroines-journey-the-progress-of-an-imperfect-pilgrim/; see also *If Women Rose Rooted: The Power of the Celtic Woman.* September Publishing, 2016. June Singer, Foreword. In Chinen, Allan B. *Waking the World: Classic Tales of Women and the Heroic Feminine.* New York: Tarcher/Putnam, 1996.
7. Christie, Douglas E. *The Blue Sapphire of the Mind: Notes for a Contemplative Ecology.* New York: Oxford University Press, 2013, p. 14.
8. Loy, DR (2012). "The New Bodhisattva Path". *The Huffington Post.* Retrieved from http://www.huffingtonpost.com/david-loy/the-new-bodhisattva-path_b_2166676.html. Macy, Joanna Rogers and Molly Young Brown. *Coming Back*

to Life: Practices to Reconnect Our Lives, Our World. Gabriola Island: New Society Publishers, 1998. See also Jean Boulton on tipping points. Boulton, J., Allen, P. & Bowman, C. *Embracing Complexity*. Oxford: OUP, 2015.

9.   Mead writes on Elder Tales at https://elderflower ing.wordpress.com/. Matthiessen, Peter. *The Snow Leopard*. London: Picador, 1980.

Chapter Fourteen

Epigraphs: Lopez, Barry. *Arctic Dreams: Imagination and Desire in a Northern Landscape*. New York: Charles Scribner's Sons, 1986, p. 257. Shepherd, Nan. *The Living Mountain*. Edinburgh: Canongate Books, 2011, p. 96.

1.   Maitland, Sara. *A Book of Silence*. London: Granta, 2008, pp. 26–27. The reflections on silence in this chapter are also informed by Lees, Helen E. "The Outdoors as the Source of Silence: Access, Curriculum and Something Relational." In *Philosophical Perspectives in Outdoor Education Conference*. Moray House, Edinburgh University, 2–4 May 2012. Cooper, David E. "Silence, nature and education." In *Attending to Silence*, edited by Henny Fiska Hagg and Aslaug Kristiansen. Kristiansand: Portal Forlag, 2012.

2.   Lopez story is quoted in Cooper, David E. "Silence, nature and education." In *Attending to Silence*, edited by Henny Fiska Hagg and Aslaug Kristiansen. Kristiansand: Portal Forlag, 2012.

3.   Matthiessen, Peter. *The Snow Leopard*. London: Picador, 1980, p. 183.

Chapter Fifteen

Epigraph: Dalrymple, William. *In Xanadu: A Quest*. London: HarperPress, 2010, p. 220.

1.   Kolbert, Elizabeth. *The Sixth Extinction: An Unnatural History*. London: Bloomsbury, 2014.

2. Eisenstein, Charles. *The More Beautiful World Our Hearts Know is Possible*. Berkeley, CA: North Atlantic Books, 2013.

3. Teaching of Buddha: Crook, John H. *World Crisis and Buddhist Humanism. End Games: Collapse or Renewal of Civilisation*. New Delhi: New Age Books, 2009. Teaching of Tao: Hinton, D. *Hunger Mountain: A Field Guide to Mind and Landscape*. Boston & London: Shambhala, 2012, p. 104. Flesh is as Grass: King James Bible, Isaiah 40:8 and 1 Peter 1:25, as adapted for Handel's *Messiah*.

4. Fortey, Richard. *The Hidden Landscape: A Journey into the Geological Past*. 2nd ed. London: The Bodley Head, 2010, p. 250.

5. Maxwell, Gavin. *Ring of Bright Water*. London: Longmans, Green and Co., 1960. pp. 9–10 in 1963 Pan edition.

Chapter Sixteen

Epigraph: Adapted in the style of the Met Office Marine Shipping Forecast.

1. Fortey, Richard. *The Hidden Landscape: A Journey into the Geological Past*. 2nd ed. London: The Bodley Head, 2010.

2. Coral's bower anchor, for everyday use, weighs 30lbs; a CQR anchor looks a bit like a plough, is drop-forged for strength, and has a hinged shank, allowing it to turn with direction changes rather than breaking out of the sea bottom.

Chapter Seventeen

Epigraph: Fortey, Richard. *The Hidden Landscape: A Journey into the Geological Past*. 2nd ed. London: The Bodley Head, 2010, pp. 23–24.

1. Some aspects of my meditation on time were stimulated by a paper by my friend Bill Torbert. Torbert, William R. "Mathematical Intuitions: Underlying the Integral Meta-Paradigm of Science Named 'Collaborative Developmental

Action Inquiry'." 2014. Draft paper available from the author.

2. There are two Scalpay islands in Scotland, one in the Inner Sound, one in the Outer Hebrides south of Harris.

3. Snyder, G. *The Practice of the Wild*. New York: North Point Press, 1990, p. 94.

4. Hinton, D. *Hunger Mountain: A Field Guide to Mind and Landscape*. Boston & London: Shambhala, 2012, p. 105.

Chapter Eighteen

Epigraph: Nicolson, Adam. *Sea Room: An Island Life*. London: HarperCollins, 2001, p. 1. The Nicolson family has owned the Shiant Islands for many years.

1. Complexity Theory: Boulton, Jean; Peter Allen and C. Bowman. *Embracing Complexity*. Oxford: OUP, 2015. Wildlife conservation http://www.theguardian.com/environment/2008/jun/04/wildlife.conservation; and http://www.theguardian.com/news/2015/jan/25/weatherwatch-arctic-little-auk-feeding-habits

2. Comment on Earth Rising attributed to nature photographer Galen Rowell.

3. Astronaut quotes taken from the video *Overview* http://vimeo.com/55073825

Chapter Nineteen

Epigraphs: Estés, Clarissa Pinkola. *Women Who Run With the Wolves: Myths and Stories of the Wild Woman Archetype*. New York: Ballantine, 1992; Snyder, Gary. *The Practice of the Wild*. New York: North Point Press, 1990.

1. Stages of pilgrimage: See Ayot, William. *Re-enchanting the Forest*. Bristol: Vala Publishing Co-operative, 2015. In identifying these three phases, William is drawing on the original work of the French ethnographer Arnold van Gennep who described pre-liminal, liminal, and post-liminal phases;

which Joseph Campbell termed Separation, Ordeal and Return.

2. Bilbo Baggins: Tolkien, JRR. *The Hobbit or There and Back Again*. Fourth ed. London: George Allen and Unwin, 1978.

3. Thomas Merton. *The Hidden Ground of Love: Letters*. London: Macmillan, 2011.

4. Daniel Barenboim, *Reith Lectures 2006*. "In the Beginning was Sound": Lecture 1. http://downloads.bbc.co.uk/rmh ttp/radio4/transcripts/20060407_reith.pdf
Traditional Chinese music: Thien, Madeleine. "After the Cultural Revolution: what western classical music means in China." *The Guardian Review*. 8 July 2016, https://www.theguardian.com/music/2016/jul/08/after-the-cultural-revolution-what-western-classical-music-means-in-china

5. Thoreau, Henry David. "Walking". *Atlantic Monthly* (1862). Available at http://thoreau.eserver.org/walking.html; Snyder, Gary. *The Practice of the Wild*. New York: North Point Press, 1990, p. 98; Macfarlane, Robert. *The Old Ways: A Journey on Foot*. London: Hamish Hamilton, 2012.

6. Mathews, Freya. *For Love of Matter: A Contemporary Panpsychism*. Albany, NY: SUNY Press, 2003, p. 21.

Thank You

1. YouTube videos of Coral's voyages are at: https://www.youtube.com/watch?v=VOmXFMNrYGE and https://www.youtube.com/watch?v=AsKq_a8P7bc

EARTH

BOOKS

ENVIRONMENT

Earth Books are practical, scientific and philosophical publications about our relationship with the environment. Earth Books explore sustainable ways of living; including green parenting, gardening, cooking and natural building. They also look at ecology, conservation and aspects of environmental science, including green energy. An understanding of the interdependence of all living things is central to Earth Books, and therefore consideration of our relationship with other animals is important. Animal welfare is explored. The purpose of Earth Books is to deepen our understanding of the environment and our role within it. The books featured under this imprint will both present thought-provoking questions and offer practical solutions.

If you have enjoyed this book, why not tell other readers by posting a review on your preferred book site. Recent bestsellers from Earth Books are:

In Defence of Life
Essays on a Radical Reworking of Green Wisdom
Julian Rose
Julian Rose's book has the power to lift the reader into another dimension. He offers a way to break through the destructive patterns of our consumer-obsessed society and discover a simpler, more fulfilling way forward.
Paperback: 978-1-78279-257-4 ebook: 978-1-78279-256-7

Eyes of the Wild
Journeys of Transformation with the Animal Powers
Eleanor O'Hanlon
The ancient understanding of animals as guides to self-knowledge and the soul comes alive through close encounters with some of the most magnificent creatures of the wild.
Paperback: 978-1-84694-957-9 ebook: 978-1-84694-958-6

Simplicity Made Easy
Jennifer Kavanagh
Stop wishing your life was more simple, and start making it happen! With the help of Jennifer Kavanagh's book, turn your focus to what really matters in life.
Paperback: 978-1-84694-543-4 ebook: 978-1-84694-895-4

Safe Planet
Renewable Energy Plus Workers' Power
John Cowsill
Safe Planet lays out a roadmap of renewable energy sources and meteorological data to direct us towards a safe planet.
Paperback: 978-1-78099-682-0 ebook: 978-1-78099-683-7

Approaching Chaos
Could an Ancient Archetype Save 21st Century Civilization?
Lucy Wyatt
Civilisation can survive by learning from the social, spiritual and technological secrets of ancient civilisations such as Egypt.
Paperback: 978-1-84694-255-6

Gardening with the Moon & Stars
Elen Sentier
Organics with Ooomph! Bringing biodynamics to the ordinary gardener.
Paperback: 978-1-78279-984-9 ebook: 978-1-78279-985-6

GreenSpirit
Path to a New Consciousness
Marian Van Eyk McCain
A collection of essays on 21st Century green spirituality and its
key role in creating a peaceful and sustainable world.
Paperback: 978-1-84694-290-7 ebook: 978-1-78099-186-3

The Protein Myth
Significantly Reducing the Risk of Cancer, Heart Disease,
Stroke, and Diabetes While Saving the Animals and the Planet
David Gerow Irving
The Protein Myth powerfully illustrates how the way to vibrant
health and a peaceful world is to stop exploiting animals.
Paperback: 978-1-84694-673-8 ebook: 978-1-78099-073-6

This Is Hope
Green Vegans and the New Human Ecology How We Find Our
Way to a Humane and Environmentally Sane Future
Will Anderson
This Is Hope compares the outcomes of two human ecologies;
one is tragic, the other full of promise...
Paperback: 978-1-78099-890-9

Readers of ebooks can buy or view any of these bestsellers by
clicking on the live link in the title. Most titles are published
in paperback and as an ebook. Paperbacks are available in
traditional bookshops. Both print and ebook formats are
available online.

Find more titles and sign up to our readers' newsletter at
http://www.johnhuntpublishing.com/non-fiction
Follow us on Facebook at
https://www.facebook.com/JHPNonFiction